Who doesn't like to see what makes a leader tick? When we are climbing the corporate ladder, it can be hard to put ourselves in the shoes of founders and CEOs. Success Mindsets not only hands you their shoes, but it also shows you how to use them to keep climbing!

Paul Gunn | CEO, KUOG Corporation

Warning: This anthology is not for everyone! If you are looking for deeply philosophical thoughts, recipes for happiness, or precise ways to succeed in your career–this book may not be what you are looking for. But if you want inspiration, motivation, encouragement, and a very thorough look at how the authors' think through their tribulations, strategies, and actions daily, then this book is perfect."

Aaron Vick | Author of Leaderpreneur: A Leadership Guide for Startups and Entrepreneurs & Inevitable Revolutions: Secrets and Strategies for a Successful Business

Resiliency and a growth mindset is critical for successful leaders. This book shares stories, strategies and insights to help people strengthen their beliefs in themselves.

Matthew Rolnick | VP Strategy & Innovation at Yaymaker and Author of "Find Your Yay"

Everything begins in your mind, to change your life and to succeed and then succeed more change your mindset first and evolve it always! The authors share great life lessons worth reading and contemplating on.

Sid Mohasseb | Best Selling Author, University Professor, Serial Entrepreneur and Transformational Speaker

I enjoyed and learned from Success Mindsets. I particularly resonated with Kissinger's "Fail Forward" message. Even others that I did not buy into, taught me something and that is what it is all about!

Dennis Andrews | Founder, Scar Tissue and bestselling author of TOO BLUE!

New entrepreneurs, seasoned CEOS, millennials, Gen-Xers…. everyone can find themselves in one of these stories. Give it a read - you'll find yourself applying the advice of these entrepreneurs to your workday.

Kader Sakkaria | Chief Technology and Data Officer at Ruffalo Noel Levitz, Best-selling Author of *Chaos By Design*

Success Mindsets really energized me. If you miss networking events or motivational speakers who hype you up and get you ready to succeed, then you'll love this book.

Rick Yvanovich | CEO, TRG

From practical steps to big-picture concepts, Success Mindset has it all! Once again, Alinka has collected a great group of entrepreneurs and leaders who have important and useful tales to share. Bravo!

Kevin L. Jackson | EO, GC GlobalNet and bestselling author of Click to TransformC

The authors in this anthology have been through it all - you can find advice for any industry, any setback, and any starting point! Friends, colleagues, family members, or even a new grad could all benefit from having this book on their shelves.

Glenn Hopper | CFO, Sandline Discovery and Author, Deep Finance: Corporate Finance in the Information Age

"Six percent of the way through Success Mindsets, I'd already written down three tactical suggestions I wanted to try in my own writing career. Thirteen percent of the way through, I found my heart in my throat at one author's heart-wrenching candor. Pretty soon, I stopped bothering to keep track of when I ingested the umpteenth piece of actionable advice or energizing inspiration and simply reveled in the spectacular variety of accomplishments and contributions different derivations of a 'success mindset' could empower. Whether your goal is to become a best-selling author, financially independent entrepreneur, mission-driven difference-maker, or anything in between, Success Mindsets deserves a home on your digital or physical bookshelf."

Trevor Macomber | Marketing Leader and Co-author of Chaos by Design: Tales of Empowerment on the Path to Digital Transformation

SUCCESS MINDSETS

HOW TOP ENTREPRENEURS
SUCCEED IN BUSINESS AND IN LIFE

Alinka Rutkowska • Aaron Poynton • Anjali Sharma • Ankit "Andy" Mehta
Areva Martin • Arvind Sharma • Bryan Collins • Catherine Bassick • David Kissinger
Deepak Syal • Diana Loomans • Grace Buckler • Hans Keirstead • J.D.R. Hawkins
J. J. Hebert • Jacklyn Ryan • Jermaine S. N. Tolbert • Jeroen Kraaijenbrink
Jody Steinhauer • Karl Shaikh • Kermit S. Randa • Kirsten Stendevad • Kris Safarova
Lee Murray • Marie Wiese • Michael Oborn • Nedra J. Barr • Paul O'Mahony
Raghavan V. Venugopal • Randy Green • Rick Orford • Sara Connell • Scott Montgomery
Sharesz T. Wilkinson • Sharon L. Ross • Shawn Johal • Shiv Gaglani • Steve Ryan
Steven Seiden • Trissa Tismal-Capili • Vandana S. Puranik

Leaders
Press

ISBN 978-1-63735-092-8 (pbk)
ISBN 978-1-63735-093-5 (ebook)

Print Book Distributed by Simon & Schuster
1230 Avenue of the Americas
New York, NY 10020

Library of Congress Control Number: 2021908925

Table of Contents

Introduction

When you read the Walt Disney quote, "It's kind of fun to do the impossible," challenges become a little less intimidating. You can take a deep breath, put a smile on your face, and walk into any room with the intention of *doing the impossible.*

When you read the Ralph Waldo Emerson quote, "What lies behind us and what lies before us are tiny matters compared to what lies within us," you focus, even just for a moment. You look closer at who you are rather than at what you have or the situation you are in. You feel more powerful, and everything around you *does* seem smaller than it did before.

And when you read the Henry David Thoreau quote, "It's not what you look at that matters—it's what you see," you stop and think. The way that you view your life, your career, your successes, your failures—they are all put into perspective. You begin to be more intentional about how you see these events and how you could possibly see something else. Something more productive, more hopeful, more motivational, perhaps?

Why are these quotes so powerful? Why do we experience a shift when we hear these words of wisdom?

They speak directly to our *mindset.* There is nothing more powerful than our mindset. If we live out our lives and careers with a success mindset, it will be much more fun to do the impossible, whatever the "impossible" looks like to you.

Our mindset shapes everything around us, from the car we are driving to the amount of money we have in the bank to the people who are working beside us. Think about it. Your mindset can turn your best friend into a backstabbing enemy, or $1 into riches or rags. The cold water that you jump into transforms into an invigorating morning activity. The mountain in front of you becomes a plaything. With just a shift in thinking, your embarrassing failures become pivotal, beneficial stepping stones on your path to success.

The esteemed authors that you will encounter in this anthology may become a source of inspiration, possible connections, and a source of advice to help you achieve the success that you want to achieve. I assume, judging by the fact that you picked up this anthology, that your mindset already perceives their stories and advice as helpful.

How wonderful is it that we have the ability to transform our entire world? The house we live in becomes a castle or a prison, depending on our mindset. The workout we do at home becomes a tiring chore or an exciting investment in our health. If we can see everything around us in an entirely new light thanks to our mindset, what else are we capable of?

You may just find the answer here. This anthology contains dozens of authors who credit their mindset to their success—whether that success is in the world of cybersecurity, wholesale retail, or law. Not all of these authors started their journey with a mindset geared toward success, of course. Throughout the course of this anthology, you will read many stories about when our authors decided to make a change and embrace a success mindset. A special person, lesson, failure, success, or life-changing event may have shaped their mindset into how they see the world today. Their mind may still remain malleable, and as they've found success in their industries they welcome the idea of growing, changing, and seeing things in new perspectives.

That's the important thing to keep in mind when reading about a success mindset—it's not permanent. You do not have to live with the same perspective of the world that you had yesterday. You do not have to have the same definition of success as your colleagues, family, former bosses, or world leaders. Your mindset is your own.

Mindset is critical to envisioning the path in front of us, whether it's completely obscure or perfectly paved. With a success mindset, all paths in front of you will *lead* to success. I know that this might sound extravagant or unrealistic, especially after the world has been shaken by so much grief, devastation, and loss. Our mindsets are constantly being challenged, doubted, and tested. But that's the beautiful thing about your mindset. Even in the toughest of times, after loss, heartbreak, or failure, your mindset can still look for lessons, bright spots, and solutions.

A success mindset isn't one that believes you have already achieved success—it just continues to tell you that, no matter what is blocking your path or hindering your ability to move forward, you will make it around, under, or over until you finally reach your goal.

And if you don't think this is possible, check in with your mindset.

Putting Ideas into Motion: How a Low Point in Life Led to a Successful Mindset

J. J. Hebert

J. J. Hebert is the nine-time award-winning author of four #1 Amazon bestsellers. Hebert is also the founder of MindStir Media, a top-ranked self-publishing company partnered with *Shark Tank's* Kevin Harrington and Mariel Hemingway. Hebert has appeared in major publications including *Forbes*, *Entrepreneur*, *Inc.*, *Business Insider* and *Yahoo Finance*. He's a writer for *Entrepreneur Magazine* and a member of the Forbes Business Council. He resides in New Hampshire with his wife and two children.

You've heard the most difficult thing about writing a book is putting words on that very first page. Even by drafting an opening sentence–one that you may very well delete later–you're breaking the icy pressure of expectation and taking a step toward turning your idea into something…tangible. It's not easy, but it's something you have to do if you're going to write that book.

Entrepreneurialism is the exact same way.

Every person can have a "next great idea." We all have thoughts and ideas that could change our lives, or maybe even change the world.

I've been fortunate enough to become a best-selling author and founder of a top-ranked self-publishing company, and throughout that journey, I've learned a very simple truth: having a great idea is not enough. To be successful, you have to *act* on that idea.

No one can climb a mountain without taking the first step; likewise, no one will put your ideas in motion for you. And, like many, it took me several years to truly lean into the idea of being a creator, entrepreneur, and businessman.

In my early days, I viewed success the same way as many fresh college graduates: a good job, a fulfilled life, and someday, a happy family.

That's what landed me a job in corporate America, working in sales and living my life in a way that was dictated by other people. My company and my boss were the ones who told me when and where I should be, for ninety percent of my time.

But still, I was happy. After all, I was on a path towards what I thought was a successful life.

Everything changed in 2009.

My entire life was uprooted one afternoon when my colleagues and I were herded into the break room and informed that the business was shutting down.

Soon, I'd be jobless.

If you've ever been in a similar situation, you know it's a *lot* to unpack emotionally. Stability has been ripped away from you.

A few of my co-workers cried. Several had been with the company for their entire working lives and now had nothing to show for it. Others, like me, stood in stunned silence while our brains reeled with thoughts, weighing uncertainties and grappling with our next steps.

Even now, over twelve years later, I remember a thought in particular coursing through my brain as I wrestled with what I was hearing: *this would be the last time that somebody else ever dictated my future employment.*

And that was the moment my life changed—the moment when I decided to set my ideas in motion and stop chasing the success that corporate America defined. From that day forward, I'd pursue the success that *I* defined.

No longer would I work forty-hour weeks for the corporate machine. I'd work for *myself.*

To be fair, I was no stranger to creative ideas. At the time I lost my job, I had just released my debut novel. By no means did I have one foot out the door, but I was positioning myself to leave the company if the book took off.

Deep down, I had been itching for freedom from corporate America all along.

From the moment I started writing that first novel, I had planned on self-publishing it. I was drawn to the idea of freedom and total control that self-publishing offered.

That said, I didn't want to self-publish with another platform. Instead, I wanted to truly do it all myself. That's why I decided to start a company called MindStir Media. I would own the company and keep all the creative decision-making to myself.

And my budget?

$700.

Seriously, I started the company with a total of $700. At the time, it was basically a passion project with just a glimmer of hope that it could someday be a business capable of supplementing my corporate salary.

In the days following my sudden unemployment, I never expected that my debut novel, *Unconventional,* would take off. To my amazement, it eventually sold 100,000 copies and hit #1 on multiple Amazon bestseller lists. Suddenly, I had income from a book I had written, and instead of spending the money, I pumped the majority of it back into MindStir Media to help build the company.

As my corporate ambition transitioned into entrepreneurial dreams, I learned that there's a big difference between *wanting* to leave your current work environment and actually having the mindset that's prepared to do so. The latter is what you can think of as a "success mindset."

To me, there are three common links between all success mindsets: bravery, creativity, and a little bit of craziness.

The bravery isn't necessarily easy to come by. Of the three, it's the one that needs to be developed the most. If you're rolling the dice on yourself, you're going to face some scary situations. Your next paycheck won't come on the 1st or 15th and you might have weeks of famine before finally enjoying a feast. But bravery will be learned or developed if you chase your dreams for long enough. Take my story as an example: I always longed to walk out on the entrepreneurial limb, but I never actually did it until I got a little push.

Next, creativity comes into play every time there's a problem that arises without an apparent solution. There's not a successful entrepreneur on planet Earth who lacks creativity. I've heard that "life is a highway," but my path has felt more like a mountain pass peppered with cliffs, landslides, gaping craters, roadblocks, and angry wildlife. Sometimes, to get from point A to point B, you've got to leap, fight, create, or innovate, and the solution will seldom be apparent.

And finally, a little bit of craziness comes in handy. You have to be willing to do things that others won't. Take risks. Make tough decisions. Throw caution to the wind and gamble on yourself. There's a reason most people don't own their own company or create their own rules for life. You need to be at least a tiny bit crazy to do so, and I mean that in the best possible way. If this sounds like you, embrace it.

If you have this mindset—this delicate balance of all three traits—it's a tool that will help you navigate through any plot twists that come your way. And trust me, there will be *a lot* of them—both good and bad.

For example, losing my job was the biggest of all plot twists, but it also is what helped me grow and develop my mindset of success from the early days of MindStir Media. Turns out, when you found a company around the same time you suffer an emotional gut-punch, you learn to roll with the punches quite well.

As I've overcome roadblocks on my path to grow MindStir Media, these punches have come with considerable frequency. I've seen a lot of commonalities between an entrepreneur and a boxer: both take punches, both stagger and occasionally fall, and to achieve success, both have to keep climbing back to their feet, keep pushing, and always keep fighting.

A lot of people claim that "anybody can be successful," but that's only true to an extent. Here's the reality: anybody can be successful *if* they are willing to work, learn, and set their ideas in motion. Achieving success isn't about being lucky or being in the right place at the right time. It's about taking initiative and creating opportunities for yourself, learning from your mistakes, and constantly working on your success mindset so that you're prepared for anything that might stand between you and your destination.

I've been fortunate enough to not only land four of my own books atop the Amazon bestsellers list, but to also see MindStir Media grow significantly over the years. At this point, my company has worked with thousands of authors, including celebrities and other high-profile creators and executives. My first client, Paula Wiseman, is also an Amazon best-selling author.

And there's still room for growth. In March 2020, MindStir Media received an endorsement from Kevin Harrington, a famous entrepreneur well-known for his work on *Shark Tank*. Kevin loved MindStir so much that he ultimately decided to partner with the company. He and his team appreciated that MindStir is run by a #1 best-selling author (me); they could quickly tell, based on some initial projects, that MindStir is a trustworthy company that can help take a book to the next level.

As I went from working for an empire to creating a publishing empire of my own, I've learned a few things that I'd like to share so that you can apply them and see if they work for you, too.

First, you must create your own opportunities. It's really easy to fall into the trap of thinking "it's just not meant to be." Instead, *make it be.* Believe it or not, I didn't happen to bump into Kevin Harrington in an elevator and use a carefully prepared pitch on him during our thirty-second ride together. I wasn't that lucky, and chances are, you won't be either. Instead, I sought out his partnership and approached him as strategically and intentionally as I could: through his son, Brian. After weighing my options, I decided that contacting his son via email, who also happens to be his business partner, was the best route. But the partnership never would have happened if I hadn't taken the initiative.

Next, I've learned the value of growth and expansion. When the early paychecks start coming in from an idea you created, it's very tempting to spend the money quickly and celebratorily. Is it wrong to celebrate your success? Not at all. In fact, I encourage you to do so! But I also encourage you to invest money back into your idea to help it grow even more. For me, that meant teaming up with publishing professionals from across the country: editors, designers, marketers, and any other talent that I identified as a value-adding contribution to

MindStir Media. There's a reason Amazon took *fourteen years* to become profitable—early on, growth and expansion is the most important thing you can do for your company or idea.

Finally, I've learned that in the world of entrepreneurialism, smart gambles take place every day. Some are impactful with a lot of potential consequences: should you invest money in Project X or Project Y? What is the best way to pitch an idea to this high-profile individual? But others are smaller, and some might even say insignificant, but they all matter greatly. For example, how you allocate your time is a great example of a smart gamble. There are only so many hours in a day, and we have other things in our life *besides* work, so you have to decide what's the best use of your time. For me, that might mean figuring out how to divide my time between clients, company growth opportunities, mentoring employees, and other daily activities. For you, it might be completely different. Regardless, we *all* have to figure out what's in our best interest to help us in our personal journey to success, and then we must take calculated risks that maximize our chance of making our dreams come true.

While the journey has had ups and downs, I'm very fortunate to be in the position I am today and I wouldn't change a single thing. Instead, my missteps along the way have helped me strengthen my success mindset, and I'm convinced that if we learn from our mistakes, our losses become victories in the end. Better yet, if you follow the advice in this chapter, it might save you scraping your knee a time or two.

With that in mind, I hope this chapter gives you not only inspiration but even more importantly, practical advice you can apply to your life immediately.

If you're interested in connecting, reach out at https://mindstirmedia.com or follow me on Twitter (@authorjjhebert).

Success in a S.N.A.P

Sara Connell

Sara Connell is a best-selling author and founder of Thought Leader Academy where she helps coaches, writers and entrepreneurs become successful, published authors and in demand speakers. She has been featured on *The Oprah Winfrey Show*, *Good Morning America*, *The View*, FOX, TEDx, and *Katie* (hosted by Katie Couric). Her writing has appeared in: *The New York Times*, *Forbes*, *Good Housekeeping*, and *Parenting*. Her first book *Bringing In Finn* was nominated for *ELLE magazine's* 2012 Book of the Year. For more information, visit www.saraconnell. com.

A while back, in the time of Gwen Stefani and grunge and 90210, there was a young girl who longed to be a writer. She had read lots of books and watched some movies and she understood that the way you KNEW you were destined (allowed) to be a writer was that a teacher would take you aside and tell you that you were special and give you extra books to read. This young girl even knew which teacher would be the one to bestow this honor and confirm her destiny. The teacher at the high school was a published author himself with a few books and a column in a national paper. She trembled with excitement the day he stood in front of the classroom, ready to hand back their first writing assignment of the year. He announced there was some real talent in the room and began calling the names of the gifted young writers. The girl listened and listened. She waited patiently. "Sa…" her heart beat fast, the moment of destiny had finally arrived, "…ndy." But her name was not called. The metal desk felt cold under her hands and the teacher's voice grew dim as if the sound had been erased from the room. In one instant, her dream was no longer hers and she felt like only an outline of herself.

Because the girl was not allowed to be a writer, she went to college and studied other people's writing. After graduation she was hired by an agency where she worked as a shadow creative, where men touched her when she didn't want them to and in protest she ate less and less until her bones stuck out from her shoulders and at night she lay awake reading books she wished she'd written.

Then one day, she was traveling for the agency job and she saw a bookstore in the airport. She ran inside just long enough to grab a book off the front table. She read during the entire plane ride. She read in the taxi. She stayed up until 3 o'clock in the morning reading that book. She was astounded! The author had written her story: the story of a young woman who'd experienced trauma, who'd stopped eating and then—most importantly–she'd shared what she did to get well. The woman in the book had done what she'd dreamed without anyone giving her any permission at all.

So even though the girl didn't believe she was good enough and wasn't at all sure she would succeed, the young girl who was now a young woman left the job and began to feed her body and she started to write.

***

A faux fairy-tale is admittedly an odd way to start a chapter on the success mindset but the start of this story demonstrates the lack of confidence I had while growing up and the end illustrates that alchemical choice point–the gateway to a confident mindset and our greatness that is available to us in every moment.

That moment when I finally started writing led me to publish my first book, find a literary agent, appear on *Oprah* and be published in *The New York Times*. The journey revealed four steps that I now have used to achieve just about every goal I've set to date and have taught to hundreds of writers, entrepreneurs, and thought leaders with similarly positive results. I call the four steps SNAP. I'm going to share them with you here so you can use them to create success in anything you desire to do.

S stands for **STAY IN THE YES**.

Like Elizabeth Gilbert states in her book *Big Magic*, I believe that visions/ideas/inspiration come from somewhere greater than our thinking mind. We receive higher inspiration constantly, yet the thinking (ego) mind gives us less than five seconds before besieging us with reasons we are too lazy or old or uneducated or not *something* enough to achieve our dream.

Our first step is to stay in the Yes. I spent years depressed and avoiding my vision because I believed I needed someone else in a position of authority to give me permission to go for it. I kept asking for "signs"–making "The Universe" the authority. I love a good sign (a billboard or song or friend or interview I'm listening to that affirms exactly what I need to hear to move me forward), but what I now believe after coaching thought leaders and writers for seventeen years, is that THE VISION IS THE SIGN.

The success mindset starts with authorizing ourselves–then bringing ourselves back to that YES every month, every day, every hour. In those years leading up to writing my first book, I idolized authors and believed they knew infallibly that they were great, worthy, geniuses. Then I'd listen to interviews with them and hear that Maya Angelou and Anne Lamott and Lily King and Cheryl Strayed worried constantly that they weren't talented enough, that their work was crap, that no one would ever want to read it. I realized the real difference between Brené, Maya, Cheryl, and all the aspiring authors was that these writers kept writing–they kept going–they stayed in their YES.

N is for **NEW ROAD MAP.**

I love the phrase "success leaves clues." Our mind loves to focus on problems and position every new goal as a Sisyphean task. The ego is trying to protect us from humiliation, rejection, and failure–things none of us would happily endure, but the problem is that the safety zone and success rarely cohabitate. It is only when we forgo safety and create our new map of adventure that we summit the mountain.

My antidote to the safety undertow: **The Treasure Map**. Find three to ten people who have succeeded at your current goal. You don't have to know these people or ever meet them in person. Listen to podcast interviews, YouTube videos, read articles people have written about them, consume their memoirs or biographies. Note the specific things they cite as having been critical to their success. Once you've completed your research, circle any actions or strategies that are common amongst them.

When I wanted to become a published author I listened to hundreds of authors with different paths of meeting publishers and developing their craft, but the one thing that every single one of them said was that they had a daily/consistent writing practice. At that point, I was only writing when I felt inspired, when I had the right pen, when the lighting was just so, when it wasn't raining. As soon as I did this exercise, I started writing every day. Big surprise, I soon had a manuscript I could start showing to people. This may sound obvious (what kind of writer doesn't understand she needs to sit her a-- in front of the computer and churn out some words) but it was listening to every single person say the same thing that moved me into a motivated (success) mindset and produced critical action.

The common denominators will tell you everything you need to go all the way with your vision.

A is for **ACTION.**

This book is about mindset but to take action, I need an optimal mindset–otherwise I'll go hide under the bed or start cleaning my closets obsessively or shopping at Target online or eating frozen yogurt by the gallon instead of doing all those juicy actions I identified in my treasure map. My favorite success mindset strategy for action is what I call THE POWER 100.

I created this practice after reading an article on Literary Hub about a writer who was so tired of rejection that she decided to quit writing completely. Before she officially abandoned her dream, she got the crazy idea to set a goal of getting one hundred rejections. It was as if she were shooting the moon in the card game Hearts. If she set out to get rejections, they wouldn't be so debilitating, she reasoned. At the end of the year, she'd received many rejections but she'd also had three pieces published, won a contest, and was granted a writing residency. It was the most successful year she'd ever had as a writer. The exercise kept her in the game and it gave me new inspiration.

I wasn't brave enough to try for rejections but I was up for committing to sending one hundred submissions of my writing.

I tried the strategy and had my most prolific year of publishing ever. I tried the one hundred on other goals as well. Every time I'd do one hundred of something (income goals, sales conversations, dates with my son to become more present, connecting with friends) the same phenomenon happened—I'd far exceed what I'd done before—often beyond what I'd imagined was possible.

When we put all of our focus on ACTION (versus the results of our action) we become exponentially more focused and productive. As a writer, I went from checking my writing submission responses like a fourteen year old hoping her crush would text back, to churning out new stories and firing them off to magazines so I could move closer to my one hundred goal. I didn't have time to doubt myself and my abilities, I needed to get that next submission online. The Power 100 not only 100x our productivity, but it also creates a success mindset loop. We feel more confident because we're being the prolific, brave, motivated people we want to be. That confidence energy sprinkles like fairy dust across our websites, conversations, zoom meetings, and emails. I offer The Power 100 to all my clients—whether they are pitching articles, literary agents, publishers, TEDx, speaking stages, podcasts, or the media. To date, it always delivers results.

Focus on massive action, and the desired outcome will naturally occur.

If you want to supercharge The Power 100, I offer the P in SNAP.

P stands for Future **PULL.**

If I were only allowed a single success mindset strategy—it would be this. Put simply, the Future PULL is any method we use to experience our vision fulfilled as ALREADY DONE. Ancient Buddhists practitioners called this Thinking From the End, modern coaches might call this Future Pacing. The way I like to practice this most is like this:

Affirm your #1 goal of the moment—the thing that when you achieve it would have you doing naked cartwheels on Instagram Live. Now, if you have a friend who is not put off by weird things, call them up and tell them your goal and have a brief conversation about it as if it's a few months in the future and the goal is achieved. Only use the present tense (no I hope, or wish, or it would be so cool IF)–you are time travelling here–to the place where you've already done this thing and it's amazing, and awesome, and even better than you hoped. The key here is to generate the consciousness (energy state) and emotions of this thing as already being your reality. The subconscious mind does not distinguish between imagination and reality–so you talking, feeling, thinking, and vibrating the fulfillment of your vision day after day will eventually create a tipping point where your brain thinks it's actually happened. When we reach this state, it's only a matter of time (usually not very long) before that's exactly what happens. Future Pull acts as the drain cleaner to resistance, fear, doubt, and subconscious blocks (which by the way are the only things that can actually keep us from achieving any dream).

You can also future pull yourself. Now when I pitch a story, article, or talk, I'll send myself a YES email the same day. If I'm sending one hundred pitches, I'll send one hundred acceptances, congratulations, one hundred YES emails to myself. Of course I know I'm writing these, but there's something about seeing all those re: Congratulations! swarming my inbox that lifts my heart, keeps me going, and makes me believe it's already done. I don't have extensive hard data yet, but over the past five years, I've tracked my own and my clients' success rates and early indicators show that the Future PULL accelerates goal fulfillment by 30-60 percent.

When you STAY IN THE YES, adopt a NEW ROAD MAP, take ACTION with The Power 100, and Future PULL, you activate the magic–you become UNSTOPPABLE.

Diligence, A Family Matter

Jacklyn Ryan

Jacklyn Ryan is a designated CCIM (Certified Commercial Investment Member) in commercial real estate. She analyses numbers, reads contracts, and interacts successfully. Then a crisis happens. Our professional world is put on hold. We are thrust into a world where we have to trust the medical professions taking care of our loved ones.

Jacklyn calls herself a reluctant expert in home health care. Dealing with home health care agencies involving her parents, she learned unscrupulous agencies hire minimum wage employees, thereby increasing their profits.

Her mission is to expose fraud in senior care. In writing her book, she has learned of many families with similar experiences. She is determined to improve caregiving because it is a rapidly growing industry. Robots cannot replicate hands-on human care for vulnerable families. People are more determined that their loved ones remain home rather than moving them to a facility.

Due to her efforts, a local house representative proposed a State House Bill that all caregivers be fingerprinted and FBI Rap Background checked. This is an ongoing, real-time background check. This is a warning signal to families with aging parents and will hopefully raise the bar so our loved ones will receive better quality care. For more information, visit www. caregiverscaretakers.com.

My phone rang at 5:30 a.m. It was Dave, dad's friend. He said, "Your dad has fallen, and he's hurt bad." I said, "Ok, I'll be right there." Dad's house is within an eyeshot of my house. I got there in minutes and dialed 911. "My dad's fallen and hurt himself." I had to repeat the address three times and was switched to a different operator once. **Lesson**: A Life Alert® device would've been helpful.

He was diagnosed with a broken hip. Once he was discharged from the hospital, then rehab, I was referred to a home health care agency. I hired "First Agency." Any home health care agency should be reputable, right? **Lesson:** Always, in anything, interview three. Do your due diligence.

I naively assumed First Agency would have qualified people that would, first, arrive, secondly, arrive on time, and lastly, be engaging with my dad. After ten caregivers in eight weeks and having to unexpectedly adjust my work schedule because these people were not dependable, a woman around my age, early fifties at the time, Claire, arrived. She arrived on time, was engaging, and had a bright smile. Our family and dad liked her. Dad was eighty-two at the time and struggling with basic Assisted Daily Living (ADL) tasks after the hip fracture.

I stopped by to see dad one morning a few months later. I noticed a $900 tire receipt on the counter. What? Claire and dad were gone in his truck. I looked at Claire's tires, and sure enough, they were brand new. I alerted my family, and we arranged a meeting with dad and Claire. Because it had been so difficult to find someone to be with dad, we thought we could have a meeting with the two of them. Dad was apologetic, more so to Claire, because they got caught. I said, "Claire, if there's anything you need, let us know." Dealing with this incident upfront, we thought, would put an end to any future problems. So wrong! As we call it, they went "further underground." **Lesson**: We should have notified First Agency, and they would've fired her.

My brother and I shared the Health Care Power of Attorney (POA), but I always handled everything. A few years earlier, I had taken dad to have quadruple bypass surgery. Later, he broke both hips at different times, and I sat with him at the hospital every time. My dad was an alcoholic and heavy smoker. One evening, he drank so much, he fell and was rushed to the hospital. This was all under Claire's watchful eye. He went through the trauma and hallucinations of detox.

He had literally burned up his esophagus. The doctor told him, "If you drink alcohol anymore, you will die."

At First Agency, Claire and another caregiver, Mary, cared for dad. Mary later moved to "Second Agency." Eventually, at First Agency, we began missing bills. Later, there were billing errors. We learned the comptroller was billing for overtime and embezzling the difference! I had previously met the owner, so I copied him on questions about the billings. I last heard the police escorted the comptroller out in handcuffs. That is when we asked Claire about transferring to "Second Agency."

A year later, dad had leg surgery due to plaque in his arteries. Alcohol was no longer thinning his blood, and cigarettes were clogging his arteries. There had been some previous minor incidences that caused me to become even more suspicious of Claire. I cringed when I overheard Claire telling him that "no one but me can take the best care of you!" Much time had already passed, if I confronted Claire about anything, I know dad would have defended her, and it would push me further away from him. Why? Because dad had disclosed to his friend at one point, if he were younger, he would've married her–dad was in love with his caregiver!! I had a sense of powerlessness. It was an impossible situation.

Over time, so many stories were told to me about dad and Claire that I had to decide who was the more guilty? Claire, for manipulating dad? Or me, for not telling my brothers. I could not bear the burden any longer of hearing and knowing so much.

In 2017, dad wanted to go to Jackson Hole for this eighty-fifth birthday. Claire let the family know, and one of my brothers arranged the trip. Actually, Claire had claimed the trip was her idea because she and dad had planned to go by themselves. I guess she realized that didn't look right. My brother arranged the trip with two private airplanes to carry all twenty-three family passengers to celebrate dad's birthday in Wyoming.

After returning from the family trip that Claire was a part of, my brothers, myself, and two other caregivers met with Second Agency to tell them of Claire's manipulations. Dad had paid for her grandchildren's summer camp, Claire's son was living in dad's rental house and paying rent money to dad that he would then give to Claire. Additionally, he made one caregiver take him to Claire's house so they could visit while she was off duty and away from him! Dad felt like he just had to be around her and call her often. Claire bragged to the other caregivers about the trip and gifts she received from dad. Claire always spoke negatively about the other caregivers and of me. How do low-life people make themselves feel more important? By putting other people down. Claire, at one point, told me that she had been in jail a few years earlier for meth charges. Remember that smile? Her teeth weren't real!

I brought up to the agency that Claire had disclosed she had a jail record. The agency owner showed me her background check. I will never forget that. They had accepted Claire's transfer, knowing she had a record! He was not apologetic. He just smiled. They did not want to lose this account.

The Second Agency had a meeting with Claire, and our family had a meeting with dad. A few days later, dad wanted to blame me for all the trouble. Why? Because I was the closest to him. Abusive people always hurt those closest to them.

The Second Agency put Claire on notice. She signed an agreement not to violate the terms of "not speaking negatively of others," "not accepting money or gifts," "to notify me promptly of any health issues with dad," and a whole list of other regulations. She was not fired. One of the honest caregivers quit. She couldn't believe Claire would remain after everything was disclosed! **Lesson**: When running a business, be honorable. Even if it costs you money and the loss of an account. Good people get hurt otherwise, and you will lose, if not the money, your reputation.

Three years have passed since that meeting. For a while, things seemed on track. Sometimes, I would stop by their office and talk about things I thought they might not be aware of about Claire. I believed they cared.

In 2020, because I took pictures of three receipts that totaled about $400 of groceries in two weeks to feed a skinny little man and texted them to Claire, asking, "Do you have enough groceries to last a while?" Irritated by this, she convinced dad I was after his money. He removed me as his Health Care POA without discussion. I suspect I was also removed because I highlighted daily care sheets where something was missing or questioned odd spendings. The Second Agency was tired of me keeping an eye on dad and their caregivers.

The other honest caregiver was later fired because, as she disclosed to me, "the agency just doesn't care to hear the truth and deal with the issues." Everything the other caregiver told the agency was soft-pedaled to my brothers. Once I was removed, communication ceased. **Lesson:** Do not become friends with people who care for your loved ones. When a company receives over **$200K annually** from one account, do you really think they care? The national cost of care per year is $4,000 per month. Around-the-clock in-home care averages $16,743 per month. **Lesson:** Always be critical of where information is coming from, particularly if the source is biased.

My brother, who took over as POA, lives thirty minutes away. One time when dad had fallen, it took him two hours to arrive. I was there in minutes but could do nothing. Dad was hurt, but my brother told him to wait on him to arrive. While we waited, I told him I could've had him to the hospital by now, but he removed me as POA. I asked dad why. He replied I was after his money. I told him I didn't need his money. He replied, "I know that." No, none of this makes sense.

A year has passed since being removed as dad's Health POA. There is not a solution to my personal story. We get along better because I only see him a few minutes once a week. He cannot blame me for anything, and I have resolved I cannot worry about him as he made his own decisions. However, let me transition into what I am working on to improve the situation for others.

By profession, I'm in commercial real estate. I am licensed in the states of Texas and Arkansas. When renewing my Texas real estate broker's license in early 2020, I had to complete extra paperwork after finishing my continuing education. It was called the FBI RapBack background check. I thought, "What's this?" I researched it and why it was a requirement in Texas. FBI Rapback is an ongoing, real-time background check. It is not only required upon employment or once a year. It is ongoing, real time! Think of it this way: suppose a caregiver was selling drugs and was arrested but had a good job. They might have enough vacation time, or sick leave built up to handle taking off for court dates. The employer would never know. However, with ongoing, real-time background checks, the State Police would notify the employer. This was implemented in Texas because the

Real Estate Commission learned that felons were involved in real estate transactions! **Lesson**: If there's a problem, you need to be diligent in finding the solution.

I have been fingerprinted in both states, another requirement of being licensed in real estate. Caregivers in Arkansas are not fingerprinted! I contacted many legislators and finally got one's ear. This is only because he is familiar with family caregiver issues. He has proposed a House Bill that all caregivers of daycare, teen facilities, and senior care be fingerprinted. He proposed implementing the FBI Rapback Program. Fingerprinting might pass. The State of Arkansas Police database needs to be upgraded to coincide with the FBI database. So this might be presented again later.

I am contemplating running for state legislature in the next election. The legislature in my district was not very encouraging but sympathetic to my issue. People are more determined than ever to keep their loved ones in their own homes rather than moving them to an assisted living facility. It is very important to have a family discussion about how your loved one wants to spend the last quarter of their life.

Documents need to be in proper order. My mother had a trust, but neither my brother nor I could review it until she passed. Yes, everything was split equally, but the one page I needed was…blank. There was not a list of accounts, names, and phone numbers. I chased documents for six months before everything was closed. **Lesson**: Get documents in order.

You can review senior care resources on my website and find a site to hire a caregiver directly, avoiding an agency. You can pay for a background check. I find better-qualified caregivers on this website than paying an agency $20+/hour when they pay their employees around minimum wage. There is a resource featuring a newsletter that offers guidance and blogging forums to ask questions. **Lesson**: Do research! Don't wait for a crisis to happen, be prepared. There is a free questionnaire that addresses some legal questions and how to qualify an agency/caregiver on my website: www.caregiverscaretakers.com.

This is not your typical business chapter, but it is something you might have to deal with unexpectedly. We are dealing with businesses that we think should care. Some do, some don't. If you find a qualified, caring caregiver, treat them like gold because they are. Just be cautious!

The Wondering Expert, or How to Have Success Without a Plan

Jeroen Kraaijenbrink

Jeroen Kraaijenbrink is an accomplished strategy educator, speaker, writer and consultant with over two decades of experience bridging academia and industry. He empowers people and organizations to discover, formulate, and execute their future plans by providing them with strategic guidance. In doing so, he enables them to realize their greatest ambitions.

Drawing from cognitive psychology, humanism, martial arts, Saint Benedict, and a wide range of other sources, he is the author of numerous articles on strategy, sustainability, and personal leadership and five books: *Strategy Consulting*, *No More Bananas*, *Unlearning Strategy*, and *The Strategy Handbook*, a two-volume practical guide to strategy. He is an active *Forbes* contributor where he writes about strategy, leadership, and how to help you embrace the complexity and uncertainty of this world.

He has a PhD in industrial management, teaches strategy at the University of Amsterdam Business School, and has helped many midsized and larger companies across the engineering, manufacturing, healthcare, and financial services industries.

Jeroen is the originator of the *Strategy Manifesto,* envisioning what strategy could and should be like in order to live up to its promise to provide effective guidance to 21st century organizations. For more information, visit www.strategymanifesto.com.

I'm the strategy guy but for most of my working life, I didn't have much of a vision or any goals other than being successful. That may sound rather awkward, but I'll explain why it isn't. In fact, it reflects what has become one of the key elements of my view on strategy: that strategy—and anything else in life—doesn't necessarily start with a clear vision, mission, or goals. These unfold while wondering and wandering around from day to day, week to week, and year to year. And yet, there is a strategy.

This might sound familiar to you, probably not the exact details but the lack of conscious direction in my career path. When I was a college graduate, I was given the opportunity to do a PhD, so I did a PhD. Four years later, I was given the opportunity to become an assistant professor, so I became a tenured assistant professor. And once I was on this trajectory, I didn't have to think much about my goals anymore: as assistant professor you are supposed to aspire to become a full professor, have a job for life, and appreciate a reliable income and pension. And for that you need to do one thing: publish like crazy in the best journals in your field. So, that's your goal and that's the journey I embarked on.

Looking for Impact (and Recognition)

Once I was an associate professor, though, things changed. I started to rethink my career. The next step would be becoming a full professor. And then? Would I be happy? My conclusion was that I wouldn't. On the contrary, it actually frightened me because it would mean that my entire career was already set in stone and in a direction that didn't really fit me. But if this would not be my career, what then? Does that sound familiar?

While working at the university, I had been involved in its startup incubator and I also had begun to do a little bit of executive education. What I loved about this work was the immediate impact it had. Instead of waiting and hoping for accepted journal publications and citations, I suddenly had an immediate visible impact on the life and work of entrepreneurs and managers. And, not unimportantly, it also gave me immediate recognition and appreciation of a real person who was happy with how I had helped them. Something I apparently needed dearly.

From there on, my ideas about my career changed quite radically. I wanted more of this: more impact on more managers and entrepreneurs, thereby helping more organizations to become more successful (and thereby also making more money with less effort and less stress). So, I stepped out of the world of academia. Not at once, and never fully, but I gradually left university and became an entrepreneur myself: an independent strategy consultant and trainer.

What It Took: A Wondering Expert Mindset

Leaving a tenured job at a university raised questions for the people around me. Why leave a respected job and the opportunity to become a professor? And why would you leave the comfort and certainty of a tenured job and take so much risk? But it never felt like that. For me, the real risk was ending up in a job where I would be unhappy. For me, making the step felt like *reducing* risk. The right mindset, I believe, is to look at the big picture to weigh risk and to factor in your opportunity costs: the risk of *not* doing something.

Making the decision meant that I had to figure out things myself—because suddenly my goals weren't given anymore. I had never been a consultant or entrepreneur and had never really thought about what I wanted "to become." I still don't really know. And maybe that is the key: don't focus on where you want to end up, but focus on who you are and what you can do next.

I like to call this the "Wondering Expert" mindset. The expert part is most obvious. For me, it means that I am fully invested in business strategy as my one and only topic. I study it, I teach it, I coach it, I write about it, I train it—I live it, you may say, and have for over two decades now. The heart of this is that I do as many different things as possible, but all focused on one single topic: strategy. This has enabled me to develop deep, and at the same time, differentiated knowledge and skills.

The wondering part means always being open and willing to stop one thing and start another. Throughout my career thus far, I've started a lot of different things and stopped just a few less. And that's the point: never give up exploring and trying out new things. And never think you are there, know it all, or should proceed along a chosen path just for the sake of having invested in it. Stay a novice, curious and eager to learn—wonder.

A Wondering Expert mindset also means a third thing to me. It is not just an outward journey to look for new things you can do. It is just as much an inward journey, discovering your unique perspective on things. What I have found is that focusing on your intuition and following your unique view on the world (the world of strategy in my case) makes you far more interesting and valuable than becoming just another commoditized expert. And it feels much better, too, because you start to see that you, as a person, have something to bring to this world and that people respect you for who you are, not for what you have copied from others.

No One Said Things Would Be Easy

My career is not one great success story. In fact, I've never really seen it as a success—until recently. As I said, I've stopped many things and this was not because they were so successful. I've tried to team up with others to form a venture not once, not twice, but four times and each attempt was equally unsuccessful—with the exception of the last time, which was by far the least successful of all and ended up in quite an aggressive breakup. Furthermore, riding the COVID-19 e-learning wave, I've invested heavily in developing an online learning platform, which I have stopped, too.

But none of this felt like a failure or a waste of time. It mostly felt like a relief and opportunity to do the next thing based on the experience I gained and that fitted me even better than what I did before. As the cliché goes, I learned a lot. But more importantly, each thing I tried served as a stepping stone for other, better, more interesting activities and brought me in touch with helpful new people. For me, the key to a success mindset is to keep on finding out what success looks like to you and update your ideas about it along the journey.

What I found and still find most challenging throughout this journey is to insist on being the Wondering Expert—especially the expert part. Self-doubt is undeniably my biggest pitfall. Am I doing the right things? Who am I to call myself an expert? Can I do this? Shouldn't I have clear goals like everyone is telling me? And, why can't I be normal?

Very unproductive thoughts, but very real to me. And very core to the whole Wondering Expert mindset as well. After all, the whole idea of it is to keep on wondering and develop your own unique perspective on how things are and on how they should be. This means that this mindset is both precious to me as well as a burden.

But the precious part weights far more. Because it works for me. It has brought me where I am and even though being successful hasn't been part of the vocabulary while growing up, I can now confidently say that I am successful in what I do and that my approach can be one of the roads to success.

The Role of Luck

I've been lucky. Not in the lottery or casino sense that great unexpected things happened to me. I mean in the sense of being privileged. Even though my parents were both working class and had not overly much to spend on their four children, I am a white male, living in a wealthy country, with the ability to go to a good school and university and choose the life that I want. And I've also been lucky with the intellectual and cognitive abilities I've been born with, so the preconditions for success were there.

But besides these preconditions, I believe that the primary source of my personal success is mindset. Yes, skills and persistence matter, but there are many people with better skills, and certainly with more persistence. One might even say that part of my Wondering Expert approach is giving up when things become too hard or unpleasant. And yet, I believe it is this mindset–the willingness to try new things and leave old things behind–which has brought me the most.

The Three Things I Learned

I don't know whether I can vigorously recommend my approach to success to everyone. After all, a key part of the mindset described is to do things in your unique way–which includes not following common advices that may have worked for others. But, since it worked for me, there are probably others for which it will work too, especially experts in their particular fields. So, based on what I learned, here are my three takeaways.

1. **You don't need goals to be successful.** It is an accepted belief that you need to set ambitious goals and need persistence to be successful. That may indeed be one road. But my own journey has shown that without goals and without that level of persistence, you can be successful too. If you have the drive to move on, to move forward, to do better than today, then your goals will unfold throughout the journey. As long as you feel the urge to be successful, you will find a way.

2. **Discover and leverage your uniqueness.** Your uniqueness is the only thing in this world that you can bring which others cannot. Therefore, finding out how you are different in terms of knowledge, skills, viewpoints, or anything else, and leveraging this uniqueness is a key ingredient of success in both business and your personal life. It makes life more fun, relaxed, and rewarding.

3. **Dare to stop, especially if you are invested in something.** I've seen too many people stick to their habits, jobs, and lives and become dissatisfied, frustrated or otherwise unhappy. They have chosen the comfort of certainty about what they have over the uncertainty of something new and possibly better. I don't mean to radically break with the past. I mean to pivot, change, dare to take the next small or bigger step that you believe will be better, even if you don't know where you will end up.

And Now?

Adopting the mindset described has helped me a lot. Not just in business, but also in my private life. A key reason for this is that instead of asking *Why?* I tend to ask *Why not?* Why wouldn't I move to another country (and move back again), why wouldn't I quit my job and become independent (and get another job and quit again to become independent again), why wouldn't I try and write a book (and write a few more), and why wouldn't I welcome a foster daughter into our home (and agree to let her go once it turned out that worked for the best).

This mindset has also shaped how I work with clients in my strategy consulting work. My entire approach to strategy as I teach it, apply it, and write about it in my books, is built around the principles described above. In a world that is as complex and uncertain as ours, strategy is not about insisting on predefined goals, about mimicking what others do, or about following the trends in society. These are important, but more important is discovering the inherent uniqueness of your organization and leveraging it in a flexible way, moving away from the obstacles that pop up, and riding the opportunity waves that come your way.

In this sense, life and business aren't that different and I believe the same mindset can bring you success in both. Therefore, I try to practice as I preach and preach as I practice. Live your life as you think it should be lived and embrace the opportunities that come to you.

If you'd like to learn more about me or my work, you can google me (there's just one Jeroen Kraaijenbrink), connect via LinkedIn, or visit www.jeroenkraaijenbrink.com.

You Can't Be Everywhere

Marie Wiese

Marie Wiese is the author of the award-winning business book *You Can't Be Everywhere,* a book she wrote in 2016 to help small business owners tackle the web. She founded Marketing CoPilot in 2006, an award-winning digital marketing agency that has helped hundreds of companies turn their websites into lead generation and sales machines.

She is a growth advisor with start-ups at innovation centers in Ontario, Canada, host of the podcast *Women Talk Tech* and an instructor at the University of Toronto where she teaches business presentations and public speaking.

Marie resides just north of Toronto, Canada, in the hometown where she grew up. She has three children, two grandchildren, and a wonderful 1978 VW Camper Van called Louceel that she drives every weekend with whomever wants to climb onboard. For more information, visit https://marketingcopilot.com/.

1969. Let It Be.

There was a lovely blur outside the window. The car I was travelling in with my mother, brother, and aunt was making a 300-mile voyage on a warm June day in 1969. My family was moving, and I was packed up with my brother and our belongings in the back seat.

I do not recall what was playing on the radio, but I learned later in life that my mother loved John Lennon. I imagine in my mind the lyrics to *Let It Be*.

My mother was driving and talking to her sister in the passenger seat. One minute she was there. Then she was not.

Glass, metal, tumbling, and deafening silence.

This car accident claimed the life of my mother and brother. I was five years old. My mother was twenty-three and my brother was two. My father, who was not in the car, was devastated.

The "accident," as we later came to refer to it, became the source of my ambition. It was trauma that formed my ideas about what success meant. When you lose something important early in life, you chase success as if your life depends on it. You need to stand on your own fast. You cannot rely on the things most people rely on as you grow into adulthood.

I survived. Survival became a theme that I confused with success. It became a race to see if I could overcome the next hurdle. This desire to succeed went uncontrolled and unchecked for many years.

The accident did quite a number on my leg, breaking my femur and requiring me to walk with crutches for several months, but I was young and recovered physically very quickly. After the accident I lived with my grandparents. My father moved in with his parents in a neighbouring town and began rebuilding his life.

Before long, I could run again. I found that when I did, everything except what I was running toward fell out of focus. Everything and everyone else around me melted into a blur. The blur helped me forget.

Basketball became a focus. Singing became a focus. Grades in school became a focus. I launched myself into each activity so everything else fell away.

My father remarried. I returned to live with him and his new wife. They had two children of their own. I liked them best when their faces were a blur in the bleachers or auditorium. My new family celebrated my successes both on the court and in the classroom. They provided fuel for the fire by being hard on me and demanding the best.

Neither my father nor stepmother brought up my mother or my brother in conversation.

My university was carefully selected to be a comfortable distance away from my father and his new family. I excelled academically at university as I had done in high school. I sprinted my way through my studies, letting campus life whiz by. By the time I bolted across the convocation stage, I had secured a respectable job in public relations and unlike my university pals who were taking time off to travel, I was working two jobs and pushing myself and my resume towards constant new goals.

I climbed through the ranks two steps at a time, and by twenty-nine, I was a director of marketing at a large bank. Getting promoted was straightforward: when a higher-up asked for something, I said yes to everything and then got it done.

For nearly a decade, I kept running and passing through my life in a not so lovely blur, in constant motion of ticking all the boxes and being everywhere to have it all. At twenty-five, I married my husband Dave, had two children, bought and renovated two houses, and had tripled my starting salary by the time I was thirty.

I was proud of my success. I ran to the next challenge two steps at a time so the rest of the world could be a blur.

Until I tripped. Metaphorically.

My life then became a series of car wrecks from which it got harder and harder to recover emotionally, physically, and mentally.

2000. A Hard Day's Night.

In 2000 I went down hard, and it took me two years to get back up.

In 2000 I was thirty-five. I had just given birth to my third child, and it was one of the loneliest and toughest years of my life. During my pregnancy I was diagnosed with a bowel condition that put me in and out of hospital. I spent a month of my pregnancy in the hospital losing weight and trying not to give birth prematurely to my baby girl. They induced me at thirty-four weeks. Six weeks following her birth I had bowel surgery that did not go well. I was unable to get out of bed for the next two months and unable to hold my baby. A year later I had to have another round of surgery.

Despite this, I was determined to go back to work three months after giving birth. I missed the blur, that shapeless wash of energy that drove me toward success. I missed being everywhere.

I had invested as an employee in the software company I was working at, trying to capitalize on the dot com boom. In 2001 we took a double whammy. The bottom had fallen out of the tech sector and the anchor clients we had to help grow the business in the US market were based in the World Trade Centre. The combination of 9/11 and the dot-com bubble burst scared the preferred shareholders, and they held a fire sale.

I lost my investment. I lost my bowels. I lost my ability to be a mother to my children. Suddenly, it was 1969 all over again and I was in the back seat of a car watching the crash in slow motion.

I had been running so hard and for so long that people standing next to me felt uncomfortable, almost invasive. I wanted to keep moving forward, but the combination of emotional, physical, and mental exhaustion held me down.

I thought about everything I had achieved. The success I had celebrated in my life. And suddenly I was acutely aware of having nothing. The corporate racetrack on which I had been running belonged to someone else. If I was going to run, I wanted the race to be my own.

2004. Strawberry Fields Forever.

With the loss of my health and my business investment, I convinced my husband to sell our house in the city and move to the country. I wanted to move the kids to give them a come-home-when-the-streetlights-come-on kind of childhood. I wanted them to enjoy the freedom of rural life.

A move to the country would be good for everyone.

I threw myself into country life with the same energy I gave to everything. I started my own business. I managed the building of our new home. I learned to snowshoe. I put my kids in sports and activities that had us out of the house six days a week. I did what I always did except now I was doing it between farms of strawberries and open skies.

I had changed my surroundings. I had not healed my mind.

2014. While My Guitar Gently Weeps.

My mindset until 2014 was to go as fast as possible to get to the next step. Although there had been a myriad of signs to slow down and even stop, I did not see them. I just kept moving to embrace the blur.

In March 2014, my husband was diagnosed with a rare, tumour-based cancer treated with invasive surgery. I took six months off to look after him while keeping the momentum rolling on the home front. For the first time in my life, I could not fight through the situation and get to the other side. Too much was out of my control.

Over the next seven years, I almost lost my business due to financial mismanagement and the strain that constant periods of time off took to look after Dave. The recurrence of his cancer meant he was in the hospital consistently from 2018 onwards, moving towards inoperable cancer that robbed him of his quality of life but not his will to live.

2021. Here Comes the Sun.

It is 4:00 a.m. and I am in bed crying.

My husband is next to me snoring lightly, barely audible above a howling windstorm outside. I do not let people see me cry. I was taught early on that tears are best kept private; that they are for damsels in distress, not for successful businesswomen. We did not talk about the "accident" and we certainly did not cry publicly.

The roar outside is reduced to a dull drone in a still room. The only other sounds come from a dying man's restful breaths.

And a tired woman's ragged ones.

My husband's chest lifts and falls beside me; every time a gust of wind beats at our bathroom air vent, his mouth twitches beneath his grey-flecked beard. His type of cancer takes most people within eighteen months of their diagnosis. He has survived seven years and believes it is because of me. My survival skills have sustained us both.

Whenever I work early or late, which, thankfully, happens less than it used to, I lie down on the single bed in my office that doubles as a couch. It is hard to sleep in there, though. I worked hard to give my office a sense of movement and energy. It has a brilliant blue wall with lots of light and pictures. Pictures dedicated to the family I have and the family I lost.

Thanks to Dave, there is no longer a blur. Just startling clarity. I understand quite painfully what my life is about to become. I understand the decisions I must make, the conversations I must have; with friends, family, my children, and myself.

All that running has come to a grinding halt and I can now sum up in one word the definition of success: *resilience*.

It is not the running to avoid pain that makes you successful. It's slamming right into it like a brick wall and having a moment of clarity that no matter what you do, no matter how many seven-step books you read, success happens when you least expect it. It is not a formula. It is a life lived with resilience.

It is the ability to watch the sun come up day after day and be tough enough to go on.

My husband is a tough guy. He has been positive all the way through his various operations and cancer treatments. This man who I love, who quietly watched me through my own blurry life, needs me now.

My children's father is dying. I watched my mother die. Fifty years later I finally understand. It is an echoed lamentation from my own childhood that cuts deep.

Now, I realize what I mistook for success was merely a reaction to trauma. Ticking the boxes is not success.

When I think about the times I felt I had not quite made it; when I aimed high but fell short it was not the conditions that were flawed. It was me. I was flawed. Broken. And I needed to heal.

Perpetual motion meant success to me; stopping meant death. If I never stopped, maybe, somehow, I would keep my mother alive and I would never have to face that pain.

The pain my children are going to learn firsthand.

So now, I have stopped. I am still. I will stand on this path with them, only moving forward when they are ready. Waiting for them and moving forward with a confident, purposeful step, that's real success.

I will look pain in the eye and acknowledge it. Acknowledging my pain, the pain of others around me, and being able to say it out loud.

Resilience allows us to move forward each day. Embracing the pain of life allows us to be successful.

My success stems from my pain. Embracing it allows me to do anything, be anything, and face every day for the rest of my life.

Success is a Lifelong Attitude

Sharesz T. Wilkinson

Sharesz T. Wilkinson is an active Forbes Councils member, strategic advisor, and international executive communication expert.

She works with leaders, organisations, Fortune 100 companies, and ambitious individuals in business, entertainment, sports, and politics around the world on how to maintain top-level performance and get results during challenging times.

Sharesz T. Wilkinson represents The Speech Improvement Company (TSIC) based in Boston, has worked with the White House, and taught at Harvard and Massachusetts Institute of Technology (MIT).

A multiple award-winning international speaker, author, entrepreneur, investor, and philanthropist, her contributions have been published on various platforms including *Forbes*, BBC, Thrive Global, *Authority Magazine*, and *Hollywood Weekly*. She was interviewed in VoiceAmerica Influencers, EPN, Positive Phil Show (US), and more.

Sharesz T. Wilkinson is an Executive Contributor for *Brainz Magazine*, and the co-author of multiple published international books. Among the international awards received are the "Visionary Leader Award 2021," the Global Woman Economic Forum WEF 2018 Award "Exceptional Women of Excellence," and the "Humanitarian Fellow" Award from Rotary. She was further a nominee for the 2019 Tällberg/Eliasson Global Leadership Prize. A Senator in the Grand Assembly of the World Business Angels Investment Forum (WBAF), she is also a member of the Global Woman Leaders Committee. For more information, please visit her Forbes Executive Profile link at

https://profiles.forbes.com/members/coaches/
profile/Sharesz-T-Wilkinson-Strategic-Advisor-
International-Executive-Communication-Change-
Expert-The-Speech/e51c94ea-29a7-4a69-9d2c-
462502d34956

I saw the movie *Cry Freedom* in the late 80s. It impacted me deeply, and I promised to myself that I would make a difference with my life wherever I went—and so I did.

In order to learn to stand up for myself and others, I had to go through very rough and tough life experiences. I was destroyed at least once on every imaginable level and rose like the phoenix out of the ashes time and time again. Life taught me how to be resilient and flexible, how to become zen, get a grip on my thought processes and emotions, how to become mentally strong, and do things when I was afraid, regardless of how I was feeling.

In my last year of university, I was a high-flying student as well as athlete, plus I was already working on my first paid job assignment before graduation. When a big car carelessly rear-ended a stationary and rather small car, all that came to an abrupt ending. What ensued was a one-hundred percent invalidity, years of tremendous suffering, and the loss of nearly everything that meant something to me in life, including my self-esteem. An endless legal battle for my rights followed, which I finally won—nine years of barely holding on through all the massive changes, losses, and pain, as if my life had turned into an out of control freight train.

As if all this was not enough, I eventually found myself in an abusive relationship with two babies, and no support. I felt alone, completely abandoned, and absolutely terrified. What saved me was the thought of my children and what future I wanted them to have, what role model I wanted to be for them. The image I had in my mind looked entirely different from what we were living through at that time.

If circumstances do not change, we are forced to change ourselves. I mustered all my courage and not only left the relationship, but my country, my company, and everything else I knew to move to a faraway tiny island where I hoped to recover together with the kids.

Little did I know back then that this was only the beginning of a very adventurous journey which would eventually culminate in me summiting/achieving the top in business acumen and international accolades years later.

What guided me throughout was my faith and the conviction that God had a plan for us, and even if I did not know at the time where it would lead us, I consistently did the work at hand of raising two small children as a single mother. I slowly regained my health through countless surgeries and medical treatments, and kept fighting for over two decades to get justice and rebuild a professional career.

I continuously read, attended courses and trainings, did research, looked for mentors, and studied new topics when the kids were sleeping. For years, I worked into the wee morning hours, and got up early to get the kids ready for school, often going far beyond my physical capacities, bearing unfiltered pain as I could not function with painkillers.

Success is not a destination, it is an attitude in how we deal with and overcome challenges in life.

We had to start over three times on different continents before we finally found a place to settle, receive the necessary paperwork, and manage to build a sustainable future. The adversities and fear at times seemed unbearable and insurmountable. I was heartbroken and exhausted.

Further, I experienced that the more I tried to make a difference, the more resistance we encountered from our environment. Little did I know that this resistance was the very process that would prepare me for great things to come. As Henry Kissinger said, "A diamond is a chunk of coal that did well under pressure."

This is when I learned that we only have to make it through the next five minutes, one breath at a time. We are rarely in serious and immediate life danger. As long as we are aware of this fact and keep breathing, things will eventually get sorted. Just keep going.

I further learned that in order to go fast, we have to go slow. This is a completely counterintuitive approach in our fast-paced world.

Due to my health issues, my damaged body acted as a regulator which did not allow me to overdo things. If I did it regardless, I would suffer dire consequences, and be bedridden with unbearable pain for days on end, not being able to function.

I eventually and very painfully learned over time to respect my physical limitations regardless of the reactions of my environment—and have faith in life and the best possible outcome if I just kept diligently working towards it step by step by step, being kind to myself.

My grit and perseverance came from my upbringing as an athlete. I did ice figure skating since the age of four and had an unusual childhood. My schedule was planned throughout the years with school work, trainings, and competitions. I had barely any spare time left to just be a normal kid. I knew what it felt like to bite my teeth from a very young age onwards, what it meant to have delayed gratification, working relentlessly towards a goal even if I literally fell down countless times, bruised and with freezing feet and bleeding ankles. I knew what it took to continue regardless of pain and hurt, to perform at a very high level during challenging times, and make it all look effortless, easy, and graceful.

The feeling of having finally made it through after decades did not hit me until both my children went for their university studies overseas and were in their second year. I felt like having completed a lifelong marathon, and finally having a moment to myself to breathe, to relax, to enjoy, and to celebrate all of our successes and achievements.

That year, coincidentally, I received the "Exceptional Women of Excellence Award" at the Global Women Economic Forum in New Delhi, India, for my professional work. When I first received the email, I thought it was a prank. It only sank in a few days later that I would have to travel to India to personally receive this prestigious award on stage in front of hundreds or thousands of people from over 150 different countries.

Years earlier, I was honoured with the Rotary Humanitarian Fellow Award in a small and humble ceremony for my contributions in helping to build up the Rotary Education Fund in Malaysia, a passion project of my heart.

Since the day I saw the movie *Cry Freedom*, and made myself a promise, I have striven to make a difference to the people I met in my daily life and environment in whatever way I could. The principle of kindness and giving back, often exceeding what I could actually afford, stuck with me as a life principle to counteract all the injustice and violence I observed in so many places I had experienced and travelled to.

These two awards seemed to me like an acknowledgement for my relentless efforts no matter what, and over decades, to reach my goals and make a difference. What seemed impossible became, in the end, a logical consequence of everything that I had endured and lived through.

If I had a choice, I believe I would have chosen a less painful and less lonely path than the one I had to walk. I would have appreciated the knowledge I've acquired later in life at a much younger age. I would have loved a normal childhood and family life. Humans naturally want to avoid pain and seek pleasure.

One thing that kept me going was this thought: if I can make it through the first highly challenging fifty years of my life, the next fifty will be joyful, happy, light, and healthy. I was willing to bear all the difficulties and hardships, although many times giving up seemed like the easier and more bearable option. It felt like a bargain and a promise between me and God. I wanted to gain at least some illusion of power over my own life.

The biggest three takeaways to share are simple truths.

The first one is the foundation of our life. Focus on your breath and keep breathing. Breath is life and without it, we can't survive. It is crucial to take deep breaths daily to breathe in life.

The second one is to keep going step by step by step. No one jumps up a mountain. It might not be sexy to do something with a lot of patience, commitment, grit, belief, and perseverance, yet in my experience it is the only way forward. There is no such thing as overnight success.

The third one is of equal importance. Our attitude in how we do anything and everything determines our outcome. Commit to excellence, do and give your best, even if it is just washing the dishes. Every action has a consequence that ripples through our life. Take care of the little steps and they will amount to big leaps over time!

To date, I have received eleven international awards, have been interviewed on a variety of platforms, have travelled to more than fifty countries around the globe, stayed in twelve, and lived three lifetimes in one.

Did I expect any of this to happen? Not in my wildest dreams. I had set the intention of wanting to travel, to discover other cultures and languages, when I was a student. Never did I envision the adventurous life that I've led thus far nor the profound impact it has had on so many people.

I never made my work about myself since that young promise—I did not chase fame, money, or glory. I had to work with coaches to overcome my fear of going public. My work was always dedicated to being of service to others, to make a difference, for decades in the shadow, often without reward or acknowledgement. This required a very strong faith and a clear purpose. I am happy to have had both, oftentimes not knowing what the future would bring, nor how we would survive.

If we can value life and how to build up, give back, and support each other, the world will be a very different place. We all can start today, with who we are, and what we have, right here, right now, making one small difference at a time.

Please connect on a platform of your convenience via https://linktr.ee/stwilkinson or info@stwilkinson.global.

How to Move the World

Shiv Gaglani

Shiv Gaglani is the co-founder and chief executive officer of Osmosis.org, a leading health education platform with an audience of millions of current and future clinicians as well as their patients and family members.

Shiv's primary passion is developing innovative and scalable solutions in the fields of healthcare and education. To this end, he curated the Smartphone Physical, which debuted at TEDMED, and the Patient Promise, a movement to improve the clinician-patient relationship through partnership in pursuing healthy lifestyle behaviors. Shiv is an avid writer who has written two educational books, *Success with Science* and *Standing Out on the SAT and ACT*. He is a regular contributor to *Forbes*, which named him to their 30 Under 30 List in 2018.

After graduating magna cum laude from Harvard College in 2010 with degrees in engineering and health policy, Shiv began his MD degree at the Johns Hopkins University School of Medicine (from which he is currently on leave) and earned his MBA from Harvard Business School in 2016. In his spare time, he enjoys spending time with his family, snowboarding, skiing, running, and flying.

"Give me a lever and a place to stand, I can move the world."

I think about this quote from Archimedes when I reflect on the decision to leave the Johns Hopkins University School of Medicine to start my company, Osmosis.org. To believe in this quote, and to apply it to your own life and personal mission, requires a success mindset. It also requires an understanding of how to balance two dichotomies: scale versus direct impact and opportunity versus strategy. With the right leverage, the right place to stand, and a success mindset, one can move the world.

Prevention and Education Will Move the World

There was little question about whether I was going to pursue a career in healthcare. My mother is a physical therapist and my father is a doctor. As I shadowed him at the hospital he worked at in South Africa, I saw how he was making a difference in the lives of his patients and their families. At the age of five, I knew I was going to follow in his footsteps.

Fast-forward sixteen years to when I began medical school. I was intent on pursuing surgery given my background and interest in biomedical engineering. But within the first six months, I could see that there was an opportunity to place the world on a lever, so to speak. As I shadowed one of the surgeons, I met a patient with terminal lung cancer. The patient, only in his 60s, had to go into hospice.

This patient had started smoking forty years prior and never stopped. I found myself thinking about the financial and emotional costs to both the patient and his family. How could this situation be avoided? What if we went back in time forty years to educate the patient and encourage him to never start smoking? I began getting really interested in preventative medicine. Education and prevention were the levers and the place to stand. By focusing on this path, we could move the world.

This was the mindset shift that in part led me to co-found a health education platform called Osmosis.org with my medical school classmate, Ryan Haynes. Osmosis empowers the world's clinicians and caregivers with the best learning experience possible, featuring thousands of short and engaging educational videos ranging from why one should get vaccinated to how to perform Cardiopulmonary Resuscitation (CPR). The mindset shift toward prevention and education was just the beginning of the journey. In order to make our goals a reality, we had to tap into a true success mindset.

The Johns Hopkins University School of Medicine begins with a year and a half of preclinical curriculum before students enter the even-more demanding clinical rotations. At that year and a half mark, Ryan and I found ourselves making a critical decision. Either we were going to stop working on our idea, or we would take time off, defer med school, and try moving the world with Osmosis.

Fortunately, we were able to de-risk the decision by gaining acceptance into a tech startup incubator called DreamIt Health. We now had capital, access to partnerships, and the ability to build a team. On the other hand, we were already safely on our path to becoming physicians at Johns Hopkins. This is where it's important to note how important education is to me and my family, given our history. My grandparents were refugees; my parents and I are immigrants. Education is a secure path to climbing the economic and social ladder. Had I earned the right to take a risk? Could I land on my feet if Osmosis didn't work out?

When you have a success mindset, the answer is yes, and not because of blind faith. A success mindset is one that believes that very few decisions are irreversible. And no matter what decision you make, you will find opportunities for growth along the way. With this mindset, we left medical school, knowing that if it was meant to be we could get back on the path.

Very Few Decisions Are Irreversible

Two of our medical school classmates helped illustrate this point. One started school as a single mother who had just had a baby six months prior. She had been working as a bartender to make ends meet while completing the premedical coursework. Another classmate immigrated from Eastern Europe, earned money through gig economy work, and became an electrician before saving up enough to apply to medical school. Meeting these incredible people served as a reminder that very few decisions are irreversible.

My mother, Vanita, also inspired me with this attitude. She's a physical therapist who started her own very successful practice. As she was working on her license, she also learned how to start and run a general merchandise shop when we lived in Africa. Most recently, she taught herself how to invest in cryptocurrency and knows more about the space than virtually anyone else I know. Watching her take risks and dedicate herself to lifelong learning provided a solid foundation for my success mindset.

I have already learned so much from taking the risk and leaving medical school to start Osmosis. I've had to ask myself questions about the impact I want Osmosis as an organization, and me as an individual, to have.

The answer can in part be influenced by understanding the two dichotomies that I mentioned earlier: scale versus direct impact and opportunity versus strategy.

Scale Versus Direct Impact

A physician has a profound personal impact on each of her patient's lives, though it's severely limited in scale because she is trading time for that impact. Conversely, a scientist who spends years in a lab may not be directly impacting the lives of patients, but if she discovers a new compound that can save lives, she can massively scale her contributions to the world. I've found this dichotomy to be true of many professions; for example, a teacher (who makes a high direct impact on students on a low scale) versus an education tech entrepreneur (who makes a low direct impact on students on a massive scale).

This idea has influenced the decisions that we make at Osmosis. I have found the scale to be incredibly gratifying. It's an amazing feeling to wake up and see that thousands of people from the other side of the world have been learning through Osmosis. This is success for me. That being said, I do miss the one-on-one impact that I could make if I finish med school. Entrepreneurship can be lonely. You spend a lot of time working to make the impact that you see for yourself and your company. Spending time directly working with patients or clients can also be gratifying and illuminating.

Having a success mindset allows one to balance this dichotomy and remember what they are working towards. In the case of Osmosis, the more educated and empowered people are to take care of their own health, or the health of their loved ones, the fewer clinicians are needed. The more education that people can access about preventative healthcare, the less they have to spend on healthcare costs down the road.

Opportunity Versus Strategy

It's often said that one should enjoy the journey, not just the destination. Entrepreneurship is like taking a road trip with a destination in mind. For example, say you're driving up the Eastern United States from Florida to Maine. While that may be your strategy, it can be incredibly gratifying to keep an open mind and be opportunistic to other routes, even if they involve detours. Say your favorite artist is having a concert in Nashville— do you go out of your way to go see them? My view is that as long as I'm having fun with the people in the car, and learning and growing along the way, while still keeping the strategic direction in mind, I can take time to be opportunistic. Nashville, here we come.

My senior quote in my high school yearbook was: "*If you have enough pieces of wood in the fire, one of them is going to catch.*" This echoes another of my favorite quotes from dual-Nobel Laureate Linus Pauling: "*The best way to have a good idea is to have a lot of ideas.*" I didn't go to medical school to become an entrepreneur. Medical school was one opportunity, one idea. Entrepreneurship was another. If I had zeroed in on the original strategy that I built for my career, I wouldn't have taken the opportunity to start Osmosis with Ryan. This is the balance between opportunity and strategy. Once you have a strategy and move closer to your goal, you can't take all of the opportunities available to you.

In the early days of Osmosis, I had problems seeing when to pursue opportunities and when to stay focused on a singular strategy. Many entrepreneurs do. I was grinding all day, every day. But keeping my head down and only focusing on the strategy that I have built leaves very little room for exploring new opportunities. What's more, it leads to burnout.

Successful entrepreneurs like Bill Gates carve out weeks, if not months, each year to be more opportunistic and creative. During this time, Gates doesn't open his emails related to Microsoft or the Gates Foundation—he just reads. Leonardo Da Vinci did something similar. He built in ample time to be creative and incredibly opportunistic. As he followed his curiosity and opened his mind to different possibilities, he discovered things that he could strategically apply in his paintings and inventions.

Da Vinci mastered the balance between pursuing opportunity and strategy.

Stability and a strategic routine can support you on your journey toward any goal, but the world around us is always changing. Marketing today is so different from marketing ten or even five years ago. The healthcare and education industries are changing rapidly. On the other hand, there are certain truths about human behavior, such as the need for community, that haven't changed for millennia. Entrepreneurs have to tap into all of these things to see where disruption is possible and how people will respond to their offerings.

As your business grows, the best way to balance between opportunity and strategy changes, too. Osmosis has grown so much since we left Hopkins. What started as an educational tool for 120 of our classmates has now been used by tens of millions of people around the world (www.osmosis.org/world). More people know us, and more opportunities are coming our way. But we can't let all of these "pieces of wood" catch fire or we won't be able to focus and control our business.

At the center of this balance, between both opportunity versus strategy *and* scale versus direct impact, is our mindset. Every choice that we make comes from our success mindset. Every risk that we take is determined by our mindset. The place where we stand and the leverage we use will be determined by our mindset. But I am confident that because this success mindset is at the center of all of our decisions, we will move the world.

You can find Shiv Gaglani on LinkedIn (https://www.linkedin. com/in/shivgaglani/). For more information, visit www.osmosis.org.

You Can't Take It With You

Jody Steinhauer

President and founder of The Bargains Group, Jody
Steinhauer has mobilized her award-winning discount
wholesale and promotional products company to
revolutionize the business landscape for good. She has
been the esteemed recipient of many awards including
The Business Leader of the Year Award, Canadian
Woman Entrepreneur of the Year Award, and Canada's
Top 40 Under 40. As a Canadian female entrepreneur,
Jody uses her network of resources and leveraged buying
power to aid every company and nonprofit agency that
she touches to maximize their buying dollar.

Pioneering her belief of "giving back makes
great business sense," Jody is a tireless advocate and
founder of the charity Engage and Change. Its two
annual initiatives, Project Winter Survival and Project
Water, help thousands of homeless survive the extreme
weather conditions while engaging individuals in active
philanthropy. Inspired by the impact her charity has
made, Jody launched the social enterprise Kits for a
Cause. Jody has created a turn-key, fun, and engaging
program for businesses to engage their employees
while solving local community services' needs for
resources and creating massive impact simultaneously.
Her model of "brokering goodness" has worked with
some of the top industry leaders in both the corporate
and philanthropic spheres. Jody resides in Toronto,
Canada, with her husband, five children, and dog.
For more information, visit bargainsgroup.com and
kitsforacause.com.

I received a phone call I'll never forget from a woman I had
worked with a few years before. She was a very wealthy
woman who had been in a C-suite position of the company that

I was working with. Her voice was panicked on the phone. She said, "Hi, Jody. I'm calling you from a shelter, and I owe you an apology. I never understood the work that you did. I thought you were nuts. My husband beat me up last night and stole the keys to my Mercedes. I had to call the police and flee with my children. I'm in a shelter right now. And thank God for you, because I was just given something that made me feel really good–a clean pair of underwear. And you know, that gave me hope that somebody actually cared."

The Bargains Group isn't a company that is making millions in real estate or dominating global markets. Kits for a Cause isn't going to solve the homelessness crisis. In my business, I'm just giving someone a pair of underwear, but phone calls like this remind me that giving someone a pair of underwear makes me successful. All of us need to feel good in bad situations–all of us need hope. If we have hope, it's one step forward to everybody being successful.

This might not be the chapter you're expecting to read. Sure, I'm fortunate that I've been able to grow a thriving business. My business doubled during the pandemic. We work with the Canadian government, Bank of America, and huge corporations. But I don't see my business as successful because we bring in a certain amount of money. I see it as successful because we are helping the homeless and teaching other people how they can help, too.

They Have Dignity

Let me explain. After working in the fashion industry for many years, I ended up going out on my own and finding the world of discount. The Bargains Group was born thirty-three years ago. Everything was done the old-fashioned way, through relationships and phone calls. I was a big discount shopper, and I didn't have discount wholesalers as competition in the market. At the time, I was just having fun.

A few years into running The Bargains Group, I was doing my volunteer work, and I had this euphoric moment that I'll never forget. I was behind the scenes at a very high-level fashion show that was benefiting a homeless shelter. In between dressing models, I struck up a conversation with a woman named Mary Brown. Mary told me that she was responsible for clothing the youth at the largest homeless shelter in Canada. Naively, I said, "That's so cool." I was under the impression that Mary was a volunteer, sorting through the big dumpsters that sat in supermarket parking lots where people could donate clothes and household items. But that's not what Mary did for a living. In fact, she was disgusted that I assumed she sorted through garbage. Mary was a paid employee, she told me, and she didn't sort through shit. She told me that her job was purchasing clean socks and underwear. Why? Because kids on the street are just like you and me. They have dignity.

Mary went on to tell me about her typical day: she worked a fourteen-hour day at a shelter, went home, put her kids in a car after serving them dinner, drove to the local discount department store, found the store manager, negotiated a discount on 1,000 pairs of socks, checked out, loaded up the car, loaded up the kids, drove home, unloaded the car, unloaded the socks, woke the kids up early, got them to reload the car, dropped the kids off, drove down to the shelter, unloaded everything, went to the accountant, and got reimbursed. I was exhausted to hear all of that, but I asked her how much she paid for the socks. She told me, letting me know with pride that she got a 10 percent discount from the store manager. Little did Mary Brown know, The Bargains Group supplied those socks to that store. I said, "Mary, I think I can help you."

I gave Mary my card and told her that the next time she needed socks to call me. She could get the socks for 80 percent less and I would deliver them to her door. If she wanted anything else, I'd be happy to donate more to her company because she was doing such incredible work.

At first, Mary was skeptical. She asked if the socks I was selling her were stolen! But that's what The Bargains Group was already doing—supplying stores with discount products. I wanted her kids to feel incredible and to hold onto that dignity with clean socks, underwear, and anything they needed. I wanted to help Mary help more kids, too. To me, this a was success.

After a month of using us, Mary called me and told me that she saved so much money from using The Bargains Group that she hired two social workers to run two more programs. And then she said to me, "Can I tell other people about you?" She started telling people all over the country about what we did and how we could help shelters. People started calling in and ordering from all over. I wasn't just happy to have new customers–I was so happy to work with them. Working with someone at a shelter is very different than retail buyers. Everyone was nice. They spoke kindly. They were respectful. They sent us flowers and chocolate and they asked if they could pay us early. Not only did it make me feel great because I heard the stories of the impact we were making, but it also made my team feel amazing that we were doing this work. When you do things and people treat you well, you want to do more. We were onto something.

This inspired me to pivot my business. How could we help these people more? You can't make money selling to charities– it's not a predictable, scalable business. But what we could do is reconfigure our business so that we could help more shelters when they called and needed our help alongside the retail stores. So that's what we did. The more we helped, the greater we felt. Then we branched out into clothing, winter clothing, socks, and underwear. We branched out into housewares, bedding, linen, hygiene products, Christmas gifts, toys, and volunteer gifts. We opened up a new division of custom logo promotional products and catered to charities, walkathons, golf tournaments, and fundraisers. We kept growing and growing, and a lot of this had to do with the fact that we were ahead of our time.

When I started working with homeless shelters, I knew I was ahead of my time. No one was interested in corporate social responsibility. When The Bargains Group started putting together survival kits for the winter and summer, business leaders thought I was crazy. They told me people living on the streets were garbage, even though they could have easily been a relative or a friend who was down on their luck.

But then I started getting calls five or six years ago from businesses that needed my help. They were freaking out because they had no idea what to do for their "Impact Day." No charities would work with them because, frankly, companies that showed up for a day to paint a wall or serve food weren't making the impact that they thought they were. So when I took these calls,

I asked leaders the basic questions. I asked them if they had a cause—and usually they didn't. I asked them if they had a budget—and usually they did. I started to realize that I could change the world with these budgets, all while making these businesses feel awesome. I could teach them how to market their work to leverage their brand. So, we opened up a separate social enterprise called Kits for a Cause. Kits for a Cause is just growing like wildfire. It's group team-building with massive impact. Over the past year, we became virtual because of COVID-19 restrictions, and everybody is coming to us. We're changing the way people give and changing people the way people are doing volunteer work and philanthropy. This, to me, is a success.

Kits for a Cause started as a social enterprise, and I wasn't going to make a big pile of money from it. I'm not trying to make a big pile of money, because my reputation as a philanthropist and someone who wants to help is most important to me. Your reputation is the most important thing you own. My father instilled this lesson in me from an early age: it doesn't matter who you are. It doesn't matter whether you're Bill Gates, Warren Buffett, or someone with a few cents in your bank account. It doesn't matter whether you have a Mercedes or your Mercedes was just stolen from you. We're all going to the same place, and you can't take it with you.

I've had so many opportunities to make huge money with both The Bargains Group and Kits for a Cause, but I would be doing things that would potentially jeopardize my reputation. I just got a call from a massive retailer who asked why I had never called them. I told them that I didn't have salespeople and that all of my product was in my warehouse. They couldn't believe it. They asked me, don't you want to sell your product to us? I said, "Maybe, but I'm not motivated by money." I can thank God that because I've stuck to my reputation and the success mindset that my father had instilled in me so early, I can choose who I sell to. If I know there's a shortage of ladies' underwear for my shelters, for example, I don't care how much a retailer pays me for it. They're not going to get it. To me, success is about helping those that can't help themselves. My success is not how many millions of dollars I have in the bank. I do well for myself, but I need to feel like I am fulfilling every part of my soul. This means giving, mentoring, being a great role model, and influencing other business leaders on how they can help people who may be struggling or down on their luck.

I've Always Wanted to Help

You don't need me to tell you that people don't always understand how people become homeless. They don't think about the single mother who is leaving an abusive husband with no money of her own in the bank or the man who just completed a twenty-year prison sentence and doesn't have any family or even updated clothes to help him get back on his feet. And because people don't understand how people become homeless, they don't understand what it takes to get them back on their feet. I know what it takes because I give that to the people I meet all the time.

Take this couple that I met. They were having a hard time and were thrown out of the local shelter. One was schizophrenic. I let them come and stay in the back of my building for a year. They pitched tents and we brought them food and my entire company adopted them. When the weather dropped, I knew they wouldn't be comfortable in the tents so I got them a hotel for the winter. I contacted social workers to connect them to the long-term help they needed. This couple called me two days ago and said, "We're so excited. We got our first home." They've just signed a year lease. This isn't just a mindset that has run my business for thirty years–it's who I am. I just want to see progress for people who just need the opportunity. If you have hope, support, and opportunity, you are closer to success and so are the people around you. For this couple, at one point success was a tent. Their idea of success currently is to see their daughter who was taken away and is in foster care. To them, that year lease is a step closer to that success–it's more valuable than a million dollars.

I know people with millions of dollars who, in reality, have nothing. I know people, like the couple I helped out, who got a tent and felt like they had everything. That's what I try and teach everybody around me. This is what a success mindset is all about. It doesn't matter where you came from, it doesn't matter where you're going, it doesn't matter what you drive, or how much you have. What matters, whatever you have, is what you do with it.

Lessons from Horace and Aristotle

Lee Murray

Lee Murray is an award-winning author-editor from Aotearoa-New Zealand (*Sir Julius Vogel*, *Australian Shadows*), and a double Bram Stoker Award®-winner. Her works include military thrillers, the Taine McKenna Adventures, supernatural crime-noir series The Path of Ra (with Dan Rabarts), and debut collection *Grotesque: Monster Stories*. She is proud to have edited seventeen volumes of speculative fiction, including internationally acclaimed *Black Cranes: Tales of Unquiet Women*, an exploration of otherness and expectation by horror writers of Southeast Asian descent, breakneck military monster fiction in *Hellhole: An Anthology of Subterranean Terror*, and *Baby Teeth: Bite-sized Tales of Terror*, featuring nightmarish tales based on the creepy things kids say. Her books for kids feature space travel (*Conclave 7*), time travel (*Battle of the Birds*), and coping with your baby sister when you accidentally cause a zombie apocalypse (*Dawn of the Zombie Apocalypse*).

Lee is co-founder of Young NZ Writers and of the Wright-Murray Residency for Speculative Fiction Writers, HWA Mentor of the Year for 2019, NZSA Honorary Literary Fellow, and Grimshaw Sargeson Fellow for 2021 for her poetry collection *Fox Spirit on a Distant Cloud*. Read more about the author at leemurray.info.

My story starts with two tiny frogs. Imaginary ones. Named Horace and Aristotle, they were the main characters in the made-up bedtime stories my dad would tell me; two bumbling yet endearing personalities who lived in the creek at the bottom of our street. Life can be perilous if you're a frog; there are roads to cross and cats to outsmart, and even reaching the counter at the ice cream shop can be tricky. But, bracing themselves for adventure, Horace and Aristotle would catapult themselves off the washing line, or surf across the road on a sheet of corrugated cardboard, the two loyal friends always working together to solve problems and make it safely home. Dad was a great performer too, giving his characters' quirky voices, and adding humour and drama to his tales. I loved those stories. I dreamed of growing up and becoming a storyteller.

But life happened, and I got blown off course, choosing instead to study science and management, to live and work abroad, and marry and raise a family. It wasn't until I reached my forties, when we returned to our beachside home in the Land of the Long White Cloud, that I returned to my love of story. It was my husband who suggested that I become a writer.

"Stop talking about it, and give it a go," he said. I'd supported his career, so he was pleased to invest in mine.

So, there it was. I had no excuse not to go adventuring. Here was my chance to write that promised novel. Only, now that the time had come to follow my dream, I felt as small and as vulnerable as those tiny frogs. Nevertheless, I dived in; I completed some creative writing courses to gain some confidence, joined a monthly writers' group, and acquired my first writing credits in some local magazines, all while writing my first novel.

Persuaded by that old adage "write what you know," I wrote a zany romantic comedy, drawing on my experience of running twenty-two marathons. The novel was too long, and the cover was awful, but was a great starter book for learning about writing and publishing. On the way, I also learned that light-hearted stories involving wardrobe malfunctions and cupcake deprivation, while fun to write, weren't going to sustain me, despite women's fiction being a highly lucrative genre. Instead, I wanted to write more meaningful stories, addressing issues that resonated for me personally. Things like fear, otherness, and oppression. And that realisation led me to speculative fiction and horror, specifically monster fiction, because "monsters are living breathing metaphors."[1] At least, that's the view of filmmaker Guillermo del Toro. These metaphors are well-known by now: zombies as a stand-in for the global pandemic, kaiju for nuclear war and globalisation, and Frankenstein as a symbol of scientific hubris, for example. By battling such monsters on the page, we create a measure of distance, of safety, allowing readers (and writers) to analyse, evaluate, perhaps even discover viable solutions for the things that haunt us. How might Horace and Aristotle have reacted when faced with a wily neighbourhood cat, for example? And if those plucky little heroes could outwit a monster more than ten times their size, then why not us?

It was just a few years into my writing adventure and already I'd proven I could write a book, and I'd also discovered my genre. It was time for a new goal. I decided I would write the best New Zealand monster fiction I possibly could. After all, what better place to conjure monsters than New Zealand, a land overrun with orcs and *taniwha*, gods and demons? The land itself has an uneasiness to it. Consider this passage from *The Woman at the Store* (1912), a short story by iconic writer Katherine Mansfield:

"There is no twilight in our New Zealand days, but a curious half-hour when everything appears grotesque–it frightens– as though the savage spirit of the country walked abroad and sneered at what it saw."

It was while I was out completing a long distance run in the New Zealand bush, where that "savage spirit" walks abroad and sneers, that I dreamed up the idea for the story. Unlike our Australian neighbours, New Zealand has no dangerous wild creatures. The terrain can be treacherous, and the weather fickle, but we have no venomous snakes or saltwater crocs. The best we can do is a timid little spider and some overlarge crickets. Nothing that can kill you.

But what if there were?

Filled with excitement, I went home and opened a Word file, labelling it Global Blockbuster. An ambitious goal, and one I didn't really expect to achieve, but Dad, my favourite storyteller, always said, "Aim high." As the hero of my own story, it was to be the inciting incident that truly set my writing career in motion, and the impetus for my best-selling novel *Into the Mist.*

This is where Horace and Aristotle hop back into the story. Because if I were to have any chance of producing a global blockbuster, I knew I would have to catapult my writing skills to the next level. I would need to take a global approach to branding and publishing, which meant gaining a better understanding of my genre and the wider literary industry. Even more than that, I would have to become a writer deserving of a global readership. Just as my dad's imaginary characters Horace and Aristotle had always worked together to overcome obstacles and make it safely home, I realised that if I were to achieve my real-life goal, I was going to need help, and a lot of it. (There's a reason *With a Little Help from my Friends* is one of The Beatles most enduring tracks.) The only way I knew to gain industry knowledge, build a brand, and enlist the help of other writers, was to be generous with my own time and skill. So, about the time I labelled my file Global Blockbuster, I decided on the word "kindness" as my goal-setting catchphrase. Turns out, kindness is a strategy that works.

To begin with, it enabled me to improve my craft. Already a member of numerous critique groups and writer's forums, I volunteered to read and critique other people's manuscripts. I raised my hand again and again.

"Send it through and I'll take a look," I said. "Happy to help."

There was never a lack of takers. I spent hours reading and editing other people's work. I brainstormed plot lines, fine-tuned query letters, and helped perfect titles. Sometimes, people failed to reciprocate. It didn't matter; by analysing other people's work, I was learning new skills and earning the respect of my peers. And everything I learned, I put into practise in my book.

Little by little, I was surrounding myself with a community of genre professionals. I extended my strategic kindness to include manuscript assessment, literary judging, guest editing, mentorship, and literary events management—almost entirely unpaid work. Yet every time I helped a colleague present their first panel, pitch their story, or submit their first manuscript, I'd gain something: a helpful contact, resource, or new friend.

Sticking with my policy of kindness, I became a champion for my genre, commenting on speculative fiction at public appearances, in the media, and online. Everywhere I went, I promoted my colleagues. People sometimes question the wisdom of this, but in my view critical mass is important: getting works that resembled my own work into readers' hands could only help to grow the genre. Keen readers might get through two or three books a week in their preferred genre—more than I can write in a year–and if they were reading one of my colleagues' books, I hoped they might one day take a chance on me.

At home, there was a bigger problem. While technological changes were making global markets more accessible, New Zealand's own readership was retrenching, our largest cohort, older female readers, preferring literary fiction and cosy mystery titles. It occurred to me that for a sustainable career as a *New Zealand* writer of monster fiction, I would also need to inspire a passion for genre fiction in younger readers. To that end, I joined forces with my friend and colleague Piper Mejia, author of *The Better Sister and Other Stories*, establishing Young New Zealand Writers, a volunteer group offering development and publishing opportunities for school students. Focusing on genre topics, and using vehicles like free writing competitions, student conventions, and anthology projects, the programme has developed thousands of young readers and writers. It's been no small task, not the least because participating students each receive customised feedback on their work. Over the past decade, that feedback would amount to several books. We were building a cohort of new readers, but not without a significant investment in time and energy.

I'll admit, at times I felt as disillusioned as poor Horace at the ice cream shop, jumping up and down at the counter like… well, like a frog…yet never high enough to be spotted by the vendor. I could relate. Horror fiction is poorly supported in this country. While readers love it, our funding organisations, publishing companies, and literary festivals tend to ignore genre writers, and booksellers and libraries rarely stock genre books. From time to time, I would focus on those negatives, or I would compare myself to writers of other genres, people who I perceived were doing better than me. Dangerous thinking for an anxious Piglet sort with depressive tendencies. Worse, being a "kind" writer was becoming so embedded in my identity that I found myself prioritising other people's work over my own. I was sabotaging my own goals and getting seriously frazzled in the process. In Dad's story, Aristotle swooped in on a curtain cord to help his friend; in my story, friends and family swooped in to remind me of the importance of balance.

"Be kind to yourself," they said.

My military monster thriller, *Into the Mist,* was released in 2016, outselling all the other titles in the publisher's stable in its first year, and prompting the publisher to demand a sequel. Never actually reaching "Global Blockbuster" status, it remains my breakout novel, gaining national and international award recognition, and establishing me as one of the country's foremost writers of speculative fiction.

My community-building work has paid off too, earning me New Zealand's Sir Julius Vogel Award for Services to the science fiction, fantasy, and horror community, the Horror Writers Association's Mentor of the Year Award, and an Honorary Literary Fellowship from the New Zealand Society of Authors.

"There's seldom anyone more helpful or supportive than Lee Murray," writes horror reviewer and author, Steve Stred. "Such an incredibly kind person in my writing journey…."

My own writing journey may have had a wobbly start, but I'm on the way now. In fact, in May 2021, I was awarded two international Bram Stoker Awards®, horror's highest accolade, for superior achievement in the "fiction collection" and "anthology" categories, the first New Zealander to achieve this. I wish Dad had been alive to see it. I wish he'd seen how his bedtime tales have shaped my life, and the lessons I've learned from his two tiny frogs. I think he'd be proud.

Why not make this success mindset work for you? Take a leaf out of Horace and Aristotle's book. Seek out others of your species, people with like goals, and share your journey with them. Be generous with your time and skills. Embrace kindness as a guiding principle to grow your network and your knowledge. Celebrate other people's successes, and never be afraid to swing from the curtain cord to help a friend achieve their goal; they might just help you get your own ice cream. Focus your mindset on kindness and community and you'll have all the tools you need. Then brace yourself for adventure, and catapult off the washing line on a trajectory to success.

Success Begins in Your Mind

Ankit "Andy" Mehta

Ankit "Andy" Mehta is a co-owner and partner at the Bristol Group, a nationwide Mergers & Acquisitions (M&A) Advisory and Business Brokerage firm. He works with lower middle-market business owners to sell their businesses to strategic buyers and private equity groups. The Bristol Group brings together decades of expertise in structuring business transactions and valuations. Working across a national network of offices, their individualized approach guarantees that every client receives the requisite personal attention to meet their needs.

Prior to co-owning the Bristol Group, Andy worked in M&A advisory at national consulting firms for twelve years, completing over a hundred transactions advising business owners, private equity groups, investment banks, and strategic buyers.

Andy earned a Bachelor's Degree in Economics with University Honors from the University of Michigan and completed executive accounting and leadership programs at the University of North Carolina. He is a Certified Valuation Analyst (CVA®) and a member of the National Association of Certified Valuators and Analysts.

To learn more about Andy, and how he can help you exit your business at a premium, connect with him here: https://www.linkedin.com/in/andymehta/.

A New Adventure

It takes courage to pursue your dreams.

In February 2020, I decided to launch an M&A advisory and business brokerage firm. I had been working in the M&A industry for over twelve years. I was already an expert in my field and earning a stable six-figure salary. But I was hungry for more. I wanted the freedom to dream big, set my own goals, and devote myself to pursuing those goals.

So, I left my comfortable job to launch a business.

Despite my experience, starting a business was a huge financial and professional risk, not least because of the significant challenges, such as the disastrous COVID-19 pandemic, that were thrown in my path.

However, with a success-oriented mindset, I was prepared to meet the challenges. In the process of doing so, I built a thriving business, substantially increased my income, earned industry recognition, and redefined what success means to me.

Invest in Yourself

Your mind is your greatest asset. The most profound changes in my life have come from investing in self-development.

As I stepped out of my comfort zone and launched my business, I set out to develop myself. I wanted to be the absolute best. To do that, I needed to have a growth-focused mindset and commit to continuous self-development (despite already having extensive industry experience). That is when I discovered mindset training.

Every day I allocated time to watch webinars, listen to podcasts, and read books. I found digital mentors in motivational speakers and mindset trainers such as Les Brown, Tony Robbins, Bedros Keuilian, and Jay Shetty, to name a few.

I listened to interviews and read biographies by CEOs, entrepreneurs, and athletes who had achieved remarkable success in their careers. I wanted to learn from the best.

I listened and I evolved.

Everything was on track until disaster struck.

Business Launch Hit By The Pandemic

In March 2020, just a month after I left my stable corporate job, the pandemic hit. A public health disaster declaration, the first one in Texas since 1901, was issued, locking down the state and sending the economy into a severe recession. The American economy declined by 31 percent in the second quarter of 2020. This was the worst contraction ever recorded.

The M&A industry came to a screeching halt. There was far too much uncertainty and panic in the market for business transactions to get completed. As a new business, we were ineligible for COVID-19 assistance from the government. Furthermore, in-person networking, which has traditionally been the lifeblood of marketing in the M&A industry, immediately ceased.

Suddenly, I found myself facing the absolute worst-case scenario. I was now heavily invested in my new business, had zero clients, and found myself facing a public health crisis and an economic recession of historic proportions.

Contrary to conventional wisdom, I refused to abandon my business, compromise on my goals, or lower my standards on the clients I chose. The more challenging the situation, the more motivated I became to succeed.

Focus On the Things You Can Control

I decided to not worry about what I couldn't control. Rather, I chose to adopt a mindset of positivity, growth, adaptability, and ownership. I would hold myself accountable for my goals, irrespective of what was going on around me.

Successful entrepreneurs do not let people, circumstances, or obstacles derail them. Rather, they confront the situation head-on, adapt, evolve, and create the outcome that they seek. For me, this meant choosing purpose over pleasure and adapting my lifestyle, actions, and networking to focus on my goals.

I worked harder and smarter to adapt to the new COVID-19 reality. In practice, this meant taking my business and networking activities online. I rewrote my marketing plan to make it 100 percent remote–using a blend of emails, telemarketing, and mailing hundreds of hand-signed letters every week.

Unfortunately, it soon became apparent that this strategy would not produce results quickly enough. I needed to sign clients immediately. It was time for a new approach.

An Adaptive Mindset Pays Off

In the pandemic world of disrupted industries and virtual meetings, I needed a more targeted and personal strategy. I had to focus on the limited industries that were still operating at full capacity and get the attention of the owner or the CEO. I searched online for all nearby businesses that were deemed "essential" and remained open for business. Once I had a list of them, I conducted extensive research on each business and its owner in order to write highly customized emails to them. Painstakingly, I repeated this process thousands of times until I achieved my desired outcome.

Impressed by the amount of research I had done, several prospective clients responded and initiated dialogue.

Within a month, I signed clients with businesses worth millions of dollars. This far surpassed the expectation of what could be achieved so soon after starting a business amid a recession.

However, this success did not come without challenges. In July, one of my largest clients insisted that I secure them an all-cash offer for their business with zero seller financing—and they wanted the transaction completed within four months!

For context, less than 10 percent of all businesses are sold for all-cash and less than 30 percent are sold within four months. Not to mention that we were in the midst of an economic crisis. Statistically, the odds of success were less than 3 percent.

Common sense warned me to stay away from this deal to avoid wasting time and money. However, if you desire to be the best, you must take calculated risks. Once again, I adopted a success-oriented mindset and decided to ignore the statistics. I was fired up by the high-risk and high-reward nature of this transaction and decided that failure was not an option.

Over the next four months, I worked as hard as I could, and I got the deal done on time—with a terrific buyer and an all-cash offer. My client was absolutely thrilled! Since then, the Bristol Group has completed dozens of transactions on behalf of our clients.

As a new business owner, not only did I survive a severe recession, I thrived! In recognition of my deal-making abilities,

I received an award from the M&A Source at their 2021 Deal Summit. Having extensive M&A experience helped me navigate this journey, but there is no doubt that my achievements were a direct result of my success-oriented mindset.

What Is a Success-Oriented Mindset?

I firmly believe that a person will only go as far as their mindset allows them to. Successful people have one thing in common—a success-oriented mindset. Below are the four principles that form the basis of this mindset:

1. *Growth.* Welcome challenges and view them as an opportunity to get better. You are comfortable with being uncomfortable. In other words, you strive to step outside your comfort zone and push your boundaries. You are motivated by the opportunity to aim higher, be better, and achieve more in all aspects of your life. You welcome feedback as a catalyst for growth and truly believe that you are capable of achieving your goals.

2. *Ownership.* Take ownership of everything associated with your goals. Recognize that your life is a product of your thoughts, decisions, and actions. There is no room for excuses, feeling victimized, or for blaming other people or circumstances. You focus your energy on creating the results you seek. You have complete control over the life you live and the level of success you achieve.

3. *Adaptability*. We as humans aspire for a comfortable and stable life, but with stability comes stagnation. If we are stagnant, we will never reach our full potential in a constantly changing world. When unforeseen challenges arise, you focus your energy on finding solutions. By viewing change as an opportunity for growth, you can use it to drive motivation and progress. It is essential to expect and welcome challenges, adapt to them rapidly, and trust that change will result in a better version of you. Adapt to win, rather than to cope.

4. *Positivity.* Strive to see things from a positive perspective and you can transform every situation into a positive outcome. Positivity is contagious. It will filter into all aspects of your life and to those around you. Replace negative people with those who share your values and purpose, turn off the news, and delete social media. Feed your mind with positive inputs to uplift your thoughts, actions, and—as a result—outcomes.

Find Mentors

You don't need to reinvent the wheel. Instead, find mentors and leaders. Seek out resources that can teach you about successful mindsets and improving yourself. In today's digital age, you have all the knowledge that you need at your fingertips. A few mindset books that I recommend are *Man Up* by Bedros Keuilian, *Inner Engineering* by Sadhguru Vasudev, and *The Secret* by Rhonda Byrne.

Develop Self-Discipline

In order to be your best self, you need to develop self-discipline and take extreme ownership of your life. You should be disciplined with your health, mind, and time. It is critical that you hold yourself to an organized schedule and prioritize working on your goals. Through self-discipline, you will be able to perform and achieve at your highest level.

Dream Big

Success starts with a dream. Never let your decisions be driven by fear. Successful people do not limit themselves because they are worried about failing. Instead, they are driven by what makes them come alive!

If your dreams and goals do not motivate, excite, and scare you in equal measure then they are not big enough. You must find the sweet spot between being ambitious and realistic. Fear, glass ceilings, and limitations are nothing more than constructs of the mind. Adopt a mindset of growth and shatter them.

In the face of challenges, I turned to what I had learned about mindset and success. For me, adversity proved hugely motivating. I wanted to fight for my goals and dreams. It is necessary to adapt and reassess–but you should stay true to your objectives. Throughout the turmoil of 2020, my goals did not change. The only thing that changed was how I was going to achieve them.

This is what separates success from failure.

Success Is Not a Singular Achievement

Mindset is the secret to my success and the success of my mentors. Within twelve months of launching a nationwide M&A advisory and business brokerage firm, I had developed a strong client base, substantially increased my income, and earned industry recognition–all during a severe recession.

The impact of mindset on my life is not measured by my business alone.

During this time, every facet of my life improved. As I was smashing my business goals, I was also setting personal records in the gym and achieving my long-standing fitness objectives. Most importantly, my success did not come at the cost of my family. Instead, my work-life balance has been better than ever. I am a better husband, father, son, brother, and friend–and my mindset inspired those around me. My wife Ginny was promoted to a leadership role at work, smashed her own fitness goals, and published her first children's book.

Investing in your mindset will transform your life. Success is not a singular achievement, rather it is the sum of every facet of your life.

Success is living a meaningful, purposeful, and fulfilling life in pursuit of your dreams. It is achieving your goals and having inner peace with who and where you are in life while being excited about the journey that still lies ahead of you. It all begins in your mind.

I wish you success.

To learn more or inquire about exiting your business at a premium, you can reach me directly at andy@bristol.group.

Failing Forward

David Kissinger

David Kissinger, Registered Nurse (RN), is the founder and CEO of NurseNow Staffing, www.nursenowstaffing.com, the fastest growing nurse staffing agency, specializing in decentralized clinical research, in the nation. Under David's leadership, NurseNow grew exponentially, reaching over $4 million in revenue in its first year.

David's thirty-year career in healthcare started with him serving as a hospital corpsman in the Navy. After his service, David became an RN, focusing his efforts on patient-centered care. In addition to serving as the director of nursing for a leading healthcare system and the executive director for the Northwest Ohio office of one of the largest homecare companies in the nation, David also contributed to the success of two healthcare IT firms. His contributions in consulting, project management, and leadership development at maxIT and Sagacious Consultants directly impacted their growth and led to the successful acquisition of both companies.

When he is not working, David enjoys spending time with his wife, Tallie, and their four children. He also gives back to his community by volunteering at his church and serves as the vice chairman of Gateway Youth Development.

When I was about eight years old, I collected baseball cards. A true entrepreneur from the beginning, I thought it would be a great idea to set a card table out on our front lawn and sell those baseball cards to people who drove by our house. Instead of tons of sales, what I earned that day was a blistering sunburn. I realized quickly that I had not considered everything that would go into this business venture—and that the cost of turning into a lobster was not worth the sale of a few baseball cards for a quarter apiece.

It was a failure, but it was the first time I "failed forward." The day may have been a disappointment, but I learned a valuable lesson about developing a pathway to profit: profit shouldn't cause you more harm than what you can potentially earn. This lesson took me one step further on my entrepreneurial journey, which would eventually lead to my position as the CEO of NurseNow Staffing.

Quite a few years after my baseball card venture, I found myself unemployed, as a nurse, in the midst of the COVID-19 pandemic. That sounds ridiculous, and it is. Before the world was turned upside down, I had worked for four different employers. What I realized during the pandemic, however, was that I was casting a vision that was not shared by the companies I worked for. I wanted to see nurses paid a living wage. I wanted to see nurses paid weekly. I realized that my vision was not going to be fulfilled in any companies that already existed. The only choice I had was to build a company on this vision, and gather people around me who wanted to see that vision fulfilled.

So, on August 2, 2020, in the heat of the pandemic, I decided to start a nurse staffing company. I believe that nurses and the work that nurses do is valuable, and I also believe that they need to be compensated well for that work. So that's what I set out to do. But like my baseball card venture, I had a lot to learn about running a business. I had to fail forward a few more times to create the success mindset that I have today.

You Have to Have Faith

NurseNow Staffing started with one nurse, in one nursing home, in the state of Kentucky. Her first invoice was for $812.50. And as I wrote out that invoice I thought, "Wow, this is a legitimate business. This is a real company." It felt awesome. I got out a cigar and a bottle of scotch, and I celebrated our first invoice.

But entrepreneurs know that building a business is rarely cigars and scotch. I quickly realized that one of my biggest problems was going to catch up to me as the business grew: I needed to have the ability to pay people before I got paid. I wrote an invoice for $812.50, but at the end of that week, the nurse wanted–justifiably!–to be paid right away. That invoice was just a piece of paper; it wasn't a fully completed payment. I needed to go find actual money so I could pay the nurse before the invoice was completed and the business got paid.

At first, this wasn't an issue, as we had put some money aside to fund the early days of the business. But as the company grew– and it grew quickly–I realized that I needed to have more money than our own savings to be able to ride the growth trajectory that we were on. I started to approach several different people thinking that they would see an investment as a great opportunity right away. As it turns out, not every person was willing to loan me money.

Several people told me exactly how little my company was worth. They told me that my business plan was a failure and the company would never reach the million dollars in revenue that I had envisioned. But these people didn't have the same faith that I had in the company.

This was a bit of a crossroads for me–a pivotal moment many entrepreneurs experience. What do you do after repeated rejections? How do you continue to step into the possibility of failure time and again? Keeping in mind the early lessons of my life, I decided I needed to keep the mindset of "failing forward." I realized I could only turn failure into success if my mindset was right. And in order to correct my mindset, I had to have faith.

I've always been a person that believed in things that no one else thought possible because of my faith. The definition of faith is to believe things that others don't believe are possible. It is with this mentality that I approach not only the company I'm leading right now but also every area of my life. When you have faith, all other things are possible. I have faith in myself, faith in my instincts, faith in my gut, faith in my heart, and faith in my mind. Faith permeates every part of me, and that's why I have been able to find success by failing forward.

Two Letters

You need faith when you are staring into the abyss–you have to believe that there's a way out of where you are at that moment.

My company reached that point when our growth sapped all of the resources that we had in our savings. I had put everything into the business; but each week, I had to make payroll. I wasn't going to compromise on that. NurseNow Staffing pays weekly because nurses deserve to be paid weekly.

By refusing to compromise on the pay schedule, I put myself in a tough position. I needed, in a way that only a business owner who's starting out and starting up can understand, to raise money. If we didn't make payroll that week, the company was done.

I called an investor and I left it all on the field. I told the story of NurseNow Staffing, of the vision that I had for solving this problem that nurses are facing all around the country and the world. We had the capacity, with an investor's help, to make a difference.

And then I just shut up.

I knew that if I talked first, I would lose. And I would lose a lot. We needed to cover payroll for the next thirty days. At the time, I thought this was an enormous ask; after all, I was asking an investor for a sum much higher than any amount that I've ever made in my life.

The silence felt like an eternity. And finally, after what seemed like forever, they said "OK." That was it. That's all they said. Just those two letters.

I had been trying to get to "OK," those two letters, for almost three months. And I knew that when they said "OK," that meant that everything was going to work out.

Of course, I had no idea that what I thought was a full month's worth of payroll turned out to be about two weeks' worth. Later that day, someone told me they needed nurses–up to one hundred nurses, to be exact. And they needed them at the end of the week.

To fulfill that need, we started calling and emailing and texting every single nurse we knew as fast as we could. Over the next three weeks, we ended up onboarding over forty new nurses. That meant I had forty new nurses who needed to get paid before I got paid–and I was back to square one with the same solvency issue I thought I had solved a few weeks earlier. Entrepreneurship, I was quickly learning, was a series of solving problems and facing the risk of failing forward. To get the investments I needed—much larger than what had felt like an enormous ask just one month prior—I had to tell the story to more people. But I saw this as an *opportunity* and not another setback. The story of our company is not just about me; it's about nurses caring for patients. And that's a very important story to tell—one that is worth the challenges and roadblocks and moments of staring into the abyss that entrepreneurs face so often. And there is no better time to tell that story than when nurses have given so much of themselves as they have in this pandemic that our world has faced.

I was able to get those two little letters again, now knowing that it wouldn't be long before I faced another set of challenges.

When I started NurseNow Staffing, I dreamed that someday we would make a million dollars in revenue. I thought that if things went well, that maybe in two or three years we might achieve a million dollars in revenue. But by the end of December 2020, we had created nearly a million dollars in revenue—in less than four months. This is just the cherry on top to my larger vision. Giving hundreds of people the opportunity to make a living wage and a positive contribution to our world is a great privilege and a great honor. Walking away with the knowledge that I am able to see out my vision and my revenue goals certainly beats walking home with a sunburn and quarters in my pocket.

Because I've Failed, I Can Succeed

I haven't succeeded in everything I've ever done. There is a lot of failure between my first business ventures and my first million dollars in revenue. I stood on the brink of failure many times as I pitched NurseNow Staffing to people who didn't believe in me and investors who slammed their doors in my face. Still, it's possible that what I'm doing right now with the company might be my greatest failure. I can't know for sure. But I am hopeful that each time I fail, I am going to have the opportunity to reach back, persist, and continue to strive for ultimate success.

And that's what a success mindset is: the willingness to fail, learn from failure, and persevere in the face of adversity. For me, this success mindset had to be learned over time. I couldn't possibly have been as confident twenty years ago as I am today because I hadn't yet experienced the challenges of the last twenty years. I failed. I learned. And then I put that knowledge to work so I could succeed.

Life is a series of experiences that we can either learn from or not. The choice is ours. And this is the true value of experience in life, failure, or otherwise–it is an opportunity for us to increase our confidence as we gain more insight. As we look back on how we've failed and what we've overcome, we understand the increasing amount of things that we can handle. Asking investors for a sum larger than any of my previous yearly salaries was daunting–until I was able to not only do it but also go back and ask for more. I wouldn't have approached investors in the first place if I hadn't been on the brink of failure–and succeeded–before.

The irony of a truly great success mindset is that it's really all about the willingness to fail. It's a cycle: Fail. Learn. Succeed. With every opportunity that comes my way, I will continue to be willing to fail forward, keeping in mind that as long as I persevere, the end of the cycle is always success.

Unfinished Success

Areva Martin

Areva Martin is an award-winning civil rights attorney, advocate, legal and social issues commentator, talk show host, and producer. A CNN legal analyst, Areva co-hosted the syndicated talk show *Face the Truth* and Emmy Award-winning *The Doctors*. Host of the web-based talk show *The Special Report with Areva Martin*, she is a regular contributor on *Dr. Phil, Good Morning America,* and *World News Tonight*.

A best-selling author, Areva has dedicated her fourth book, *Awakening: Ladies, Leadership, and the Lies We've Been Told,* to helping women worldwide recognize, own, and assert their limitless power.

Areva is the founder of Special Needs Network, Inc., California's premier autism advocacy organization. She has raised millions of dollars for autism, and has played a leadership role in advocating for state and federal laws to eliminate disparities in state funding for individuals with disabilities. She is also founder and CEO of the digital health technology company, Butterfly Health, Inc.

A Harvard Law School graduate, Areva founded the Los Angeles based civil rights firm, Martin & Martin, LLP. Her extensive business experience has positioned her as one of the top female entrepreneurs of the 21st century.

When I started my career, "success" was all about being in control of my own destiny and being an entrepreneur. I wanted to be my own boss. But because of my zip code, familial structure, race, and gender, I started my career with my hands and feet tied behind my back and a one hundred pound weight on my neck. I knew I would have to work twice as hard to get there.

So how *did* I get here? I have launched and run four successful businesses, employed hundreds of people, and built a media platform to advocate for underserved families, women, and children. I've accomplished all of that despite the fact that women—and women of color in particular—face almost insurmountable obstacles when we try to start a business. We face barriers to getting capital, racist and sexist tropes that say we are not as qualified as white males, and more.

I encountered these obstacles from the moment I sent in my first job application. But even when I was doubted, judged, and criticized, I held onto a particular mindset that says there is no such thing as failure—just unfinished success.

My Story

I grew up poor, living in a St. Louis housing project with my grandmother and my godmother who worked multiple jobs, including one as a janitor. My earliest work experiences were helping my godmother clean offices at night. At ten years old, I would travel to the wealthy suburbs outside of St. Louis and watch her work at big law firms and accounting firms.

Watching my godmother wasn't a tragedy—it was an inspiration. I was raised to believe that even though someone might have more than me—more resources, connections, money, etc.,—I could even the playing field through hard work. That perspective carried me through college, law school, and every entrepreneurial venture that I've been a part of.

When I came out of law school, I thought the job was done when I applied for my dream job at a powerful law firm. I had graduated from Harvard Law School at the top of my class—why wouldn't they hire me? I was competing with a classmate of mine…and watched as my dream fell out of my hands. She was offered the position and I ended up taking the "next best thing job." I wasn't crazy about the opportunity even though it offered a high salary and was located in Los Angeles. My story could have stopped there, but from the moment I took that job, I told myself that I never again wanted to find myself applying for work, knowing I'm very well qualified for it, and for some very notable, subjective, unknowable reasons, getting passed over for someone else. Every woman, especially women of color, knows exactly what I'm talking about. We are constantly overlooked for promotions, working as the "only" Black woman in the office, and subject to microaggressions that are ignored by supervisors and managers.[1]

I vowed, from that moment forward, to have more control over my career and build a space where I wouldn't have to experience that kind of rejection or discrimination.

But it's not easy to get everyone on board with that path when you share your goals with your peers. Not many people look at a Black woman from the projects in St. Louis and see a budding entrepreneur or a managing principal of her own law firm in a big city like Los Angeles. I know how others perceived me as I spoke my goals and took action to achieve them. In 2020, the ABA Profile of the Legal Profession reported that only 37 percent of the attorneys in the United States are women and only 5 percent are Black—and this is considered progress from when I was starting out as a lawyer. For a Black woman like me, having a job in a corporate Wall Street firm at all was seen as "beating the odds;" owning a firm was seen as impossible. They were wrong.

In Los Angeles, I had no one to vouch for me, either. I was a relatively young lawyer with limited legal experience. I had never run a business before. I had not gone to business school or taken any business management or accounting classes. And like many Black entrepreneurs, I had no investment capital. In fact, I was just getting out of law school, and I had heavy student loan debt. Getting a bank loan was out of the question and no one in my family had the money to help me start my first business venture. (I was the first person in my family to graduate college, first person to go to graduate school, and the first person to get a law degree.) A lot of my salary from my "next best thing job" went toward my loans, not savings or investing. Needless to say, I was defying odds and stepping out in a lot of firsts.

For casual observers, I was just a young lawyer with a dream. But for me, I was a woman on a mission with a dream

---

[1] Sarah Courey, et al. "Women in the Workplace 2020," (McKinsey & Company, 2020) www.mckinsey.com/featured-insights/diversity-and-inclusion/women-in-the-workplace#

that was backed by the mindset that took hold from those early days following my godmother around to her shifts as a janitor. I didn't stop until my law firm became one of the largest African American owned firms in Southern California. Not getting the job of my dreams wasn't a failure–it was just unfinished success.

Being Fearless

At the core of this mindset is *fearlessness.*

I would never let the fear of failure change my course. At times I felt rudderless. I had no roadmap or manual to follow, no guide or mentor to direct me. I didn't have financial resources to fall back on when things were tight. But I didn't let the deficits deter me. I was no stranger to personal sacrifices and I wasn't afraid of making mistakes and learning from them.

That meant separating myself from people and influences that tried to dissuade me from leaving my cushy corporate job and striking out on my own. I purposely limited my conversations and my interactions with those people. Achieving my goals allowed no room for people who had negative or discouraging things to say.

But I didn't have to be alone. Surrounding yourself with like-minded people who lift you up and believe in your dream is really important to overcoming unfinished success. This is true of the team you build around you, too. As a female entrepreneur, developing a strong and supportive team can help you achieve your professional goals and open up a world of choices, such as having a family and a lifestyle that restores and inspires you.

Having other people who are driven, ambitious, and share your values will help you when you hit low periods; they can offer helpful advice when you encounter problems and challenges. They'll be a source of strength for you–and you'll need that strength as you work your ass off.

Work Ethic

I have never shied away from hard work. Just like my godmother taught me, I showed up early, stayed late, and worked weekends. Through sheer grit and determination, I was going to do what I needed to do to start my own law firm and be free of corporate expectations and obstacles. By day, I shadowed a senior lawyer in court and met with clients. In the early evening, I went to networking functions and then spent hours working on legal cases, writing briefs and letters, and doing legal research. My "days" lasted from nine to midnight.

As I got my law firm off the ground, I worked every weekend without fail. Days were shorter–from ten in the morning to five or six in the evening. But every weekend, I worked. Fortunately, these long hours didn't feel like work. I loved it. I loved knowing that I was getting closer to the freedom I had envisioned for myself. I loved knowing that I was beating the odds. I loved knowing that through my work as an entrepreneur, I would help people in the legal space (and later the nonprofit space, through my media platform, and in the healthcare space, too).

Today, part of working hard is working smart. We are in an era where work looks very different because of technology. By being strategic, you can accomplish much more at a faster pace. And that leaves time for play–because my mantra is business before pleasure, then pleasure all the time. You'll be reaping the benefits of that hard work by diving into the things that bring you joy.

Your Mindset Is Your Key To Success

After I started my law firm, I started a nonprofit. Then, I started a media company. And now I have a healthcare tech company. I've started four businesses, and although I have learned a lot about management, leadership, and the industries where my businesses are operating, my mindset has remained a constant. Being fearless, with a stellar work ethic, will help you reach success no matter where you come from, who your parents are, or how easily you can access the resources that traditionally have put people (specifically white, wealthy men) on a fast track to that same level of success.

You also have to be willing to stumble along the way. And you will stumble. You will encounter all types of unfinished success, rejections, and the doubt and discouragement of people who would hold you back. You have to be the kind of person that eats "no" for breakfast, because you're going to get told "no."

"You can't."

"No, I can't help you."

"No, you can't do this."

"No, this has never been done."

"No, we don't want your services."

People will tell you "no" because they don't like the way you look, don't have connections to your family, or don't believe that someone with your background will ever make it in your industry. Those rejections can look like failure, but having a success mindset gives you the mental strength, fortitude, and flexibility to brush off "no" and push forward to "yes."

Even though I didn't look like I belonged in health-tech incubators or at the head of multimillion-dollar companies, my drive and fearlessness are what connects me to many successful people in business. Not everyone shares their unfinished successes once they have hit their targets and reached their goals; but I'm here to tell you that successful businesspeople have all endured periods of highs and periods of lows. We have had to stick it out for years at a time as we hone our craft and build our business.

Adversity and Opportunity

As my professional life was taking off, my law firm was growing, and I was creating a family of my own, I encountered a life-altering challenge I'd never imagined. My two-year-old son Marty was diagnosed with autism.

The diagnosis was devastating for our family, and our future suddenly seemed uncertain and frightening. But as I fought to access the services for Marty and resources for our family, I learned that many families who have children with disabilities—especially families of color—are underserved, ignored, and neglected by our healthcare systems.

Fear and uncertainty made way for determination and commitment. Instead of stepping away from my professional life, I would double down on my efforts—not just for my own family, but for all families enduring that unjust system. I pushed forward in my advocacy, established a nonprofit organization, leveraged my media platform to advance my cause, and found a new definition and level of success.

We're Not Statistics

I often think back to growing up in that St. Louis housing project. I think back to the time before I had any thought of ever having financial success or being considered a successful entrepreneur. No one expected me to be a successful businesswoman, thought leader, or influencer. And although money is important to everybody, that's never been my primary motivation. When I reflect on my journey, I think more about how I was supposed to be a statistic. I was supposed to be another person who didn't break out of the cycle of poverty. Women of color face consistent barriers that are *intentionally* placed to keep us at home and away from financial independence and success. We have grown up listening to lies about what we are capable of and what choices we should make in life. The secret to success is rejecting those lies, defining success for ourselves, fearlessly leaning into our strengths, working our asses off, and never giving up on our dreams.

I'm deeply proud of my story. And every time I share it, my greatest hope is that some young girl growing up in a poor neighborhood and encountering the obstacles I did will hear my story and realize that it doesn't matter where you start your journey—it's the middle and end that count. The roadblocks and setbacks are simply unfinished success.

PPE Wars: What COVID-19 Taught Me About Business

Aaron Poynton

Aaron Poynton is a businessman, entrepreneur, and consultant. He's the CEO and founder of Omnipoynt Solutions, a full-service high-technology strategy consulting and professional services firm in the aerospace and defense, national security, and health and safety markets. Aaron started his career in the military before transitioning to business. Initially working in the corporate world, he later transitioned to entrepreneurship, creating several companies and nonprofits. Aaron has conducted business in about fifty countries and has driven over $1 billion in contracts and revenue. He is a contributor to Forbes.com and is a member of the Forbes Business Council.

The Calm Before the Storm

On a warm and sunny morning on March 11, 2020, I sat near the poolside café of the Sheraton Jumeirah Beach Hotel in Dubai. Facing the beautiful Persian Gulf drinking an Arabic coffee, I admired the Palm Jumeirah in the distance and watched the skydivers float in under the canopy, touching down near the International Marine Club.

My cell phone buzzed; it was a message from a client. "We're going to need to cancel our meeting," it read. "Things are really getting worse here, and the borders may close soon. I suggest you get home while you can." As I pondered what to do, my phone buzzed again. This time, it was a news alert: *The World Health Organization declares the COVID-19 outbreak a pandemic*. "Well, shit," I said, "I guess it's time to go."

I spent the next few hours canceling meetings and reworking airline tickets to return to Washington, DC. "I'll probably be back next month," I told the young woman as she checked me out of the hotel. "You know, when this whole COVID thing blows over," I continued. Little did I know. My flight home was eerie; I sat in coach and had an entire section–about one-quarter of the plane–to myself.

After landing at Dulles, I experienced another eerie, twilight-zone moment. As I left the airport and drove toward the Capital Beltway, the regular bumper-to-bumper traffic was replaced with a wide-open road. I waited for zombies to lumber onto the highway, and I kept looking for Will Smith and the German Shepherd from *I Am Legend*. As I sped home at a record-setting pace, my denial turned to disbelief. Hundreds of questions swirled through my head, but I was confident that I was prepared for whatever came my way because I had built a mindset for success.

The Inner Explorer

As a young boy, I was a Boy Scout, specifically the senior patrol leader. I was an explorer–discovering caves, traversing forests, and soaring down rivers. I knew all my knots, had a sash full of merit badges, and eagerly performed first aid on anyone with even so much as a paper cut.

I took this foundational experience and mindset into young adulthood when I served in the US Army, and later to the business world. I worked in diverse and progressive roles with companies large and small, usually gravitating toward more challenging entrepreneurial roles, such as sales. I never stopped exploring and learning due to an innate and obsessive curiosity.

I went on to earn several advanced degrees. I studied business at Duke and conducted postgraduate business studies at Harvard Business School. I traveled the world studying business, read hundreds of case studies, and developed a global network of friends I could turn to for any business advice.

At Harvard, I studied Sir Ernest Shackleton, the Antarctic explorer who braved the harsh elements to attempt to reach the South Pole. His third attempt on the appropriately named ship, *Endurance,* is a seminal example of leadership under uncertainty. With Shackleton's principles enshrined in my ethos, I could handle any challenge. Or could I? While these experiences and learnings served me well, the one case study that was missing was leading and conducting business during a global pandemic. COVID-19 was uncharted waters.

The Shit Hit the Fan, and There Was No Toilet Paper

I sat on the head—literally—with no toilet paper. I found a creative way to get out of that situation. It had happened before—panicking people, making a "run" to the grocery store, emptying the shelves of toilet paper, milk, and bread. Typically, this was an acute situation, such as when the weatherman called for a Nor'easter. Within a few days, the shelves would be restocked; we never "really" ran out. But this time, we did. Walmart—out. Costco—out. Giant—out. Amazon—out. Wait, what? Amazon is out of toilet paper? That's not possible. I mean, if Jeff Bezos can fly to outer space, I'm sure he can find a way to make more toilet paper.

Toilet paper was the first commodity, but other items quickly followed. Hand sanitizers, hand soaps, diapers, tissues, water filters, canned foods, over-the-counter medicines, board games, and even bidets—all out of stock. The combination of irrational hoarding and supply chain challenges due to border closings were to blame. But what came next was more serious. We were out of critical medical supplies and personal protective equipment (PPE). Nasal swabs, nitrile gloves, and isolation gowns—out, out, and out.

Made in China

Unfortunately, nothing is made in America anymore—US manufacturing has been disappearing for years as globalization has accelerated and America has transitioned to a service economy. America has become less attractive for manufacturing due to cheaper foreign labor costs. This change didn't happen overnight but gradually occurred over decades. While Americans blindly indulged in first-world luxuries and distractions, China was taking over the world. In the 1980s, China's manufacturing started to soar, surpassing the manufacturing capacities of industrial powers one at a time. In 2010, China surpassed the US to become the number one industrial powerhouse. Today, it is estimated that Chinese suppliers produce 80 percent of Walmart's merchandise. This is why the US ran out of just about everything during COVID-19.

But when it comes to PPE, it's not just China; isolation gowns are made in Turkey and Mexico, nitrile gloves in Malaysia and Thailand, and so on. Traditional supply chains broke down as each country engaged in a bidding war for limited supplies, driving up the prices and creating a new gray market. It was literally a free-for-all, "wild west" trading environment. The reliance on foreign supply was a major wake-up call as the fragility and vulnerability of America's supply chain became blindingly obvious. However, for every shift in market dynamics, an entrepreneur exists to fulfill an unmet need, which is where I came in.

The Call to Duty

During my last call to duty, I served in the US Army post-9/11 as a biological officer, helping protect America from weapons of mass destruction. In many ways, this new call to duty was very similar: COVID-19 was a biological threat. My training and experience helped me frame COVID-19 as a war—and I took on a warrior mindset—not against a hostile country or terrorist group but a microscopic bug.

"PPE Warriors" popped up on my WhatsApp account. I was added to a new group. "We need six million masks ASAP," it read. I went to work; I would not sit on the sidelines of a global pandemic when I knew I could help. "I've got them in New York," I replied. And that was the beginning: I had become the modern-day drug dealer of PPE. Armed with a WhatsApp account and lots of caffeine, I spent the rest of the year filling the void where traditional supply chains failed.

High-drama negotiations with hostage-like "proof of life" videos of supplies and million-dollar wires to strangers were customary. We had trucks racing across the country to get supplies before we were outbid. We had inventory robbed from warehouses. We were coordinating with folks at the Department of Defense and the White House to help get our airplanes landing permits in foreign countries where travel was prohibited–all in just an ordinary day.

It was crazy. In one sobering moment, we were trying to close a $400 million glove deal on a Zoom call in the middle of the night. One guy joined shirtless and was all tatted up, wearing a baseball cap backward. Another toothless guy joined from a Caribbean island, trying to get us to transfer our deposit offshore. *Was I being "punked"?* Such was a stark contrast to my typical suit-and-tie boardroom negotiation.

Travel was nearly impossible, but we still had to vet our sources and conduct on-the-ground logistics operations. Vietnam, Turkey, and Korea–here we come! Flying from continent to continent, our team spent the night on the floor of quarantine holding centers. We had a group of "goons" watching over our precious inventory like hawks in Turkey. We were strapped to the back of mopeds zipping through Ho Chi Min City traffic to get government stamps on our documents. When cargo planes were in short supply, we desperately leased a passenger jet and stuffed medical gowns into the overhead bins and under the seats.

We were legit, but the market was shady as shit. Charlatans, fraudsters, and crooked brokers were everywhere; avoiding them was like walking through a minefield. We were on a roll, avoiding all the traps. And then, "We've been scammed," my partner said. I felt like puking; we were halted in our tracks by a fraudulent transaction through Dubai. Our money was gone–millions of dollars stolen by a fake company through a sophisticated international scam.

Working with the FBI and Thai police, we tracked down the bastards: a deceptive wannabe businessman in Dubai and a Thai woman and two African men in Thailand. In paralyzing suspense, we watched a video of the Thai Police conduct a raid on the criminals' hotel room in the middle of the night. Armed men burst through the door wearing police gear and, ironically, PPE. Two of the criminals, caught in bed, were stunned like deer in headlights. The crooks were there, but the money was gone. It was just another day in the world of PPE wars.

A bumpy start didn't dismay us. In fact, the challenge called more people to the team. I made no promises of riches or fame—just the opportunity to contribute. It reminded me of Sir Shackleton's famous advertisement to attract crewmembers to the *Endurance*: "Men wanted for hazardous journey. Low wages, bitter cold, long hours of complete darkness. Safe return doubtful. Honour and recognition in event of success."

We learned, improved, and never gave up. Our determination paid off with more orders. At the peak of the pandemic, we were flying two Boeing 787 cargo jets full of critical supplies to the US every week. Smooth as butter and with military precision, we delivered hundreds of millions of items flawlessly. When the government notified us of an acute national shortage of testing consumables, we answered the call with all hands on deck. We secured another airplane and rushed deliveries to the front lines like lives depended on it—because they did.

Reflection

"Would you do it again?" someone asked. "You bet your ass I would," I replied. In one year of the PPE world, I learned a lifetime's worth of business skills. It was stuff that you can't read about; you have to experience it.

I learned how to better read people and honed my "bullshitting" detection skills. I learned the importance of integrity and the consequences of situations created by those without it. I learned how to better operate under intense, battle-like pressure. I learned to follow my instincts and intuition, never straying far from my core principles. I learned how to strike a balance between risk and reward. I learned that having a success mindset with grit and determination is the biggest determinant of success. I learned that some people you revered suck and that other people you undervalued are worth their weight in gold.

But why? For what? As the great entrepreneur and explorer of our time, Elon Musk, said, "If something's important enough, you should try. Even if the probable outcome is failure." From failure, you learn. Initially, we failed a lot, so we learned a lot. Yet, our wins eventually offset our failures. But what's most important is knowing that we played a tiny part in the most important mission of our generation.

Winning Can Be Life Changing

J.D.R. Hawkins

J.D.R. Hawkins is an award-winning author who has written for newspapers, magazines, newsletters, e-zines, and blogs. As one of only a few female Civil War authors, she is a two-time winner of the John Esten Cooke Fiction Award (*A Beautiful Glittering Lie* and *A Rebel Among Us)* and the B.R.A.G. Medallion. Her books include *A Beckoning Hellfire* and her ongoing *Renegade Series.* Her nonfiction book, *Horses in Gray: Famous Confederate Warhorses*, has been published by Pelican Publishing. Ms. Hawkins is a member of the United Daughters of the Confederacy, the International Women's Writing Guild, Pikes Peak Writers, and Rocky Mountain Fiction Writers. She is also an artist and a singer/songwriter. Learn more about her at http://jdrhawkins.com.

One of the biggest goals I had set for myself was becoming an award-winning author. However, my initial goal was to write a compelling story; one that, to my knowledge, had never been told before. I never imagined I'd be a Civil War author, but after winning a trip to Gettysburg, Pennsylvania, I was inspired to write such a story. The trip was sponsored by Boyd's Bears, a teddy bear company which, at that time, was headquartered in Gettysburg. The company flew my son and me to Baltimore and drove us by limo to Gettysburg. We were treated like royalty! Seeing the enormous battlefield, the train depot where President Lincoln traveled to and from to give his Gettysburg Address, and all the reenactors and artifacts gave me inspiration, which led to writing my first novel. The story centers around a typical Southern soldier, and why he decides to fight for the Confederacy. It describes the impact that the Civil War had on individuals and families. Success came when I wrote the novel, which has now become a series.

Returning to Gettysburg later on, I saw firsthand how enormous the battle really was. I was asked to participate in the authors' tent at the 150th anniversary reenactment. Over 65,000 reenactors were present, along with nearly a thousand horses and 400 cannons, some of which were originally used at the battle. People were dressed in period costumes, and they held a dance, a period church service, and a ladies' tea. It was like going back in time. One couple even got married while wearing 1860s costumes! Reenactors ranged from typical soldiers to officers, including General Robert E. Lee and General J.E.B. Stuart. After attending this event, I knew my imagination was right on track with what I had researched. It was as though I was witnessing the actual battle, and it was amazing.

In order to write my first book, I had to develop a mindset which included diligence and discipline. I set aside a specific time each afternoon to write, and edited what I had written later in the evening. I did all this while working, because I have a devotion to my craft and wanted to see it through. Since I was working, it was a challenge to adjust to odd writing hours late at night (fortunately, I'm a night owl), and to keep my imagination planted in the past. In order to do this, I listened to period music while writing, laid out pictures of people dressed in period clothing, and studied unique forms of speech from that time period. This was difficult and frustrating at times. I think authors who write in the present tense have an easier time of it than historical authors do because they don't have to worry about accurate descriptions of corsets, for example.

I also needed to travel to the various battlefields described in my story. Because I live in Colorado and grew up in Iowa, I had never actually seen a Civil War battlefield (until I won the trip to Gettysburg), so I had to make sure the way I described the terrain, the buildings, etc., were precisely accurate.

When I first started writing the novel, I didn't understand the complexity of the Civil War market, or even how the publishing industry worked. I just wanted to tell my story, and I was compelled to do so by conducting a large amount of research. I couldn't modify my mindset in this respect, but only wanted to enrich and expand upon my characters. In my opinion, writing and acting are comparable. One of my favorite actors is Johnny Depp, and not just because we have the same birthday! I appreciate his talent because he takes each character he portrays and carries him over the top to the nth degree. From Edward Scissorhands to Captain Jack Sparrow, Johnny knows how to elevate his characters, making them relevant and memorable. This is what I try to achieve with my characters. In some instances, the characters took control of my ideas and changed the plot, so when an author says their characters wrote the story, it's true!

When I first began writing, I really had no one to walk me through the process; I had to figure it out for myself. Although I received suggestions from people, for the most part, I was on my own. For me, the best way to begin was to make an outline of the entire manuscript and detail it, chapter by chapter. At times, the undertaking seemed daunting, even overwhelming, but I persevered by taking it one day at a time. I had the fortitude to complete what I started, and I have always been that way in everything I do. It's never been acceptable for me to not finish what I started, and I'm definitely not a procrastinator.

Many plot twists were encountered along the way, not only in my books, but in real life as well. As I stated before, the characters sometimes took on voices of their own, sometimes even speaking to me subliminally, and changed the course of the story. They also changed the dialogue many times. I imagined how the characters would react in certain situations, and what they would say. My initial intention was to write one novel, but the idea expanded into a series, which I call the *Renegade Series*. One book turned into two. Then I wrote a sequel, and went back to write a prequel. The fourth book is due out this year, and there will be five books total in the series. In real life, I encountered many obstacles, including moving seven times, dealing with the deaths of my parents, and my husband's job changes and retirement. It became challenging trying to find the right time during the day to write, because my husband is home now and is distracting. But I wouldn't have it any other way!

On my journey to becoming an award-winning author, I have encountered numerous obstacles and low points. At the top of the list would be receiving bad reviews. This is always ego deflating, to say the least! Thankfully, the good reviews have outweighed the bad, but it's still a blow when it happens. Every author I know has received rejection letters. Many famous books were originally rejected by agents and/or publishers, such as *Gone with the Wind*, *The Life of Pi*, *The Wonderful Wizard of Oz*, and *Moby Dick*, to name a few. Stephen King's *Carrie* was rejected thirty times. One friend, who is now a best-selling author for his contribution to *Chicken Soup for the Soul*, received so many rejection letters that he wallpapered his bathroom with them! Although I received a few bad reviews, I didn't give up. In fact, it made me more determined to become a better writer, so I persisted, and it paid off.

Other obstacles I've encountered include having my book get delayed because the publishing company I was going with folded. Believe it or not, we were ready to go to print when the company closed, so I had to search out another publisher, which took about a year. The publisher of my nonfiction book is now Pelican Publishing, which is a traditional publisher and has been around for years. This also happened to me when I was getting ready to publish the third novel in the *Renegade Series*. I have encountered personnel changes with publishers, and have dealt with increased costs with some of my self-published books. One publisher got angry with me for sending out review copies and dropped me completely! Luckily, it didn't take long for me to find my new and current publisher, Westwood Publishing, with which I'm very happy. Because of all these growing pains, I realized that I could succeed, regardless of the high rate of rejection, and changes in the publishing industry.

I learned many things from overcoming these obstacles, but the most important thing was I received verification that I am an excellent writer. This happened before I won any awards. When I started writing my first novel, I asked several family members to read the manuscript. All of these people said I had a good story and that I was a great writer. There's nothing like validation to motivate someone, and this was incentive enough for me to keep going, believe in myself, and never give up. Like any career, there are ups and downs, good experiences and bad, but with a success mindset, anything is achievable. I credit my success one hundred percent to all of these attributes: luck, talent, writing habits, persistence, and perseverance. The lucky part had to do with winning a trip to Gettysburg. They called it the Boyd's Bears Family Reunion. I never expected it, but that's how a trip to a teddy bear family reunion changed my life, and eventually led to my becoming an award-winning author. In fact, I was voted second best author in Mississippi next to John Grisham by the DeSoto Tribune!

The greatest milestones I have achieved so far are receiving numerous awards. This never would have happened if I hadn't published my first novel. Although I am not Southern, I learned a lot by writing from the Southern perspective, and I wouldn't have changed any of it.

Three takeaways which made a vast difference to me are perseverance, confidence, and dedication. These three things made me successful, and I believe anyone who has these same attributes has the ability to be successful as well. I have persevered by conquering my obstacles and completing my projects, my confidence in knowing I was capable of creating a work of art and of being the best I can be at my craft has paid off, and my dedication to thoroughly research and accurately communicate gained knowledge about my topic has been rewarding in so many ways.

To sum it up, the role my mindset plays in my life is essential to my success. My determination has gotten me to where I am today. Winning awards and receiving positive reviews is validation toward my success, as well as making money at my craft.

Please follow me, and feel free to contact me at http://jdrhawkins.com.

Minding Your Castle

Jermaine S. N. Tolbert

Jermaine S. N. Tolbert is a Detroit, Michigan, native currently residing in Austin, Texas. He began to spawn attention from music industry executives after posting *YouTube* videos in 2007. In 2010, he had an unfortunate incident that forced him to walk away from a music recording opportunity with two-time Oscar nominated and multiple Grammy Award winner, Pharrell Williams, to re-develop mentally from the traumatic experience of being abruptly admitted into a local psychiatric medical facility in Southfield, Michigan. It happened just days before his life-long dream of signing a recording deal became a reality.

After being diagnosed with paranoid schizophrenia and depression, and being ignorantly recommended prescribed medications from doctors–ultimately receiving no help, Jermaine has miraculously used "knowledge" as the catalyst and means to surmount what others would dare to peer into–a microscopic look into the self. He was able to climb back to mental adroitness. Today, Jermaine's focus remains while pursuing his life's work in mental health advocacy, and personal success through proper brain training. To receive a free download of the first five chapters of Jermaine's book *Remind Me To Think: The Genius Behind Crazy,* and/or to pre-order your physical copy, visit https://bit.ly/3z8DnPM

I have a background in music, have shaken hands and rubbed shoulders with countless celebrities, and have little formal education in psychology–just the letter grade A in a course I once took in college. So, what do I have to offer touching anything in the realm of thought? I've written a solo book entitled *Remind*

Me To Think: The Genius Behind Crazy, perhaps suggesting that I've probably done little in that regard.

The underlying question is: why have I been chosen to give words here for you to carry as having weight? There have been and will be many books written by PhD-caliber professionals on the topic. What have they left out of the conversation that makes me inclusive in the dialog to be able to offer sage advice? Could it possibly be that most only have a theory in such a matter, while I have the actual practice of overthrowing crippling thinking?

Well, I'll have you know that my education gained from living in a psych ward qualifies me to speak on such a thing.

All the factors that opened the avenues for my life to journey into the music industry—on the brink of a recording contract with a two-time Oscar nominated, and multiple Grammy Award winner—are the same factors that drove me into a schizophrenic, depressive, suicidal bubble. What were the factors? It all came down to my knack for soundly thinking.

In my personal case, the medication that was suggested I take for what was diagnosed as schizophrenia and depression was ignorantly recommended. It was grossly ineffective. In the end, with no actual help from experts, I was lucky enough to regulate my own mental adroitness.

A Mind Is a Fortress

There are many perpetrators of sound thinking. They come in the form of other people's opinions, self-doubt, fear of success, understanding what's realistic (and what's not), and too many others to name. The only way to recognize these perpetrators is through knowledge—the catalyst for rationality. My breakthrough to freedom from two mental health diagnoses had little to do with a corrective drug. The journey taught me a great deal about what mental health means, and subsequently how it eludes the perfectly *normal.*

We easily fall prey to small minds, and even our own defective brainwork, because we have not properly fortified our mentalities for anything or anyone that presents a blockade or impediment to progressive thought—including our own ignorance. We quickly and easily give up our power and intellect by what we allow or don't allow into our minds. How fluidly we fall short of greatness! To fortify the mind takes gumption. It takes fearlessness. It takes a will to reposition our cognitive frame of reference.

Jim Rohn, the once great orator, voiced it best for us when he said, "Everyday, stand guard at the door of your mind." The door of the mind is just as important as the mind itself. It acts as a gatekeeper, opening to invite in and throw out what's necessary to live our best lives. And likewise, it closes to shut in and keep out those same frameworks. In other words, your mind is a fortress.

In order to function on the level you were meant to, one must first adopt this understanding. Your fortress must be guarded at all costs. Keeping out negative thoughts and protecting life-altering ideas and strategies is a must. One could (unknowingly) be subjecting their livelihood, or God-given purpose to demission on account of a vulnerable entryway. I've learned this the hard way. I went as far as, after unlocking my quarters, finding every potential intruder (in all forms), and tossing them the keys. I pointed out every crevice of my domicile to them, and provided the supplies to widen the cracks for scalable damage.

So, where did the shift come in? How was I able to transform myself from a suicidal wreck to a seemingly steel castle of a mentality? It was no easy feat, to say the least.

A Mind for the Big Leagues

One distinct afternoon, I had recently been on the phone with my oldest brother who lives in Jacksonville, Florida. I was crying my eyes out to him about how I wanted success so badly. I knew I wanted it, but couldn't seem to harness the gifts and capabilities I'd been complimented on throughout my life. My charisma, my singing agility, my passions, nor my intentions could crack the pavement of the ground I wanted to tread.

Just a few years prior, two childhood friends and I started a group; we were on the brink of signing a major recording contract with Pharrell Williams. Pharrell has been nominated for an Academy Award not once, but twice. He's a multiple Grammy Award winner, and a recent judge on NBC's hit TV show, *The Voice*. I'd spent nearly ten years before the opportunity to work with him creating and perfecting notoriety for myself as an elite singer in my hometown of Detroit, Michigan. After some internet videos that I posted spread, my notoriety spilled over into other states, even some other countries. I believe that was initially how I got on Pharrell's radar.

Things didn't turn out the way I had hoped as a result of my mental conflicts. I was admitted into Providence Hospital's psychiatric center in Southfield, Michigan, twenty minutes from the west side of Detroit, where I'm from. This occurred at the most inopportune time in my life—at the moment a deal was implicitly underway.

Pharrell gave us a call just a couple of days after my ten-day stay in the hospital. The group and I had spent over a year creating the music that would accompany us on our debut project. He was sending us all to Miami, Florida, to meet with him and music professional, Andre Harrell. Andre Harrell was a music industry legend (may he rest in Heaven), noted for upstarting the careers of Sean "Diddy" Combs, Mary J. Blige, and many more, so the fellas and I were super excited. Adversely, I knew I was in no condition to go. My thoughts were all over the place. I didn't know if I could trust myself to be copacetic in such an unpredictable environment.

The guys had no insight into the battle I was facing at the time. I ultimately had the power to skyrocket our movement or bring it to a grinding halt. I felt horrible! I felt completely insignificant, and a disastrous failure. I had absolutely no clue how or if my life (my mind, really) could or would ever return back to what I thought was normal. It was the hardest, and most important decision I'd have to make in my lifetime, and I sensed it very clearly. I declined the trip, and any further participation in the group, to secure my mental faculties. I gave the guys my apologies, and asked for their prayers.

Coincidentally, after having that conversation with my brother over the phone, I saw an advertisement online about how rich people became rich, and suddenly an upturn materialized. By this point in time, I was in a much better head space since spending time in a mental health facility but still light years away from the mindset I now hold. What I would call a perseverance mindset.

A Mind for Knowledge

The video was by a gentleman named Tai Lopez, an established entrepreneur and multi-millionaire. The message couldn't have come at a better time. It was a godsend for a surety. He didn't speak on some get-rich-quick scheme or anything of the like. He plainly declared, "The No. 1 reason (why) the wealthy are wealthy is because of knowledge." He went on to say that the founder of Facebook, Mark Zuckerberg, is rich because he knows something the rest of us don't. How stupid does that sound? Well, as a matter of fact, it didn't sound stupid at all. *Wow!* I thought.

"If anyone other than Mark Zuckerberg knew how to build Facebook (or anything close to it), they would."

Right then it hit me like a ton of bricks!

The guy mentioned that all the other creators of wealth and success attained such because of a knowledge base others *don't* have. What he was getting at is that excellence is not a matter of luck. He kept on about seeking knowledge daily in whatever specific area one wishes to excel. He said to actually execute, or to do those things after learning them, and one's life would follow those performed actions as a result.

My crying eyes became a pool of joy coupled with a childish, wonderstruck grin. I thought surely I could use this technique to climb out of the mental hole I was in. I began devoting my waking hours to studying health, wealth, love, and happiness per his advice. He said those were the pillars life should be built on– "the pillars of the good life." He said to gain knowledge in those four areas on an indefinite basis, and watch life open up in ways only the imagination could see. I wasn't so stupid that I couldn't hear the wisdom in what he was saying, that's for sure. I read book after book, and listened to one personal development seminar after another.

In a matter of one month from when I had begun to fill myself, knowledge had become my No. 1 pulling force–Empire State Buildings above what music could have ever done for me. Not only had knowledge *found* the roots of what was said to be schizophrenia, and depression, it uprooted them in exchange for replacing itself there, igniting a fire in me. It stormed in and reprogrammed my brain, offering a new lens from which to see. It triggered a laser focus through which I was able to observe, and *feel* each growth spurt in my thoughts in real time. That quickening birthed an entirely new passion in me. Instantaneously, all I wanted to do was to wake up wiser than when I went to sleep the night before. That was the plan of action. This is the perseverance mindset!

Ultimately, I learned I was more than what music had to offer through me. I was more than what I had to lend to it. Apparently, music wasn't big enough for the impact I knew I was predestined to have. I would never have been able to write a book to assist others in removing and circumventing calamitous thinking if it were. A book especially designed for the community of individuals living in a mental war, and the many who will face a mental battle in the future. For parents with children suffering, or parents with children that are gifted. A formula for anyone to achieve optimal brain functioning, it's for business professionals, musicians, artists, millennials, entrepreneurs, or anyone aspiring to be.

Fortification By Default

What is more important than knowledge, or at least of the same urgency, is the removal of senseless stimuli. It means nothing to gain all the knowledge in the world, but then continue to feed oneself the crap that causes negative self-talk, irrational thinking, and unwanted behaviors. Senseless stimuli come in the form of conversations, music, movies, internet videos, radio, television, books, you name it. Anything and everything that yields false, limiting, unconscious beliefs of the self falls into that category.

The idea here is that your mind is also a garden. What you plant, allow to be planted or watered, will assuredly spring forth in the physical realm. One who employs the self to continual learning while exterminating useless consumption is far out in front of the pack.

There's no doubt that knowledge provides an impenetrable steel gate for your fortress, but to give your enemies the keys to that gate is more than irresponsible.

Coaching Character to 10X Potential

Shawn Johal

Shawn Johal co-founded DALS Lighting, an LED lighting business, in 2009. He implemented the Scaling Up Growth System and led the company to triple its revenues, well into the eight figures.

Shawn went on to found Elevation, a Scaling Up coaching firm, where he works with entrepreneurs and their teams to help accelerate their growth while helping them find personal balance and happiness.

He is a Certified Scaling Up coach and the author of *The Happy Leader*, a leadership fable about transformation in business and in life. He provides a "Happiness Roadmap" for his readers and clients, teaching them how to achieve both happiness and success.

Former president of EO Montreal (Entrepreneurs' Organization), Shawn remains an active member and mentor to numerous young entrepreneurs, helping them improve as business leaders and as individuals. A finalist for the EY Entrepreneur of the Year, Shawn is also the board chair for "Champions for Life," a nonprofit foundation helping children develop their physical literacy.

I have always noticed a direct correlation between sports and business. Sports encourages us to get out of our comfort zones and to set aggressive goals toward physical achievement. This trait is transferable to business. In fact, when you talk to highly successful business people, you quickly learn athletic prowess goes hand in hand. If someone succeeds in one field, they often succeed in another. In sports and business, we need someone making sure we are performing at our highest level. We need a coach.

When we're young, not many of us look in the mirror and say, *"I'm going to be a coach one day."* It's a strange aspiration. I grew up playing competitive soccer at a very high level. I was mentored by amazing coaches (and some terrible ones, too). Coaches teach a great deal of leadership lessons. Through it all, I learned a lot about how to be successful. I've used that discipline and effort in my everyday life since. I have found my calling in coaching entrepreneurs.

As a young athlete, playing on a national championship soccer team, the most valuable skill our coaches imparted to us was the ability to visualize. The visualization techniques we learned have served me in my professional and personal life. When I reflect on the lessons learned in my teenage years as the captain of a championship team, I am amazed that I was able to commit to long-term goals. The team I joined at fourteen won a national championship when I was sixteen. Two years seems short today, but it's one-eighth of a sixteen-year-old's life. You learn the value of teamwork, to put in the extra hours, to live up to the sacrifice everyone is making. My experience as a youth athlete honed the success mindset I've carried into my entrepreneurial career and coaching practice.

Evolving Goals

I had a singular goal until the age of eighteen: become a professional soccer player. I was convinced it was destiny. You see, I have what's called, "a positivity bias." As crazy as it sounds, I have been diagnosed as seeing the world positively all the time. This may seem great, but it can be dangerous to see *everything* through rose-colored glasses. It leaves you certain everything is going to work out, but you are oblivious to the blind spots saying otherwise. By the time I was eighteen, I realized that I lacked next-level skills. The goal I was certain I would achieve was no longer attainable. Instead of dwelling on it, I moved on to different aspirations.

My next goal was becoming a documentary filmmaker. I spent five years studying the craft, ready to change the world with my docs. I soon found out how tough it is to break into the entertainment industry. When an opportunity to pursue a business career arose, I jumped on it. I realized that specifying a vocation wasn't the right goal for me. I broadened my goal to be a successful leader and coax the most from a person's potential.

That pivot to business came through sales. On a DISC assessment, a measurement of dominance, influence, steadiness, and conscientiousness, I am a "high yellow" which means "high influence." I thrive when interacting with people. Selling comes naturally to me. Growing up, I was always selling. As an excellent notetaker, I would sell photocopies of my notebook pages to classmates as study guides. I was working in sales to help pay for university. I worked in retail, both at a shoe store and an electronics store.

Soon, my first real job was as a sales rep for Rubbermaid. There, I was enrolled in a program called the Phoenix Program. They hired university students, provided us with a nice car, credit card, and cell phone in exchange for working eighty hours a week selling their products. Through the Phoenix Program, I attended three different leadership conferences. They were developing us as leaders: teaching us how to have tough conversations, how to hire people, how to fire people. These mentors looked us in the eye and taught us exactly what we needed to learn. Believe it or not, twenty years later, I'm still in touch with them.

Even then, my goals were more leadership-based than sales-based. The goal that arose from this was to be an impactful, world-class leader. The previous two goals were specific to job titles. My ultimate goal was now about who I would become rather than my title. And passing along this entrepreneurial wisdom to others would be my primary vocation.

Coaching Entrepreneurs

My latest venture is coaching. This is the business I wish to take to the next level as it combines every aspect of my life thus far into the perfect package. There are so many companies in need of guidance with strategic planning. Companies require comfort and support that can be hard to come by internally. That's how I spend my days now: working to empower thousands of companies to create their greatest strategic plans and experience what we like to call "profitable growth." Companies grow out of necessity. Profit doesn't always follow growth. We believe the only way a business can be successful, and its workers happy, is if this growth is profitable.

Coaching is a way of extending my personal success mindset to my clients. Success requires a wide array of qualities. Humanity is a quality that's completely overlooked in 2021. There is a lack of empathy and human touch as we hide behind our screens. Empathy and humanity were ingrained in me playing team sports as a youth.

Resilience, Optimism, and Empathy

Resilience is key to a success mindset. Do not let your emotions get the best of you. Determination sustains resilience. Pursuing a goal is important to me. Like I mentioned, my positivity bias makes going after a goal with reckless abandon easy for me. When you approach a project with clear eyes and full hearts (thanks, Coach Taylor), you say, "*You know what? This effort is going to succeed. I am going to put in the time and this is going to work out.*" Optimism is infectious.

My success mindset features empathy, resilience, and optimism. These characteristics fuel your efforts, but you still need emotional intelligence to drive them. Emotional intelligence is developed through listening. So many of us don't work on it. When others speak, are you really listening? Are you listening without formulating your answer? It has been scientifically proven that human beings take anywhere between one to two seconds to actually comprehend what someone is saying to us. If you don't let someone finish, you don't know what they're actually saying. Understanding your personal emotional intelligence and being attuned to what others are feeling ties back into empathy.

Breaking Free of Failure

I was privileged in the sense that my parents were hardworking immigrants who provided enough to eat and access to good schools. Those were my luxuries. I was exposed to great leaders and a willingness to put myself out there. When you put yourself out there, you're going to fail. And fail, I did. When you're a youth athlete aspiring to play at a higher level and that doesn't come to pass, it weighs on your identity. I spent the next five years studying to be a documentary filmmaker, but abandoned the plan shortly after graduation. I left it behind without really pursuing it.

Failure followed me into business as well. Our family started a company, which was taken public in 1999. The growth was amazing. Then, 2008 came. The Great Recession happened and our whole company went bankrupt. Many had invested a lot of money in the company and its failure was painful. But, like losing in sports, we had to let go of our mistakes. I learned from those failures and didn't look back.

You get the takeaway and you learn from it. Sports didn't give me what I *wanted* out of life: a career. It gave me what I *needed*: character, habits, and a growth mindset. Studying documentary filmmaking at university didn't give me the career I wanted, but I learned how to work in group projects, how to meet deadlines, how to juggle multiple projects. I may not be a documentary filmmaker today, but those tools are still with me. I use them when I get up to present before a crowd of hundreds. These experiences may have felt like failures because I didn't achieve my ultimate goals, but how these experiences shaped me as a person was quite successful.

In 2021, it's common to hear: *"It's good to fail. Failure is a teacher."* I believe that, too, but the reality is that I hate failing. Seriously. Failing bothers me. Failure is beneficial in hindsight, but when you're in the midst of failure, it's not something to be happy about. Failure drains your morale. We let it hold us down for far too long. How do you break free?

The Time-Anger Gap

There's a concept I've developed from an interview I once saw with the Dalai Lama. I call it the Time-Anger Gap. Someone asked the Dalai Lama, *"How come you're never upset?"* The Dalai Lama laughed, *"...You think I spend my days not angry? I'm always angry, but I know that by staying angry, I'm not going to be able to help these people. I have to get over my anger very quickly."* And so,

I interpreted this concept as the Time-Anger Gap. Here is an example. Tomorrow, you're driving on the highway and someone cuts you off. You get really, really mad. Some people let it ruin their day. Some let it ruin a week. Some, an hour. But the fact of the matter is, you will get over it. That person cut you off. They didn't kill you. You're going to forget about the car that cut you off. Why not reduce the Time-Anger Gap from a week to an hour to ten minutes to one minute to one second? Because you can control how long you hold onto that anger. You can't control the emotional experience of anger, but you can choose how quickly you return to contentment.

Here's an example to work on your Time-Anger Gap. Write down three random dates: April 2, February 23, and January 8. Now, write what you were upset about on those days. Struggling to find an answer? You're not alone. Most people don't remember why they were upset on any of these days, so they must have gotten over it. Why not get there quicker?

When you experience a setback, remind yourself that it will be forgotten in a week or month, so you might as well speed the plow.

Habits Versus Mindset

Habits are the actions you take in pursuit of success. Mindset is the motivation. I teach the value of high performance habits in my coaching. Personally, my habits are a bit intense. I have a morning and nightly workout routine. I visualize. I reach out to people and surround myself with positive, supportive peers. These habits have developed over time beginning with my coaches in soccer.

Eventually, I learned how to meditate and grew to understand the importance of fitness and nutrition. Habits are essential to a strong daily routine, both morning and evening. The evening routine is often overlooked. How do you spend the final hour before you sleep? Habits can be acquired and honed over time.

Habits are the muscle. Mindset is the brain. You need to utilize both for success. People with great mindsets, but zero habits, never act on that mindset. A mindset is only as valuable as what you do with it. You need the habits to make progress with the mindset. Mindset is talking the talk. Habits are walking the walk. Mindset is having a personal vision for your life. Habits are making that vision a reality.

Two Takeaways

I will leave you with two takeaways.

1. Take care of yourself first.
2. Go back to your childhood way of thinking.

When a plane is crashing and the oxygen masks drop, you are instructed to put your mask on first. Everyday examples of putting your mask on first: be sure to meditate, sleep regularly, exercise often, take care of people you care about, and surround yourself with those who bring out your best. Once you have that figured out, helping people will prove easier.

Secondly, return to your childhood way of thinking. No dream would be big enough. Society forces us to think smaller and dream selectively. I've found that the best dreamers have a childlike quality to them. They refuse to let society stop them from pursuing their wildest aspirations. So my advice: get back to thinking big.

Whatever you think you can accomplish, set a goal for ten times that. My goal is to help clients 10x their business and 10x their happiness; 10x is the number. Everyone has more potential than they realize. My calling is to help them realize that potential.

Conquering Excuses
That Hold You Back

Steve Ryan

Steve Ryan is an author, motivational speaker, podcaster, singer, songwriter, poet, actor, life coach, business coach, and entrepreneur. He has been featured in *Forbes*, *Rolling Stone*, *Yahoo News*, *NY Weekly*, *Billboard Magazine*, and *Source Magazine*. He specializes in mindset techniques that change people's lives through his The Abundant Lion channel. This includes a podcast called *Supercharge your Mindset with The Abundant Lion*, a blog, regular video releases, weekly motivation through his email list, and mindset courses.

Steve is also a Recording Academy member and a SAG/AFTRA actor with numerous IMDB credits. He has been successful in the music, entertainment, and business world. He is on a mission to inspire as many people as possible to enhance their mindset and go after their dreams. Learn about his mindset techniques and strategies to help you achieve success. Visit his mindset channel at www.theabundantlion.com.

Overcoming the Skepticism about Achieving Success

Do you ever feel like a hamster running on a wheel day to day? You dream of being successful but every unimaginable roadblock is drawn to you like a magnet. You hear of success stories but it's hard to be encouraged that it can happen to you. It all seems too good to be true unless you're one of the lucky ones or have the right connections. Have you ever had these kinds of thoughts before? You're not alone in your thinking.

When I was growing up, I was surrounded by people who had a fear-based mindset. Dreams of doing anything successful were viewed as something that only the rich and famous could have. Have you ever had people in your life who were skeptical of success? That type of environment made it challenging to stay encouraged. It was a struggle at times to have a positive mindset.

As a child, I was always drawn to entrepreneurship and doing things outside of the norm. I played strategy games and loved learning about investing and business. One of my favorite books was Robert Kiyosaki's *Rich Dad Poor Dad*. That book represented the core of how I felt and it gave hope and inspiration.

My biggest challenges were two things. There wasn't a support system that promoted entrepreneurial thinking and there weren't enough financial resources to make anything meaningful happen. This angered me and cemented my determination to find a path to achieve success.

Is this something that is holding you back; the lack of a support system or the lack of financial resources or perhaps both? Have you ever found yourself researching how to be successful and it still just seemed like pie in the sky?

Finding What Success Means to You

What is your definition of success? What would have to happen in your life for you to consider yourself successful? Everyone's definition of success can be different. The only challenge is that society often has certain images of defined success. These images are blasted into our subconscious on a regular basis through commercials, movies, music, and other mediums. The struggle then becomes defining what success means to you versus what's considered successful based on the world's point of view. My personal definition of success is to be able to do things in life that I am passionate about without finances being a hindrance or a concern.

At fifteen years old, it was my decision to eliminate any excuses or roadblocks that would prevent me from being successful. I saved all of my money while working in high school and learned about the stock market and business. After graduating high school, I went to college and worked full time while investing the majority of my income into the stock market. The goal was to generate enough income from dividends to pay for living expenses. While working, I started an online business. I quit college and my job a little over a year later at nineteen years old and had enough dividend income to support living expenses while focusing on growing business income. My journey was just beginning at that point but it didn't come without major challenges.

The Journey You Choose

Your road to success may be a different path than my own. Your mindset and how you approach life will play a major role as you're moving forward. The first step for you is to discover your definition of success. The next action after that involves developing an action plan to work towards your goal. Once you identify what's holding you back, then your next step is to develop a strategy to overcome those challenges.

My life wasn't easy after quitting my job. Although there was enough passive income for the basic necessities, it wasn't at a level to accomplish certain goals. I needed more time on a full-time basis to focus on the entrepreneurial path and that's why the decision was made to quit the job and college.

There were sacrifices made. When my peers were spending their money on unnecessary things that they didn't need, my strategy was to live below my means and have the faith that it would eventually pay off. I believed in it with every core of my being. The financial decisions made before that point helped tremendously. Even with passive income coming in, the journey was still a challenging one. The strategy that I practiced was twofold; live below my means and invest the majority of my income. It took a few years before my passive income grew to a level that I was very comfortable with.

Networking and Collaboration

If you are on the path to success, you have to believe in yourself 1000 percent. There will be moments that you will be discouraged and things will seem impossible to work. I remember all of those emotions of discouragement, hopelessness, and depression that were experienced on my journey. It felt like success would never happen but the strategy was maintained and eventually it happened.

One of the biggest factors that ultimately led to achieving my goals was having healthy mindset habits. Our mindset plays a huge role because that influences the decisions that we make. If you want to build a good support system, then research ways to network with like-minded people. A great starting point for you is to think about things that you are passionate about. Research and see if there are any organizations, groups, or affiliations that are a fit for you. Join the organization's email list and the email list of people that you can learn from or who share your interests. Eventually you will meet the right people at the right time if you put time and energy into that.

It's imperative when you network that you aren't a parasite. Imagine if a stranger came up to you and said that they wanted to take something from you, offer nothing in return, and want you to be happy about it. That would almost sound like a robbery. Consider approaching networking with an attitude that you are open to giving and things being mutual. This can be as simple as being willing to listen to someone or finding common interests to have good conversations. It's a good idea to follow up with people from time to time and see how they are doing. You will be amazed at how many people don't do that. Imagine every time you hear from someone, they are always wanting something. If you want a good support system, then be a good support system for someone else. If it is mutually beneficial for you and the other person, then they may be a good match to keep in your close network.

I practice this habit even to this day. There's always constant learning. Mastermind meetings are amazing. Every month I'm involved in multiple mastermind meetings. These are meetings in which everyone brainstorms and exchanges ideas. The energy with these types of collaborative conversations opens up the mind to think on a higher level. This also combats discouragement and fear. There have been many people along the way who contributed to my growth and I mutually contributed to theirs. Networking with people created a support system. If you create a support system, then negativity and fear will have a hard time influencing your mind. Think of it as an energetic recharge to keep you going towards your goals.

Healthy Mindset Habits

In addition to networking, developing healthy mindset habits will greatly benefit you. This can be a certain morning or night routine that helps your mind stay balanced and clear. What is something that you enjoy doing that relaxes your mind? Are there any particular activities that help you think?

My morning routine starts with one to two hours of non-negotiable masterminding time. The routine usually starts with easing into the day with some tea and fresh air. If there are any ideas that come to mind during this time, it's noted either on a voice note or an electronic note. It may be a song idea, podcast idea, book idea, business idea, or any other thought that flows into the mind. I like to research during this time, read, and do vocal warmups. The vocal warmups are a form of meditation because it involves a lot of breathing and energetically letting go. If you have a particular activity that you enjoy doing that puts you in a relaxed state of mind, then this can be used as a form of meditation. Some people enjoy yoga and other activities. The key here is for you to discover what works for you and do it.

If you have a goal that you are working on, carve out non-negotiable time to work on that goal. Non-negotiable time is time that you put aside for something without distractions and interruptions. It can be at any point of the day that works for you. The key is to chip away at your goal on a regular basis, whether it's fifteen minutes or three hours. The amount of time is not as important as making sure that you put the time in. Working on your goal can involve researching or taking other practical steps towards making it happen.

Researching and Mindset

Sometimes there will be moments things will seem like they are not working out. Your mindset will play a key role as to how you handle those moments. If you are open to learning, researching, and networking, then this will give you the information and the tools to develop a strategy that works for you. You will also get the tools to adjust your strategy as needed. If something doesn't work out, then you will be able to find another path or make the necessary changes.

Networking with people inspired me to eventually do life coaching and business coaching. An understanding of how important the support system is drove me to help others with their mindset.

My motivational speaking brand, The Abundant Lion, was in a news article during the 2021 Olympics when the issue of mental health was talked about. This article described The Abundant Lion as a mindset expert. Although I was described as a mindset expert, that still didn't stop me from continuing to network with people and to research self-improvement.

It's very easy for us to get stuck in our own bubble. Networking with people and being open to learning is a method that can be used to elevate your mindset and help you to constantly develop and adjust your strategies.

Actionable Steps to Take Today

Here are some actionable steps that you can take starting today.

1. Brainstorm and think about what success is to you.
2. Start researching ideas to work towards your success.
3. Network with other people and build your support system.
4. Establish a non-negotiable time every day to work towards your goals.
5. Have daily healthy mindset habits that will help your mindset stay balanced.

It's not impossible for you to reach your goals. Take it from someone who comes from a poor background with all the cards stacked against them. For nearly all of my adult life, I've been able to do things based on my passions without worrying about finances. My living expenses to this day are paid for through my passive income and that continues to give me the freedom to focus on ideas and things that I enjoy. I believe in you and believe that you have the ability to carve out a strategy that will work for you. If you stay persistent and keep a clear mindset, you will be on the path to success. If you would like to network, please reach out to me via my website at www.theabundantlion.com.

Work on Your Craft and Your Business Every Day

Bryan Collins

Bryan Collins is the author of multiple best-selling books including *The Power of Creativity*. He helps writers build authority and earn a living from their creative work via his books and courses. He also hosts the popular *Become a Writer Today* podcast where he interviews *New York Times* best-selling authors about their creative work.

Bryan's work has appeared in publications like *Forbes*, *Lifehacker*, and *Fast Company*. He lives an hour outside Dublin, in Ireland, with his wife and three kids.

To learn more, visit becomeawritertoday.com.

When I was five years old, I read Roald Dahl's *The BFG* and said to myself, "I'm going to become a writer." I was and still am fascinated with how creative people tell captivating stories that readers love and share.

I started writing for the newspaper at school and got a kick out of friends reading my stories. After graduation, I thought earning a living as a full-time writer started with becoming a journalist. So I enrolled in a communications and journalism degree in a college in Dublin City.

I had a lousy mindset in college. I spent far more time going out and getting drunk and high than turning up for lectures. Somehow I managed to graduate.

Then, I deluded myself. I believed because I had a degree, I was on a sure-fire path to becoming an editor of a national newspaper by the time I turned forty. Instead, I spent over a year looking for paying work. A successful journalism career in Ireland is about connections and story ideas, and I had almost none.

A Commission Is Not a Career

After many months of pitching editors without luck, a friend helped me land a gig writing feature articles for a popular Irish Sunday newspaper. A single writing commission turned into a (at the time) lucrative gig that helped me pay the bills for several months.

It was a well-known Irish newspaper, and I was delighted when friends said they saw my byline in it. So, I stopped pitching for paying work and concentrated on this single gig.

I told myself, "I've made it. I'm finally getting paid to write."

One Monday, my editor emailed to say, "I won't have any commissions for you this month, Bryan."

"What about the one after that?"

"It's not looking good. We're making cutbacks everywhere."

"What am I going to do?"

"Whatever it takes to keep the ship afloat."

Our mortgage was due, and suddenly I was scrambling for paying work.

So, I borrowed money from the bank until another job outside of freelance writing paid up. I found a day job working with people with intellectual disabilities.

One Saturday morning, I gathered up all my old journalism news clippings, stories, and notes and threw them into the local dump.

In Pursuit of One Great, True Essence

After washing out as a journalist, I still wanted to earn a living from creative work. So, I took a series of intensive creative writing classes in the Irish Writers' Center in Dublin. Every Monday and Wednesday evening, a dozen or so writers met and discussed stories by William Faulkner, Ernest Hemingway, and Joan Didion. We also shared our work with each other for critiques.

Our instructor, a balding literary author from Texas, told us: "You must write one great, true sentence."

I finally felt like I'd found a new path towards earning a living from creative work. So, I started writing every night alone in my home office, after work.

I spent a few years writing short stories and Irish literary fiction. But seeking perfection, or attempting to write one great true sentence, is like trying to throw a typewriter at the moon. It's impossible!

Instead, I should have published and shared my work and got feedback from readers and a knowledgeable editor. (That's advice I offer struggling new writers today.)

Who Am I to Write?

One day, I got the train into a job interview in PR, in Dublin City Center. I thumbed through some of my short stories that I'd spent months working on without success or publication.

It hit me.

I'd tried for almost ten years to make a living as a writer, and here I was applying for jobs that had nothing to do with writing or even creative work.

Perhaps I should give up? Who was I to write and try and earn a living as creative?

I couldn't do it, though.

At the time, I spent hours reading the popular productivity and technology blog *Lifehacker*. I decided to set up the Irish version of *Lifehacker*. I called my site *WorkReadPlay*.

I started publishing articles about saving time in Excel and the latest Apple news, hardware, and apps. To my surprise, that website attracted a little traffic.

I'll never forget the time I received my first affiliate payment from that website. It wasn't my quit job money, but it opened my eyes to a viable income strategy many new content creators overlook.

"Bryan, your review is #1 on Google," said Robbie, a friend in work.

"My what?" I walked over to his computer.

"I was Googling Lynda.com and your review came up."

"That's news to me."

At the time, I struggled to learn how to use WordPress and create images from my website. So I took a series of online courses on the online learning platform Lynda.com, now known as LinkedIn Learning.

One week I needed something to publish, so I wrote a detailed review about my experiences on Lynda.com and what I learned, liked, and disliked.

A few weeks later, a rep from Lynda.com emailed me. She invited me into their affiliate program. So I signed up for their program, and I added affiliate links to my content with a disclaimer.

Sixty days later, I received a PayPal transfer for several hundred dollars. It wasn't quit my job money, but it was enough to replace my bald car tyres. Better still, I was on track to earn the same amount the following month, too.

Finding the Balance Between Craft and Business

My hand was shaking when I took out my credit card.

It was 2014, and I'd never spent thousands of dollars on a course, much less from a person I'd met on Twitter.

What if I was getting ripped off? What if it was a waste of time?

Thankfully, Jon Morrow is an intelligent guy. Based in Austin, Texas, he helps writers earn a living from their work. Many of his lessons applied to my creative goals around 2014-2015.

At the time, I was learning that one lone Irish washed-out journalist can't compete with a massive media organization like *Lifehacker*. Content about technology gets old, fast. It's a niche I didn't have time for because of my full-time job and family life.

I learned from Jon, from other instructors, and later content marketing books and courses about what it takes to build an online business.

I closed down my first technology website and set up another blog about writing, and I called it *Become A Writer Today*. I began publishing articles about the craft based on books I'd read and interviews with successful authors.

I finally found an audience.

Over a few years, what started as a hobby turned into a side and later a full-time business. I received emails and comments from readers with questions about how they could improve their craft. I started publishing and selling books and courses. And my affiliate income increased almost every month.

Since setting up *Become A Writer Today* in 2014, I've grown the site to several million page views per year. Today, I earn money from selling books and courses. I also earn an income from affiliate marketing, which is promoting products and services that I use to other writers.

My site opened doors to great freelance writing opportunities like a regular gig for *Forbes* and some lucrative copywriting jobs. I also set up several other websites in different niches and replicated my business model with the help of freelance writers.

Some of that success is down to a daily writing habit whereby I write a little every day. Some is down to the help of other freelance writers who I commission for my websites. It's mostly down to pressing publish early and often.

I wish I'd started writing and publishing my work online sooner. I should have created my website and email list and began creating content online back in the early 2000s, instead of working in an unsuitable profession.

The most successful content creators, like Tim Ferriss, started back then. I also should have hired an editor and pressed publish sooner instead of repeatedly rewriting the same stories. But new content creators are still early and can pick from even more opportunities than when I started years ago.

Three Takeaways

My three takeaways from my experience are as follows:

1. In the morning, work on your craft. In the afternoon or evening, work on your business. It could be something as simple as writing 300 words and starting your email list.
2. Write, publish, and share your work online, where your ideal readers spend time. I don't mean sharing random updates on Facebook either. If you produce great content consistently, you'll slowly attract feedback about what your ideal audience wants and expects. That will, in turn, help you improve at your craft and build up an audience.

3. Create a place on the internet that you can call your own. By all means, grow a following for yourself on YouTube, Twitter, Facebook, Pinterest, or your social media network of choice. But direct some to visit your website and join your email list. That way, when the algorithm for these social media networks changes or the rules evolve, you'll still own the relationship between you and your audience.

Mindset Is Key for Creatives

Mindset is key for creatives. The great American playwright David Mamet said, "You've got to do one thing for your art every day, and you've got to do one thing for your business every day." That advice underpins how I approach creative work and earning a living from it.

Let's say you want to write and sell a book.

If you sit down on Saturday afternoon and try to produce several thousand words of epic prose, you're unlikely to succeed because you're out of practice or life will present a more appealing way to spend the day (believe me, I've tried). This lack of progress will put you off turning up the following weekend.

On the other hand, if you sit down at your writing desk every morning and produce 300 words a day for five or six days a week, that will multiply into over 2,000 words a week, or 8,000 words a month. Within a couple of months, you'll have the first draft of a book.

That's something you can get feedback on before publishing, selling, and turning into an asset for your business. And you'll still have time for family, your day job, or building an online business around your creative work.

Unlike years ago, creatives don't need to ask anybody's permission to host a podcast, set up a blog, or publish a book.

If you've an important message to share, a story to tell or you want to earn a good income from creative work, it's easier than ever to find an audience and earn an income from creative work.

All you need to do is start.

Claim one of Bryan's books for free on bryancollins.com or say hello on Twitter @bryanjcollins.

Leap Now

Anjali Sharma

Anjali Sharma is the founder of Narrative: The Business of Stories, a consulting firm that focuses on using strategic application of stories to solve the transformational challenges faced by today's global organizations. She is a sought-after keynote speaker trusted by international brands to find, develop, and utilize their transformational stories.

Anjali's career started in college, at the age of nineteen, when Hyatt Hotels and Resorts in India recruited her, but within a year she left India to fly for the world's best airline, Singapore Airlines. Working for an airline was a masterclass in understanding world views and the stories diverse people tell.

After working for the airline, Anjali transitioned into the corporate world and held senior corporate roles for more than a decade in Australia and Singapore, where she gained extensive experience, knowledge, and understanding of the strategic issues companies face as well as the concerns faced by employees. With this knowledge, experience, and unabated passion for storytelling, Anjali founded her firm in 2012.

Anjali currently lives in Singapore with her husband, thirteen-year-old daughter, and two rescue dogs. She is an avid runner and often runs as a pacer for marathons held in Singapore. She also enjoys reading, writing, and cooking anything spicy.

Anjali is currently running a book club on her upcoming book *Storied*. Join the book club at https://narrative.com.sg/storied-book-club/

Leap Now…Anywhere Will Do

1983. New Delhi, India.

I'm in a classroom surrounded by tiny colourful tables and chairs. But there are no other kids, just me and a teacher. She shows me a pencil and asks, "What colour is this pencil?" I smile, I know the answer, but only say, "I know the answer." She stares at me. The answer is grey. I know because it's the colour of the school's uniform. My mother has already bought the uniform. I have tried it on, looked at myself in the mirror several times, and felt good about myself. My older brother goes to the same school, in grey shorts. I know this colour but somehow I can't say the answer. It's stuck in my throat.

The teacher gives up on me and gives me wooden blocks, asking me to fit them in the right section on a wooden board. You know those things, where you fit a circle to a circle and square to a square. I grab it with confidence, fit the square in a rectangle and tell her, " I am done." The square did fit in the rectangle! It makes complete sense to me. As I'm brimming with pride, I notice my parents, peeping through a small glass panel on the main door of the classroom. They look a bit worried, but I don't understand why. I feel really good.

The teacher escorts me out of the classroom and asks my parents to see the school principal in half an hour to know if I have cleared the entrance exams or not for this school where the colour of the uniform is grey. Oh, that was a school entrance exam, we have those in India!

On the way back home, I was sad. Not because I failed. At three, it is a bit hard to comprehend failure. I was sad because I couldn't wear the grey uniform anymore.

A few weeks later, I was in another school in a red uniform. On my very first day of school, I kept asking my mother, "Can we go to school now please?" She was tired of me asking and said, "When the big hand of the clock is on six and the small hand is on eight, we can go to school." I sat in front of the clock staring. I remember the second it went from 8:29 a.m. to 8:30 a.m., I screamed with joy, " Let's go to school!" I did very well in school in my red uniform.

This story is like my DNA strand; it reveals the entire fabric of my character. Doesn't matter which school, what colour uniform, just leap into it. Whether you know the answer or not. Didn't get the grey uniform? Make the best of the red uniform.

That same mindset followed me in my career:

When I was a waitress, I wanted to be the best at serving coffee.

When I worked in sales, I wanted to be the best salesperson every week.

When I worked as a flight attendant, I wanted to be the best on my flight.

This mindset was the reason why I fully committed to each company I worked for. As a result, I rose through the ranks quickly, truly achieving my goals. The success metrics were promotions, salary raises, and titles. All this led to me becoming a director in Australia for a leading brand at the age of twenty-six. I was a successful person.

When I look back, the best way to define the mindset that allowed this success would be through a quote by Martin Luther King, Jr.

> "If a man is called to be a street sweeper, he should sweep streets even as a Michelangelo painted, or Beethoven composed music or Shakespeare wrote poetry. He should sweep streets so well that all the hosts of heaven and earth will pause to say, "Here lived a great street sweeper who did his job well."

My mindset was *just leap now, anywhere will do*. This served me well until 2012.

Leap Now...But for What?

By 2012, I was working as a business director for a global brand experience company. I was earning a big salary and had a big title. All the success metrics were in place. But something was not right, I was not as happy as I had been in my previous roles.

I questioned why my notion of success didn't feel like success anymore. This feeling lingered. With no clear answers, I felt more and more unsettled.

One day, a trivial experience brought clarity. My boss was on a business trip. I had sent him a contract to sign, a deal I had been working on for a while and I was really excited to get it signed. But the only problem was that my boss was not responding. I was feeling frustrated, the contract meant a lot to me and our monthly revenue goals. I called a colleague, who had gone on the same business trip as my boss. When I asked her, " Where is (my boss)?" She said, "He is out for a boys night." I was speechless. In that moment, there was a strong realisation that the feeling of success was not just about titles, salary, and the brands you work for. That success for me came from autonomy to keep leaping and to add value.

Now, just leaping was not the goal. I wanted to know why I was leaping and what value I was adding.

Leap Now…This is Why

I knew what I was looking for but didn't know what to do about it. One morning, I woke up worrying about the day ahead. To distract myself, I started scrolling on my phone and stumbled upon a blog by Seth Godin. What I remember the most about that blog was how it ended with the action statement "Go make a ruckus!"

Here is how he describes making a ruckus:

> *Not a disturbance, a racket or a commotion, but a ruckus. The act of making things better by making better things. The hard work of showing up with insight, assertions and kindness. The opportunity to shine a light, open a door and lead.* **Go make a ruckus** *belongs to each of us, because if we're not going to make things better, who will?*

There was something liberating about that. It gave me permission to do my best work, take risks, fail, try, and repeat, all in the pursuit to add value.

I jumped out of bed and wrote my very first blog that day. It didn't matter if anyone read the blog or not, what mattered to me was I had taken an action, no matter how small, towards making a ruckus.

That day was also the very first day I asked clients, friends, and family, "What am I really good at?" Remember, before that it didn't matter because the goal was to leap now and anywhere will do. For the first time I wanted to know why I was leaping, what value was I adding?

Every conversation I had led to one place: storytelling. I wondered if that was even a profession or just a hobby. When I started connecting the dots, I saw a clear pattern from school to college, from college to all the roles in my career; my gift was storytelling. I had just not labelled it!

Where was I going to begin?

Leap Now…But How and With Whom?

I started looking for people who were already doing what I wanted to do. There were not that many and the ones that I found did not respond to me. But I persisted.

The fact that I still had my regular job meant I could take my time. I was not feeling the pressure of being unemployed nor was I facing a professional identity crisis which gave me the mental space to persist. I highly recommend you do the same; don't stop working to start something else. Only when you feel confident that you have enough work in your dream role should you leave your current role.

When I say work, I don't mean revenue. The momentum of work is more important than revenue when you first start. Many entrepreneurs give up due to lack of motivation to persist. That energy to persist comes from momentum sparked by external conversations, not internal work. You may feel you have momentum through building a website or setting up systems but that doesn't help. What helps is external conversations with people who will engage with your service.

Finally, through persistence, I managed to form a business partnership.

I was ready to leap!

The only difference this time was that I didn't leap alone. I involved my mentor in the decision making process. My mentor and I are polar opposites. When I talked about making the business successful, my mentor talked about making sure the contracts were laid out correctly. When I talked about aggressive expansion strategies, my mentor mellowed my thinking and asked me to pace my approach.

Sometimes, it bugged me how detailed he was, how much he questioned everything, but I went along because I trusted him.

The business was on a roll from the first year but I hit the wall again.

After delivering the same work over and over again, no doubt I had become good at it, but I was feeling bored. I didn't feel I was making a difference anymore. I wasn't able to try, experiment, and do new things. I wasn't able to initiate change and make things better. I didn't have the autonomy. I discussed this with my mentor and his suggestion was, it is time for you to fly solo. "You are looking for creative freedom," he said.

I had so many mental blocks. "Oh no, how could I do that? I am only in my early thirties, without a big brand backing me up, who would listen to me? Who am I really?" But my mentor convinced me to take a leap of faith and make the change happen. I did just that, went completely on my own and have never looked back. It was one of the best decisions I have ever made. The year 2014 was a good year for me.

I was leaping, knowing why I was leaping, how I was leaping and with whom I was leaping. So what had I learned?

Leap Now…and Learn Now

I was now at a stage of my career where I was feeling complete autonomy and freedom. There was a sense of calm which created space for reflection. What had I learned from all of this?

Overcoming the 2012 low point in my career taught me the following lessons.

1. **Don't go cold turkey.** When you are feeling low, quotes like "Just do it!" "You can do it!" "You are made of steel!" and "Go for it!" will resonate with you. In times like these, these quotes create an impulse to act. Balance this intense feeling to act with logic and rationale. Don't stop one thing to start another. Wean from one to another.

2. **Complementary not supplementary.** Find someone who complements you with skills you don't have. My boundless energy is perfectly balanced by my mentor's careful, thoughtful approach. A lot of people find supplementary partners (people with the same skills) not complementary partners, which often leads to creative conflicts and one-sided business strength.

I was learning not only about the business, but also about myself.

Leap Now...With Self-Awareness

With miles to go, in 2018 I started to feel a slight sense of accomplishment with where I was taking Narrative:The Business of Stories, my eight-year-old story practice. Much of that sense of accomplishment came from the opportunities the business presented to develop self-awareness.

What did I learn about myself?

1. I have realised I am creative at heart. Heavily process driven environments are limiting for me; I have to have the autonomy to experiment constantly. I am a gardener who sows the seeds, nurtures, and then waits to see what happens, not an architect who has a perfect blueprint. But creativity on its own was not going to help, I had to develop a mindset of responsibility that complemented it.
2. I had a responsibility to and for my clients. My creative flair, when wrapped in the promise of responsibility I was willing to take for my clients, became the key to success. Be creative with clients, take them on a path unknown, but don't expect them to take responsibility for the project. You take it! No client will pay for you to test and try your creativity but they will pay for you to be creative if you take responsibility for their success

So what exactly can you learn from me?

Leap Now…Like Me

The first thing to realise is that you can't copy my biography, just like I can't copy yours. Don't let yourself off the hook by telling yourself the story that "she had a mentor, I don't"; "her business was successful from the onset, mine will not be."

The purpose of sharing my stories with you is to share the mindset that has served me well.

My mindset can be distilled into the following choices

- Take risks, but they have to be calculated risks.
- Look for teams with complementary skills not supplementary skills.
- Double down on your niche to find creative satisfaction by building new business models.

If you feel like leaping now, then you are my tribe! Let's connect. Feel free to contact me via LinkedIn at https://www.linkedin.com/in/anjali-sharma-4973a642/ or on Instagram @ anjaliStories https://www.instagram.com/anjalistories/

Toward Happier Choices

Michael Oborn

Michael Oborn was born and raised in the border areas of Idaho and Utah. The US Army sent him to Information Specialist School for training in media journalism. At Camp Zama, Japan, he managed a theater and directed live stage plays.

He is a member of the Willamette Writers Association, Portland, Oregon, and the Pacific Northwest Writers Association, Issaquah, Washington. Oborn is a retired Chemical Dependency Professional (CDP), who worked with alcohol/drug addicts and their families. While he uses the word retirement, his MacBook Pro doesn't. Together they have written two award-winning screenplays and a thriller which received Reader's Favorite Honorable Mention status. Having lived through his sweetheart's cancer surgery and treatment, Oborn claims cancer survivor status. Thirty years together and counting in the Puget Sound. For more information, visit:

https://www.amazon.com/s?k=Michael+Obor n&i=stripbooks&ref=nb_sb_noss_2

Where to start? How? A Mormon son, it was on a Sunday when you were told you asked the wrong questions and were then taught what the right questions were. You were young and you were busy being sixteen and doing things with your friends and buying your first car and then one day you were twenty-six and you can't swallow. "It" won't go down anymore. "It" had gathered and grown big while you were busy. One day it overwhelms busy and you're screwed.

Choose, choices; everything is choices.

My birth culture raised me to be dependent on a rigid, radical, fundamentalist system of beliefs. Guilt, shame, and other defense mechanisms insured my dependency. The conditioning was deep.

When I turned away from my birth culture I was treated like a traitor and looked at like a freak. Another word for it is abandonment, a longish word that sounds innocuous, but isn't. We are talking long-term PTSD, Post-Traumatic Stress Disorder.

Toward Happier Choices is a book about change. Some of what happened started years ago. Time was not a rapid healer, but it was thorough. Call me a slow study.

Several times I lost my way as I looked for a life I thought I wanted. The pathfinder, ready but dormant, lay waiting. Somewhere in another time I came across the following: *Where the attention goes the energy flows.*

I thought I understood. It seemed like such an obvious, straightforward statement; I paid little attention. No energy followed. It was not until I did the math, years later, that I got it. What we choose to think about is important. What we choose not to think about is also important. I am the chooser.

Practice was essential. Getting up ten minutes early did it for me. Guilt and shame can be excised–conditioned out of the loop–as long as it is replaced with a mindset positioned for success.

Over all the social demands of my birth culture for my time, energy, and money I am the one who gets to say *this I will entertain, this I will not*. As a result, my life became decidedly less complicated, not to mention more focused and productive.

The big question then, what do I want my life to look like? On what path do I want my journey pointed?

With aim and target a process begins. Hang on! At this point the adventure takes on a life of its own. Two award-winning screenplays and two books later the kid born dyslexic–a condition science hadn't defined back then–is still doing ten minutes a day. I was held back in the third grade. My parents had no alternative but to think God gave them a stupid kid.

Problem? How to write a memoir that is not quite a memoir? Not just my history, but where I am and those who have had an effect on my journey. How to write a progressive anthology of my process?

My choices in searching for a life worth living are reflected in my pen. As such, *Toward Happier Choices* is an accounting, a summary journal outlining what happened, and what I did to turn my life around.

I am convinced "story" is the best medium to illuminate what being human means. I found a collection of stories inside me raging to see the light of day. Each reveals and accents the human dimension in some unique way.

One of my beta readers called *Toward Happier Choices* a daring motivational narrative. Wow! What author wouldn't like to hear that?

If you like short stories, I've included eleven. I was a medic and training non-commissioned officer (NCO) at "M.A.S.H. 4077" during the time they were writing the film script for the movie. Does that tell you anything?

In another, Christopher Plummer played a decisive role in bringing me to understand the role radical fundamentalist cultures make in our lives.

For you whose lives revolve in and around fabric, you will enjoy "A Quilter's Heart."

If you are a sports type, you will especially enjoy the story about the sports journalist Jack Smith who covered and skirmished with the Oakland Raiders in the 1970s when John Madden made The Raiders the winningest team in the NFL. Jack and I met in AA. His drunk story I couldn't resist. Sober we did together.

I couldn't omit a comment about our unsung heroes, those that have and do inspire us. I call it "A Teacher's Curse."

Until I met Lady Meow, I would never have chosen a cat over a dog. An Egyptian cat gave me a whole new perspective on the feline species. I can no longer say I am not a cat person.

In the section entitled Potpourri I stick my neck out, yet again, spelling out why I believe it will be the female that saves our republic. For twenty years I've known this. Now, watching so many women elected to seats in the House of Representatives and the Senate is like watching a depressed stock finally shoot through the roof only instead of making one person rich it is making us all richer. *More women in Congress are a must.*

"My Treasury" of thirty-three quotes offers both humor and insight. I do not hide behind these. They tell me better than I can.

I comment on several celebrities: Whitney H. Houston, Robert Downey, Jr., Paul Newman, Mark Zuckerberg, as well as Christopher Plummer.

I explain why coffee is a health food drink instead of a Utah sin.

In any definition of content eclectic would not be inappropriate. Many exceptional people have had a dramatic impact on my life. I have included those without which this would be an incomplete picture of what happened and who I have become.

One notably stands out, an ex-policeman. He taught me two things. The media, while essential to our way of life, dedicates ink and sound bites primarily to events which grab our attention. The problem further exemplifies *where the attention goes the energy flows*, illustrating more keenly how we dwell mostly on the bad cop and almost completely neglect the officer who always wants to do the right thing. While the good cops far outnumber those we wish were not in uniform, our mental energy is focused on the bad cop. The reality is that without our law enforcement people the social order would be a joke. It would be chaos of the worst kind. No one would ever sleep again.

Yes, there are good cops. Estimates vary and range from 95 percent to 97.5 percent. Easily googled. About our first responders, the police, the firefighters, and support staff, we need to change our focus. These people are human beings just like us.

The other thing I learned from this ex-policeman is included in my book. Against incredible odds his is a story of the impossible and of hope and a promise; it is a story of the men and women who answer the call to serve and protect; and it is the story of those who stumble and fall. His is a story of hope and a promise and a rogue cop who went to war to answer the promise. His is a story that demands to be told.

The story about moving to Las Vegas is true although many having read it said, "You're pulling my leg." My liver was young. Wine, women, and money flowed like I owned my own vineyards, bordello, and printing press. Over ten dynamite years happened in "Sin City" before…

Rejection, abandonment work slow. At first, we deny. Without our consent it deepens, expands, and intensifies. One day I found myself looking down the barrel of a Smith & Wesson thirty-eight revolver and I knew I had run out of props. Nothing was left to hold me up. The needle was on empty. Abandonment and booze don't mix. A calculated 5,000 quarts of the hard stuff had been consumed keeping the demons at bay, attempting to outrun the empty reality that comes of having no family, no emotional foundation.

And there it is. How many of us have had to go on without our families? Cultural oppression is real. Today those who have experienced it exist in vast numbers. Tom Selleck's *Blue Bloods* is called a police procedural drama. While true, I have come to see it as exemplifying the values of family. Every episode ends with the family around the Sunday dinner table. Good on you, Tom. You and your crew do good work.

To my birth culture, can I go back? Sure, but not without re-embracing patriarchy and treating women as a support group to male authority. No! I was left to reinvent my life.

I survived the drug of fundamentalism. Now I had to take the bull by the horns and face the fact that I was a drug addict. The wonders of alcohol probably saved my life. I would have to have had a drink before I could pull the trigger. I loved my booze. I could be anyone I wanted. Alcohol was my new drug. My next nightmare was at full throttle.

With but one hanging horror this outline could here end; I have grandchildren being raised in a radical, fundamentalist culture. When I am gone my beautiful grandchildren will know of me only that which is forced through a Utah filter. This tome then also serves antidote to that rued possibility.

Thank God I did not meet the girl who meant *long term* until I had progressed enough to be part of a healthy relationship. The new me evolves daily even to losing pounds. Down fifty and counting.

I am the chooser. What I believe shapes my behavior. Do you wish change? Do you desire a different life? Practice is essential. We are the dreamer species. Blame the cerebral cortex. The dream evolves. It becomes a belief. The dreamer becomes an instrument of expression. Are you awake? Grab your ass with both hands and hang on. A journey has begun. Your better self awaits.

When animated the dream takes on the features of reality. Attentive energies drive the pathfinder. Check out Oprah Winfrey, she can tell you about passion, energy, and becoming your dream. She is the miracle. As she did for others, show after show, her life took on value. My God, look where she came from. Your better self is worth exploring.

Dedicated energy? That first ten minutes when the mind is fresh take over and launch my day. Setting my alarm became redundant. Where the attention goes the energy flows. Author unknown until doing it you become the author.

I found if I was to change my life, I had to reinvent my life. I believe we have the obligation to share our journeys. What our lives are about is important. In this, and at its core, writing is an act of love. As we do for others, life takes on value.

I reinvented my life by cultivating a mindset aimed at more successful results.

The First Thing You Need To Know To Have Success with Ease and Flow

Trissa Tismal-Capili

Trissa Tismal-Capili teaches simple steps on how to grow profits with ease and flow. She is passionate about helping entrepreneurs operate from the *State of Flow*™ and take their income to the next level without toxic hard work and overwhelm.

Trissa is a #1 international best-selling author, speaker, and certified professional coach for over fourteen years, helping thousands of entrepreneurs, and coaching multimillion-dollar business owners.

She trained and earned numerous advanced credentials from different coaching specializations including NLP, money, marketing, mindset, spirituality, and life transformation. Trissa received recognition as a top marketing consultant for a multinational billion-dollar company and has been featured on major media including Discovery Fit and Health Channel, CBS, NBC, and Fox.

As founder of the Institute of Conscious Business Leaders, Trissa is dedicated in her mission of gathering the world's foremost leaders in consciousness and business, along with helping entrepreneurs achieve true success. To learn more about Trissa, the Institute of Conscious Business Leaders, and how to grow profits with ease and flow, visit www.iocbl.com.

BEWARE: Read This Before Adopting Another Success Advice

What if I told you that following "proven" success principles can actually slow you down and stop you? I know so because I studied and followed virtually all top success advice, but essentially failed. Yes, I did achieve, but at a great price. Unfortunately, I can't say it was worth it.

It Started With A Flame Inside

For as long as I remember, I had this fire inside me to reach for the stars. My whole life I was told that I was meant for greatness. I grew up in a middle-class household in the Philippines. We were not rich, but my parents gave their all to give me everything to the best of their ability–travel, all-girls private Catholic schooling, various sports and music classes, as well as their time and full out support. They wanted me to become the best that I can be.

So did I.

At twelve years old, I stumbled upon the first self-help book I read from cover to cover, *The Power of Positive Thinking* by Norman Vincent Peale. It woke in me an obsessive passion for studying success. The thought that I could do anything I put my mind to was mind-blowing!

I set the goal to live life on my terms. Success is the freedom to be, do, and have what I want, anytime I want. Just like an acorn growing to become the magnificent oak tree it's meant to be, I wanted to achieve my fullest potential. It's the least I can do to give back and show my gratitude to my parents for all the sacrifice they've made for me.

I immersed myself in more self-help and leadership books. Soon, I graduated university with high honors in psychology and successfully launched a continuing legal education business straight out of college.

At a young age, I found myself immersed in the prestigious world of the richest and most powerful.

Devoted Student of Success

Realizing that being around lawsuits and litigation wasn't for me, I decided that I just needed to make a tweak. Since I learned that doing what you love is key to true success, I chose to find and pursue my passion. I jubilantly found life and business coaching when it was unknown. It was love at first sight! My soulmate career!

Los Angeles is now my new home and just like in the past, I set clear goals—specific number of clients, income amount, and luxuries I want. To avoid figuring out things from scratch I joined high ticket masterminds, invested in expensive mentors, received continuous training and certifications, as well as hired skilled contractors. Watching movies, TV, hanging out with family and friends, as well as traveling for leisure were exorbitance that created guilt and anxiety if I had to indulge in them. In my mind, that time could be dedicated to more study, work, meditation, exercise, or sleep. I was taught that the bigger the sacrifices, the bigger the rewards, and it will all be worth it. I can waste time later on when I can afford it.

Every day, I tried to do everything on the checklist: pray, surround myself with the people I aspired to become, self-care, eating healthy, personal improvement, business development, and so on. I understood that success didn't come easy. Winners are revered because they are willing to do things that most people aren't willing to do. They are able to do the hard things and push through them. So, no matter what problem came up, how intense the fears, how awful the naysayers were, or how tired I got, I wasn't letting myself succumb to any of it. I would tell myself, "*There is no failure, only feedback! What doesn't kill you makes you stronger!*" I held the vision of my goals and pushed past the difficulties.

Success Gone Wrong

Successful launches, reaching more people, helping dream clients, hitting my income targets, working with renowned movers and shakers…goal after goal achieved. I was grateful yet unhappy. I was too exhausted and burned out. I had to keep innovating; there was always the next thing to pursue, the next thing to overcome at work and at home.

Until one day when I couldn't push anymore. I was afflicted by a stress-induced autoimmune disease that made my face, neck, and arms burn in severe pain. The doctors said it was incurable.

I was forced to stop the hustle.

In the midst of this new-found inactivity, suddenly I felt that this time, the fatigue was worse. Without realizing it, I have been in chronic burnout and overwhelm, which I purposefully didn't give attention. I kept pushing myself, believing my will was stronger than anything…strong enough to ignore the pain of my deteriorating relationship (I was a wife and a brand-new mom) and piling household responsibilities.

But this round I was too spent and maxed out.

I thought the journey was supposed to be hard. I wasn't aware that I was inflicting trauma on my own mind and body, slave driving it in disguise of pursuing excellence. Apparently self-care, mindset, hard work, cutting edge tools, and strategies won't end the struggle…they can actually make things worse. I thought I was making the utmost progress, optimizing every step of the way. Now I saw how seriously off-track I was from my true intentions. I felt miserable. Life felt much better before I started. Clearly, I'd been slowing myself down without knowing it.

The Missing Piece

Nevertheless, I remained relentless. I had to find the cure even if the physicians say my condition is hopeless. I need to find the missing piece and figure out why I failed despite following virtually all the top success advice available.

It took some time, but I found the answer.

My disease as well as my crumbling relationship, chronic overwhelm, personal and work *problems were only surface symptoms of a deep underlying root cause*—mindset.

When I addressed my issues at its core, everything started unraveling like magic. I could see solutions that have always been in front of me but I was either resisting them or not seeing them at all. Furthermore, solutions that weren't working out for me before started working really well.

Here's what I found to be the most critical must-have mindset to achieve goals with ease and flow…

> ### Mindset #1. The inner pull to be successful is the pull to be more of your true self.
> You want to find your soulmate, make more money, win, get known, and make a difference, because you think these things will bring you happiness once achieved.

But they don't.

That inner pull you feel to accomplish and create a better life is actually the pull to be more of your true self. Embarking on a business goal or any goal for that matter is simply a vehicle to experience yourself as you truly are, which is love, joy, abundance, and infinite possibilities.

That's why "Be Yourself" is one of the most famous success quotes. Meaning…be love, be joy, be abundance, be infinite. Engaging with the projects and goals that align with your unique version of utmost love, utmost joy, etc., is what's calling out to be expressed through you.

It's not about attaining anything new once you reach your goals, but about becoming your true essence every step of the way.

Without truly understanding and adopting this mindset, you are at risk of misinterpreting every other success advice.

Mindset #2. The gold is in the challenges.

In any journey to achieve, there are twists, turns, and roadblocks. These challenges are golden. They are not there to bring you down. They are there to show you what is meant to leave. Any so-called problem that comes up is there to show you what is wanting to exit your system so that your path can be easier and flowing! Whether it's stress, anxiety, frustration, fears, hurt, or anger…*anything that's not joyful doesn't belong in your body and is meant to leave.*

Situations that feel difficult serve a vital purpose. They spotlight your "blind spots." These are your subconscious programming that interprets everything that you see, hear, feel, and experience. *The only reason anything feels hard, painful, frustrating, or scary is because of the blind spots that still exist within you.* Values, habits, beliefs, and strategies that seem positive can yield dysfunctional outcomes because they're all filtered by your "blind spots."

When an issue arises, whether big or subtle, it is an opportunity for you to see what the blind spot is and reprogram your subconscious. The key is to never ignore, avoid, or suppress (like I did), or something bigger will come up until you can no longer push it aside. Once you uncover your blind spots and transform the triggers, the situation won't feel challenging anymore! This means you no longer need to fear challenges! They are your gateway in bringing more ease and flow in your life!

Mindset #3. The process is meant to be joyful, not hard.

The whole adventure towards your personal and professional success is meant to be filled with fun, joy, love, peace, and lightness *in every moment,* regardless of the situation. This is the *state of flow.* Allow it to guide you in your choices.

If things are feeling too serious, tight, heavy, or challenging, then something is coming up to dissipate. It›s not an excuse for you to chase the next bright shiny object or completely change directions when things feel hard. See Mindset #2 above.

Being in the *state of flow* allows you to get more done in less time, access your genius, and create astounding results in both your personal and business life. This is a way of being that you can practice all day every day, so that joy, fun, and flow becomes your life. Reaching your milestones is not any more significant than any part of your journey. All of it is ever expanding joy and fun!

True Success At Last

When I embodied these mindsets, everything changed.

After ignoring the referral for a long while, thinking I've been disappointed by all the other kinds of doctors I've seen without relief, I finally opened up to seeing Dr. K at Keasberry Health Center. My allegedly incurable autoimmune disease healed. My body feels much more vibrant and energized than ever!

My relationships transformed from extremely toxic to infinitely loving, joyful, and harmonious. I feel so grateful every single day that I enjoy bountiful time with my hubby and kids, just hanging out in abundance, traveling, doing practically anything we can think of.

The drive to succeed dissolved. There is no longer anything pushing me to achieve. The inner slave driver has retired and yet I am able to *accomplish more*.

I learned to expand time and get more things done in less time. I work with the most amazing people, high-level powerful entrepreneurs all over the globe, doing what I love, and receiving generous income by just being myself.

I am now able to live the life I always wanted—a life on my terms—being, doing, and having what I truly want, when I want. Life and business are now a playful dance and adventure filled with bliss. Enjoying the comfort of material perks and luxuries are just cherries on top.

To me, this is true success…a life of ease, joy, abundance, and flow. Are you ready to have it too?

A Tale of Two Races

Scott Montgomery

Scott Montgomery, ICF-ACC, is a co-founder of Worldgate LLC, a technology consulting services firm specializing in implementing solutions that enable public sector clients to meet their information technology goals. In his day-to-day operations, Scott is primarily focused on nurturing Worldgate's client relationships and strategic alliances. In 2018, Scott completed George Mason University's certification program and became certified in Leadership Coaching for Organizational Well-being. His leadership style begins with the employees' well-being, as he strives to foster a growth and learner mindset in everyone. After earning his associate degree with honors at Northern Virginia Community College, Scott deferred obtaining his bachelor's degree in order to build his business. In January of 2020, he re-ignited his pursuit of a bachelor's degree and is now currently enrolled at the University of Virginia. Scott's first priority is always his family.

He is a loving husband of over twenty years and a hands-on father of three. In his spare time, Scott pursues fitness challenges. He has completed over fifteen triathlons as well as an Ironman 70.3.

You can reach Scott at his personal email, smontgomery@worldgatellc.com, or by calling 703-283-4524.

I've always aggressively exercised to satiate my soul. In practice, this meant that I worked out relentlessly for the last thirty years of my life. Once my kids showed up, everything changed (of course it did). Around the same time, I decided to open up my own business because I figured I had way too much free time. Between the busyness of raising young children and the creative chaos of building a company, I had no time for the gym.

Moreover, I numbed my stresses by eating everything under the sun. My focus was only on my children and my business, which both required my undivided attention. The cost was that I paid no attention to my body, and it showed. I began to suffer reflux, I gained weight, and I just felt gross. I came close to having to buy an entirely new wardrobe, which would have exploded any denial I still clung to.

Eventually, I decided to do something about it.

I started researching ways to lose weight. In the process, I learned about all sorts of interesting ways I could take care of myself. I started seeing a chiropractor who supported the so-called "IDEAL" protein diet. I stuck to it religiously, even though I white-knuckled my way through the first two weeks. I ended up losing thirty pounds in six weeks, and I was elated.

But I was far from finished.

I wanted to somehow drop the rigidity of my diet and discover a looser lifestyle such that I could eat "normally" while still keeping off the weight (or lose more). I got stuck, but then I realized that I was only looking at one side of the fitness equation. I decided to do a triathlon. I already knew that I liked them since I had finished five or six of them over the years. This time, though, I decided to go for the greatest challenge I'd ever attempted—the Eagleman Ironman 70.3. The nearest one to my home was being held in Berlin, Maryland, six months after I had made up my mind. I had half of a year to get into fighting shape. A success mindset is about setting clear goals.

I began training five days a week while I allowed my diet to be more flexible than it had been. I worked with a trainer, who helped me push what I had thought were my physical limits. It was a thrilling time—my days were spent swimming, building my company, running, raising my kids, and biking. Every time my alarm rang, I viewed it as my first trial of the day. From there, I just took the day one step at a time. If I ever started to anticipate all of the working out, business, and familial responsibilities, I emptied my mind and focused solely on the task immediately in front of me. During these six months of training, I could *feel* myself becoming stronger, healthier, and lighter. The weight kept coming off, and I had more energy than I'd had in years.

Race Day

By race day, I was chomping at the bit. My family came to support me, as they knew how hard I'd been training for these next few hours. The swimming came first. I struggled with it but managed to finish that leg of the race. Then, I took my bike out for the fifty-six mile portion of the race. Adrenaline propelled me forward, even though I was tired. As I approached mile number twenty-six, I sat up on the bike, raised my hands over the handlebars, stretched my lower back by reaching for the sky, and grabbed a drink from a drink station...I was halfway there!

The sheer ecstasy of my progress put wind in my sails. As I entered mile number twenty-seven, I noticed that a motorcycle with a race official sitting in its backseat was driving alongside of me. At first, I was confused why the rider seemed to be keeping pace with me. I gradually realized what was about to happen. Through her microphone, the official began shouting at me that I was disqualified, and that I was to turn in my chip at the bike rack and was no longer welcome to finish the race. I was so confused, but I obeyed her orders.

As I processed the message and thought through what I just heard, all kinds of emotions ran through me. I was in disbelief, and I felt so angry and helpless. In my delirium, I actually laughed. For the life of me, I could not ascertain which rule I had broken. I biked back the twenty-five miles that I had covered, mulling over how I was going to personally respond to my disqualification. Worse, I was disqualified at the furthest possible point from the starting line, so my "ride of shame" literally could not have been longer. As I rode back with every cyclical churn of the pedals, the answer started dawning on me. I decided that I would not allow myself to wallow in victimhood, and I contemplated how I could rise up from this admittedly humiliating defeat. I knew that I'd look like someone who was too inexperienced to know all of the rules, but I also knew that being an inexperienced victim didn't have to be my image in perpetuity.

Once I returned and racked my bike, I heard the system officially announce the winner.

I was still reeling over my unlucky situation as I saw the famous Andy Potts run across the finish line in first place. He is an extremely well-known triathlete whom I had admired for years. I debated whether I should congratulate him or cower and hang my head in shame. I opted for the former and embraced the moment. When he passed by me, I burst out to congratulate him on winning the race. I was a little intimidated: Andy was visibly athletic, svelte, and tall, and he wore a friendly smile. Still, he was kind enough to engage with me between his tired breaths. I couldn't help myself: I blurted out what had happened to me. His expression gave away that he was in as much disbelief as I was.

As I asked to grab the moment on camera via a selfie, he obliged, and our moment together was forever solidified in history. It was in that moment that I realized that my luck of intersecting with Andy *was* going to be my win! I may not have been able to complete the race, but I had earned the respect of a heroic athlete and the victor of the day. That was enough for me—it had to be. I could have turned away from Andy in embarrassment, but instead I chose to approach the day's winner. I did not allow what had happened to prevent me from experiencing something positive that day. Choosing to meet Andy was when everything turned for me—I knew that I *could* turn a negative into a positive, and that I *should* strive to do that for the rest of my days. A successful mindset is about deciding what success looks like to you.

Later that night, as I was walking into a hotel restaurant, the director of a Salem, Massachusetts marathon—who had also competed that day—recognized my children from earlier in the day at the starting line of my heat. She stopped to tell me how cute they were, and then we talked about how each of us had done in the race. When I explained to her what had happened to me, her eyes widened. She had never heard of the handlebar rule and told me that my next race was going to cost me nothing—she promised that she would get me a bib number at no charge. Although I never pursued this offer, it was a serendipitous encounter for which I am grateful to this day. The energy of the day remained positive—my decision to view the experience as a "good day" made it so.

One Year Later

In 2014, I registered to do the race again, this time with a friend of mine. Even though I had been disqualified in the 2013 race, I had such a fun time that I wanted to go for it again. I worked harder on my training than ever before. I was more resilient, more persistent, and more mentally fortified than the last time.

By the time the race weekend came around, I had high spirits. As we received instructions on how the race day would go from the officials, I listened very carefully–there was no chance that I would be disqualified again. Funnily enough, the rule that I had apparently broken was emphasized–I should not have lifted my hands off of the handlebars. Through their formal presentation, they explained that "lifting your hands off of the bike's handlebars endangered other bikers, since you could lose your balance, fall over, and cause the rider behind you to crash." The explanation brought the emotional memory of my disqualification back, but I was somehow electrified by the recollection of my mistake.

After the officials' presentation, I approached the podium. To my surprise, one of the officials remembered me. She gave me positive encouragement while reminding me not to make the same mistake again. I smiled at her and explained that my disqualification was meant to be. It was only because of that mistake that I enjoyed all of the experiences of the intervening months.

Later that night, we were inspecting the swim entry and found the same official talking to the moderator about the race day activities and how they were to be orchestrated. I could tell that they were friends and catching up. I exchanged pleasantries with both of them. The moderator offered that if my kids came to his podium on race day at the time of my heat, he would let them announce my start. Of course, we took him up on his offer.

My kids had a blast, and I got to kick off my second attempt at the Half Ironman to the voice of my three children counting down to the buzzer. They shouted, "Go, Dad, Go!" It did more to pump my heart than any of my training sessions.

This time, I finished the race. It was the most fun I'd had in years of triathlons. During the run, I suffered leg cramps, but I mustered through them. I realized that the *experiences* I had enjoyed because of my passion for races far outweighed any satisfaction I had about the races themselves.

I chose not to be vengeful with the official who had disqualified me the previous year, and it paid off. Had I been rude to her, she would never have provided my children with such a fun opportunity. I chose not to bask in resentment and instead walked down a positive path that led to unexpectedly fun consequences. Moreover, I turned my earlier failure into a success an entire year later. I made a mistake but chose to turn it into a positive. I hardly took a week off of training between my two races. I did not let one embarrassing day haunt me. Rather, I used it as motivation to relentlessly pursue my goal of completing a Half Ironman. One year after my disqualification, I did.

I've kept the same persistent and optimistic mindset since that race in 2014. It has helped me celebrate my marriage in unique and fulfilling ways, and it has helped me continue to raise my wonderful children into their teenage years. With respect to my business, Worldgate, it has also helped me sustain my drive for a culture in which we hold both customer and employee satisfaction as our number one priority. Finally, my persistence and optimism have aided my ability to hold long-term, valuable relationships with family members, business partners, mentors, and mentees. How beautiful a fact that, by improving my mindset through the pursuit of Ironman competitions, so many other facets of my life have been affected. I'm proud of the decisions I made to get fit and not allow one disqualification to stop me from achieving my goals. Failure is inevitable in life. Keep at it, and eventually you will succeed one way or another.

Check Your Mindset When Your Fulfillment Reads Out Loud

Grace Buckler

Grace Buckler, CIPP/US, CIPP/E, CIPP/G, CIPM, CISSP, CISA, CRISC, PMP, CDPSE, FIP, is the founder and CEO of THE PRIVACY ADVOCATE, a leading global privacy consulting firm. She's been an award-winning consultant for the United States Secret Service; senior global privacy advisor to Starbucks Corporation; vice-chair, advisory board member, and faculty member for the largest global privacy association.

Grace leverages her diverse expertise to enhance education, governance, risk management, and compliance for organizations while giving consumers the data privacy safety they deserve. She has been featured at multiple international events and in global publications including the *British-American Business Council*, *ISACA International*, *Digital Privacy News*, and *International Association of Privacy Professionals*. Grace has authored books, penned articles for industry journals, and has enriched books on European data protection law and practice, and program management. She enjoys cartoons, cooking, reading, writing, and podcasting. For additional information, please visit theprivacyadvocate.com.

Before the Moment of Truth

My goals were to have a career in television in addition to being a businesswoman and an author. Becoming a newscaster was the biggest goal of the three. I was fascinated with news anchors from an early age and always looked forward to watching the evening news. I soon visualized myself reporting the news by reading books out loud.

After graduating high school, I studied mass communication. My idea of success was to be financially secure, popular, and well dressed. My persistence led to opportunities with the campus TV, radio stations, and two major television networks. I was thrilled that my persistence and willingness to learn opened up many opportunities.

The Beliefs That Got Me to My Goals

I was born to ambitious parents who influenced my mindset for success. They believed that education was principal. This shaped my belief that the right university and the right program would help me reach my goals. I was determined to connect to the right knowledge and tools that would lead to my success. I knew that with hard work I was predestined for great things, but it would be a long road before I would realize my gifts, capabilities, and fulfillment.

The Moment of Truth

As a journalism student, I learned to get up early. That was my first moment of truth. Rising early had been a struggle since childhood, but I made the adjustment. I made strides in my program but it wasn't enough to fulfill me. Deep down, I didn't enjoy wearing the coveted press badge, attending press conferences, the formal dinners, or the rehearsed meetings with dignitaries. I felt there was something more for me although I could not put my finger on it.

Then, one of my professors demoted me to a lower-level writing course. It was at that point I realized that I wasn't great at everything I did. It was a humbling experience, but also the impetus that shaped the success mindset that would serve me for many years to come.

The Turning Point

I didn't know how to overcome this setback. I had other passions and gifts but I didn't see them as potential careers. I could have modified my mindset by learning from the challenges and victories of others with similar experiences. Today, I study the path of people I admire to assess whether their journey is a good fit for me. Since success is relative, I avoid success in an area that won't bring me fulfillment.

My Redemption Playbook

I am not the type to discuss my deepest needs with others. With the Bible as my playbook, I've always leaned on my faith to guide me. I learned how to really pray or have genuine conversations with God. It completely transformed my life. I was able to sort out my hurdles and overcome my fears. I was encouraged knowing that I had the support of the highest authority and knowing how much I'm loved.

One day, I stumbled upon the technical communication field. It didn't happen quickly. It took a couple of years, but I was sold. I felt peaceful about switching schools and my major. I lost many academic credits in the process, but my joy surpassed them all.

The first day of class came and ended with professors urging students to join the Society for Technical Communication. One of my professors shared how the program prepares students to work in the field as entrepreneurs or independent consultants. I remember thinking, "Who'd do that! I'll be an employee," not realizing this was an answer to my prayers. On my first event at the Society, I bonded easily. My relationship-building mindset and my faith prevailed throughout my journey. Soon I made the acquaintance of a very caring lady. She was a godsend. An attorney with many years of corporate experience, she mentored me and connected me with opportunities in technical communication.

The Curveball

Although I was blowing up with national, international, and academic accomplishments, the field of technical communication wasn't a bed of roses but I loved it. I was hired to intern at a prestigious federal agency, and then came a surprise.

In the job agreement, the agency promised a permanent job placement upon graduation. Excited, I awaited my office in the executive wing of the building. A few months before graduation, the department that I was supposed to join downsized. Even the brightest and the most experienced officers were let go. I lost a perfect career story as well as a supportive professional community. Thankfully, another executive office hired me in a timely decision. But just days before graduation, an executive dropped in and said, "Grace, you've done amazing things for our department. I know you're going to do even bigger things with your career, but we no longer need your services." That unfortunate news hit me like a ton of bricks. My options? Unemployment or temp jobs. I embraced both.

Overcoming Low Points

The layoff wasn't an isolated low point. Before accepting the internship, I had lost my brother. Losing him was a gigantic all-time low. Losing my hair during the grieving process was a painful blow to my self-confidence. Prior to the internship, I'd lost the confidence to pursue many other attractive opportunities. I'd become a bit of a recluse, but the internship opportunity had pulled me out into a state of hopefulness.

I overcame my grief with self-care, believing that I was worth every effort and every amount of money that it would take to get me feeling better again. A grief therapist helped me reverse my grief to a celebration of my brother's life. Still, I felt guilty about pursuing my career. Being open and accepting help through therapy and from a close friend offered me the clarity that I needed. I realized that grief had caused me to feel the need to settle for what was convenient simply because I lacked the motivation to pursue what was best for me.

Hair loss was a harsh low point. But I rose above it. My hair falling out was a real problem. I was very reluctant about accepting job interviews. This was the case even before I landed the internship. But for the internship, I'd felt better after I'd aced the phone and face-to-face interviews, and also throughout the two years that followed in that position. Not a single person made me feel uncomfortable about my hair. They were all excited about my value. This was one of the reasons that losing the internship was a hard pill to swallow. After the layoff from the internship, I agonized over my hair again. I feared starting over. That meant finding a job environment that would accept me just the way that I was. I held this belief that I had a unique value that wasn't designed to be hidden under a bushel. My impact on people's lives mattered. But I needed to take care of myself in order to deliver that value with the excellence it deserved. I habitually encouraged myself with scriptures and took prayer walks. This daily drill calmed, invigorated, and emboldened me. Later on, I consulted a haircare expert and zealously prayed for hair growth.

The internship and the promise of a permanent job placement were a big deal. Coming so close but losing the opportunity to fast track into a technical communication career was a huge disappointment. Turning to unemployment and temporary jobs at the last minute was rough. Nevertheless, I didn't complain. Instead, I fed my energy to my gifts. I overcame my disappointments by developing and actualizing my gifts throughout the low points. I became madly convinced that I didn't need to rely solely on an organization, a person, or a job description to fashion opportunities that I needed to deliver my value and purpose. So, I initiated unpaid opportunities that nourished my fulfillment. I trusted that God foreknew something that I had not yet seen. But I was inclined to be prepared when the right opportunity presented itself. I wanted to be mentally and spiritually fit for the silver lining in losing my internship. I persisted with calm and patiently honed my skills.

A Point of No Return

Survival was sweet. Nine months after the layoff, my hair had grown back. While on a temp job, I received an enormous job offer from a global technology firm where one of my contacts worked. My fulfillment landed an opportunity. I increased financially. I added to my mindset's repertoire the conviction that I could do anything with or without a strand of hair as long as I was actualizing my gifts, had faith, and was persistent.

Looking Back

Looking back on my journey, keeping an open mind, patience, and being flexible made decisions easier. I had a great work ethic and compassion for self and others. In retrospect, I needed to leave that internship. I needed to be focused, not busy. Besides, if I'd been placed in a permanent job at the internship as originally planned, I would have missed out on greater opportunities ahead.

Getting booted from my upper-level writing course was like a death sentence until I walked into a creative writing course. Its cozy ambience resembled a group therapy session. Everyone sat around a big wooden rectangular table and took turns listening or speaking. It was quite different from the techie journalism classroom setup I was used to. It was in a much older building on campus that had a woody but welcoming smell to it, like an old church sanctuary. My first story, *Creek Town,* had the professor raving about my ingenuity. She soon noticed, however, that I was sometimes so hard on myself. I'll never forget when she said, "Grace, every writer needs an editor." The things I was worried about, she said they were "somebody else's job." I learned that I couldn't succeed alone. I learned to connect with people with different gifts, strengths, skills, and experience. In any given discipline or path you need people whose unique gifts will perfect, crystalize, or edit yours. I wouldn't trade the experience of being demoted to the lower-level course. It opened my eyes to new possibilities.

Also, looking back, my creative writing professor often reminded me to "enjoy the journey." Her reinforcements helped me understand that I should enjoy the process rather than focus on perfection or the outcome.

What You Need, You Already Have

Unquestionably, my mindset has played a significant role in my success. It has instilled fearlessness. I sought validation from others because I was fearful. But I soon realized they were not perfect people themselves. Many projects that I led were available because others declined out of fear. I felt stuck with such projects but always ended up with remarkable outcomes and huge rewards. I realized that I had a unique value and as long as I didn't give in to fear, I'd succeed.

This mindset proved especially useful when I undertook consulting engagements with more than eleven federal agencies. I was the only female in the practice and was unswerving through tough circumstances. I was conscientious. Other notable accomplishments were earning the Society's international award for online instructional design, subsequently earning a technical art award from my school's communications and engineering departments, and later earning an award from a federal agency. Technical communication is a multi-faceted field with unique disciplines that I've enjoyed. Anticipating daily the possibility that I'd do something different, solve unique problems, and impact many lives while learning new things is divine.

Prior to discovering my gifts, I'd already actualized them—before I'd stumbled upon the technical communication field. For example, among other things, I conceptualized and hand coded websites. I produced and self-published a children's newsletter (in print). It circulated for more than ten years even though I had no prior publishing experience. I self-taught. I saw an opportunity and the need to bring my siloed church community together through a publication. It worked. I cherish these fulfilling accomplishments to this day. That was just the beginning. Fearlessness, coupled with the belief that I'm a solution, that I carry value, but also that I need other people's complementary expertise to succeed have been instrumental to my success during the period that I served as consultant for eleven federal government organizations including the Department of Health and Human Services (HHS); the Transportation Security Administration (TSA); the Defense Counterintelligence and Security Agency (DCSA), and other Department of Homeland Security (DHS) defense agencies where my work spanned the US, Europe, and Asia. This mindset serves me now as a principal consultant at my own firm as I offer perspectives on data privacy laws, information security, cybersecurity, and technical communication. I hold nine globally recognized certifications. I speak globally and have had the privilege of serving as an instructor for employees of law firms and corporations including

Verizon, Disney, KPMG, Kaiser Permanente, PwC, Deloitte, Booz Allen Hamilton, VMWare, Capital One, and Google. Have you discovered your fulfillment and the success mindset that'll get you there?

I recently reflected on my love for reading out loud and my dream to be a newscaster. In retrospect, that dream is becoming a reality although not in the way I envisioned it then. But narrating audiobooks is just as exhilarating. I can almost hear my eight-year-old self exclaiming, "Yay! Finally, you get to read out loud!" Absolutely! But that's not all. I get to read out loud to audiences around the world. My writing is not perfect, but I get to write speeches. I get to sleep until six in the morning. I get to be an entrepreneur and an author. Most of all, I am fulfilled. I didn't focus on my weaknesses and frustrations. I didn't resign from my aspirations. Rather, I resigned into my strengths and fulfillment where I found people and opportunities that crystalized my gifts, goals, and vision. This is possible because I adopted a success mindset.

Let's connect by email at info@theprivacyadvocate.com, my website theprivacyadvocate.com, or connect with me via Circle at gracebuckler.com.

Enthusiasm: The Exceptional Edge

Diana Loomans

Diana Loomans is a speaker, author, and success coach in the personal development field, and a modern day philosopher, weaving timeless wisdom with cutting-edge science. She offers trainings in human potential, success habits, awakened leadership, life purpose, wellness, creative writing, and more.

She offers personal and business coaching, and an innovative coach training program. Her clients include CEOs, government leaders, entrepreneurs, educators, artists, and administrators. She has consulted with leaders from Apple, Netflix, Ameritrade, PayPal, Tesla, CEO Space, Marquette University, and many more.

Diana has delivered over 1200 programs, taught at several colleges, and appeared on hundreds of media shows. She is consistently rated as an outstanding speaker.

Her popular books, poetry, and articles can be found in bookstores, posters, and websites worldwide. Diana is the founder of Conscious Culture and lives in Los Angeles. To learn more, visit www.dianaloomans.com.

Enthusiasm Sparks a Flame

> "Enthusiasm is the electricity of life."
> Gordon Parks

I've had the good fortune to do what I love as a speaker, author, and coach in the personal development field for many years. I've often been asked what the key to my success has been. In my early years I earned a college degree, joined professional groups, and read as much as I could in my field. I was motivated to gain knowledge, skill, and experience.

But what catapulted me from a curious intern to a national speaker, and an unknown writer to a best-selling author, did not happen from skill and experience alone. Time and again what gave me the exceptional edge was the magnetic power of genuine enthusiasm.

It took me quite by surprise during my first professional job after college. I landed a staff development intern position working for a large school district. It was customary for the superintendent, my boss, to meet with new employees to get acquainted.

During our meeting, he told me about a training he was creating on accelerated learning skills. I got very animated, describing similar techniques I was using as a parent, such as making sleep

learning recordings to enhance my child's learning, using affirmations to build her esteem, and playing certain types of music to positively influence her behavior.

My boss took it all in, but didn't say too much. I thought maybe I'd gone on way too long.

A few days later, he called me into his office and said, "I keep thinking about everything you're up to. What you're doing as a parent is exactly what I want teachers to learn to do with their students."

He said he received twenty or more resumes every week from people with PhDs, but had yet to meet one with half of my enthusiasm. He continued, "I'd like you to go through the instructor training, and become one of my head trainers."

I was stunned–and gratefully accepted. I spent the next several years teaching the program statewide. When I started, my speaking experience was minimal; my passion for the subject matter, along with loads of natural enthusiasm, won over hundreds of teachers just as it had my boss.

What I learned is this: knowledge and experience bring skill and credibility, but it is enthusiasm that stirs hearts and moves crowds. And the three combined is what sparked a flame and paved the way to an exciting and lucrative new career path.

Consider what will make you most influential and compelling in your field–having knowledge and experience, or acquiring knowledge, experience, and enthusiasm?

Enthusiasm is Charismatic and Compelling

"Let the winds of enthusiasm sweep through you."
Dale Carnegie

Later in my career, I was once introduced at a speaker's event as, "an orator who never fails to receive a standing ovation." I hadn't thought about it much, but it had become the truth. After my talk, I was asked by an aspiring speaker if I had a success formula.

I found myself saying, "Speak only on topics you are bursting at the seams to talk about, get the audiences personally involved, and know at least twice as much about the subject than you have time to share. This will make your talk compelling, your presence charismatic, and leave your audiences wanting more."

To further support and inspire speakers, I developed a program entitled, *The Standing Ovation Formula*, offering keys to delivering speeches guaranteed to rouse audiences to their feet.

Can you guess what one of the principle ingredients is in the formula?

If you chose enthusiasm, you guessed right.

Enthusiasm Opens Doors

"Proper enthusiasm opens every door."
The I Ching

Flash forward to my first efforts to get published. I'd written some children's stories and was receiving good feedback, but had no idea how to break into the book publishing world. I spoke to a book agent who informed me that only one out of thousands of children's writers ever get published. She finished with the happy thought that I might be better off trying to win the lottery.

This was pretty disheartening, but I wasn't that easily deterred. After browsing at a local bookstore, I got to talking with the manager. I was impassioned as I told her about my book ideas in vivid detail. She listened intently, smiled, and wished me luck.

As I was leaving, she stopped me and described a huge conference where publishers and book sellers all over the world gathered each year. "I really like your wonderful ideas. I'd like to offer you an extra ticket I have to help you get your books out there."

Thrilled, I didn't hesitate to say yes. I'd walked into a bookstore to browse, and walked out with an insider's ticket to the biggest book conference of the year. That door opened because I took the risk to enthusiastically share my ideas with a person of influence.

When you're fueled by enthusiasm, your message becomes contagious—and you will discover that people go out of their way to help you achieve your goals.

What are some ways that you can share more enthusiasm about your interests and ideas with those who have experience and contacts that may benefit you?

Enthusiasm Brings Opportunity

> "The first thing to be is excited. Be a thing of
> fevers and enthusiasms."
> Ray Bradbury

Thanks to the bookstore manager, I was soon flying cross-country to attend my first book convention. I met interesting people, and wandered the floors daily until my eyes were bleary and my feet ached. But I quickly learned that publishers were there to sell their new titles. Meeting aspiring authors wasn't high on their list.

On the last day in the final hour—and about to go home without a book contract—I chatted with a bookseller at his booth and launched into my book ideas one final time. He pointed to a distinguished publisher with white hair and a goatee, and said the man's company was seeking books with themes similar to mine.

The publisher was engaged with three professional-looking people. I had an urge to turn and walk away (run would be more accurate), but instead I took a deep breath and edged closer. Then I stepped up to the table, introduced myself, and asked for a few minutes of his time when the meeting was over.

The publisher seemed slightly taken aback, but agreed. When the time came, I gave it my all in the short time allotted.

What happened next is indelibly printed in my mind. He liked my ideas, but said he was most captivated by my enthusiasm for my work. To my great surprise, he then invited me to join him and his business-partner wife for lunch.

The next thing I knew, I was dining in a plush hotel with this power couple. They told me that after publishing many books, they now only worked with authors who were "in love and on fire with their ideas." I left with their promise to send contracts for two of my book ideas within a week.

That was the beginning of a long, happy working relationship. We published six books together, with four reaching the best-seller mark. My passion for my work, along with a dose of courage in the eleventh hour brought an opportunity that forever changed my life.

What great idea of yours is waiting to find its way into the world? How will you gather the courage to share more enthusiasm for your idea, and to create new opportunities?

Enthusiasm is Intentional and Emotional

"A clear intention and an elevated emotion
brings unprecedented results."
Dr. Joe Dispenza

I've served on the faculty of a national entrepreneurial organization, and coached entrepreneurs of all ages who present their ideas to investors. They come from every walk of life, and work in many diverse fields.

I have repeatedly observed that those with a clear intention and an elevated emotion (such as enthusiasm) have by far the most success with potential investors. Enthusiasm is a positive force of energy that draws attention and gathers momentum. It comes in a variety of styles and forms, from impassioned expression to a quiet, unyielding confidence.

Keep in mind that you don't have to be extroverted to be highly enthusiastic. When your intentions are clear and your emotions positive, you will come off with conviction, even if you are low key.

Enthusiasm Captivates Attention

"Nothing great was ever achieved without enthusiasm."
Ralph Waldo Emerson

I'm convinced that the captivating power of enthusiasm is the main reason that one of my heroes was inspired to write a foreword for one of my books, even though my wildest hope was that he'd write a simple endorsement.

The book was about the value of using humor in the learning process. Asked by a cohort who I'd choose if I could have anyone write an endorsement, a famous television host immediately came to mind. He was also an acclaimed comedian, prolific author, educator, and humanitarian. I'd recently heard an excellent speech he'd given with his grown son, and was really inspired. On a dare I called his agent, who chuckled and said that if he had a dollar for every book endorsement request he received, he'd be a rich man. I laughed sheepishly and said I understood.

Before the call ended, I described how moved I was to witness such shared joy and laughter between this man and his son as they were speaking together. It had really touched me. The agent said they were the same way off-stage, and cited examples that had both of us marveling.

As we spoke the agent's demeanor changed–and he suddenly asked for a copy of my book manuscript. Soon after sending it, I received a call with incredible news. After reading the entire manuscript, my television host hero had not only written an endorsement for my book, but an engaging foreword, too! I almost dropped the phone. And I have no doubt that his foreword helped the book become a success.

Receiving the best foreword that any author could ever wish for came about because I'd shared personal enthusiasm; not so much about my book, but regarding my authentic admiration for this man.

I've learned that more often than not enthusiasm is about sharing from the heart, rather than directly promoting something.

How to Cultivate More Enthusiasm

"The best predictor of your well-being is an enthusiasm and energy in your life."
Brian Johnson

Enthusiasm comes from the Greek word, *enthous*, meaning "inspired or possessed by God-essence." It refers to intense enjoyment, interest, playfulness, inventiveness, optimism, and high energy. Enthusiasm is not a gift that only some are born with. It's a mindset and way of life that anyone can acquire No matter what your current level of enthusiasm is, there are simple and effective ways to cultivate even more. Here are a few:

- Do something bold, brave, or new each day to get out of your comfort zone. Discovery and exploration are fertile grounds for developing more zest.
- Associate with enthusiastic cohorts who are more interested in learning and improving than complaining about the status quo. Be with those who inspire you.
- Make time to pursue your greatest passions and interests as a personal mandate.
- Strive to be in a profession you love, and you'll truly never work a day in your life.
- Stay on the cutting edge in your chosen areas of interest. It's one of the best investments of time, energy, and money you can ever make.

The happiest, most interesting people I know are those who have learned to cultivate, share, and maintain their enthusiasm. So study what you love, do work you love, share what you love, spend time with those you love, and the exceptional edge of enthusiasm will help lead to your greatest successes.

Seven Facets of the NEW Success Mindset

Kirsten Stendevad

Kirsten Stendevad calls herself a Nordic awakener of a more feminine future and illuminary leadership evolver, because she wakes people up to what needs to be the dominant megatrend of the 21st century if humanity is to survive and thrive.

She is the best-selling author of seven trendsetting books about 21st century paradigms (and has several on their way in international languages). She has taught workshops at Harvard Business School, MIT, NYU, McKinsey, AIG and international MBA programs.

At her Illumina International Leadership Academy, she transforms ambitious people with leader DNA to luminous role models who act as influential pathfinders for a bright future, at home, at work and in the world.

Check out her work at kirstenstendevad.com and her programs at illuminaryleadership.com.

On December 22, 2011–the day before my world changed–I was considered to be a great success: I was often portrayed in Scandinavian media as a female role model, entrepreneur, visionary front runner, and cosmopolitan networker. I had already influenced thousands of people as a best-selling author, keynote speaker, columnist, and tribe leader. I had a huge following of people whom I had trained in a feminine model of leadership and a feminine way of creating business success. My books had been translated into several languages and I had just started an international leadership training with people from ten countries. I was a happily married mother of three living in my dream house–a rare gem with a garden in the middle of Copenhagen–enjoying a comfortable lifestyle with friends and family, hosting parties, and traveling for adventure. I thought *success* was something that came to those who wanted it and were willing to work for it—on the inside and the outside.

On December 23, as I was preparing for Christmas with the family, I learned that my six-year-old, middle son was ill with a rare, highly aggressive, incurable terminal disease.

Less than six months later, on June 12, 2012, just as the beautiful sunny Nordic summer day dawned, I suddenly became the complete opposite of a success. In fact, I felt like a disaster who had catastrophically failed my life's most vital task.

In the ambrosial hour, just before the sun started to shine, my beloved, charming child took his last breath and died in my arms, only seven years and four months old.

After receiving our son's cancer diagnosis, his father and I had spent six months running a race against all odds to save his life in a myriad of ways. Now we dragged ourselves home from the hospital, lowered the flag in our garden halfway, and sat speechless on the sofa without a clue of how on Earth to survive this seemingly unsurvivable event.

We felt we had just missed succeeding at the three most important jobs for any parent:

1. Protect your child against evil;
2. If something bad happens, save your child;
3. By all means, do NOT allow your child to die.

Now, as our oldest son of ten silently began to build the Lego his brother would no longer need, and our youngest son of two was brought back home by his grandparents—clueless about losing a sibling for good—we had to undertake the last task any parent wants: planning our own child's funeral.

I remember that the question of why this had happened was racing around my brain, and that I kept speculating about what I could have done to prevent this outcome while my heart was bleeding and my uterus was screaming. Do you recognize some of these symptoms from situations where you missed succeeding at what was most important to you?

I am far from being the only one who has gone through such excruciating pain and encountered such failure, the other end of the measuring stick from success. In fact, most people on the planet sooner or later face sad events: they lose something or someone who was very dear to them, or they suddenly find themselves facing new shocking realities of illness, divorce, bankruptcy, infertility, homelessness, or the likes. These events feel like the opposite of success—in fact, they feel rather like the most evil downgrade.

Those of you who have been in a similar situation know that on top of your own devastation when such things happen, you have to deal with society's perception of success. When you don't live up to the common ideals, you may experience that others pity you and make you feel like a victim instead of gently being with you through the many phases of grief.

On June 12, 2012, I could not imagine that it would be possible to ever be happy—or successful—again. I simply could not envision how. It was the first time in my life when I wasn't able to create an uplifting perspective on the situation, one that could redirect my somber feelings in a more pleasant direction.

The night my son died, I made the irrational decision to go up instead of down from the experience. I thought, "One son is in Heaven now—the two others deserve Heaven on Earth. Why go down when it's possible to go up?" But I had no clue how to make this upgrade happen, and a bright future seemed endlessly far away, not to say altogether utopian.

Today I can report that it IS possible to become happy again, even after great tragedy, trauma, breakdowns, and setbacks. In my experience it's even possible to become happier and more grateful, peaceful, and loving than ever before.

Is this the NEW success mindset?

For sure, we are at a time in history when we all need to revise what we mean by "success."

Is success "having it all" in terms of status, money, and family—while feeling miserable, bored, restless, and negative? Not if you ask a growing number of "cultural creatives" who no longer feel drawn to mainstream ideals but choose to live in alignment with their own definition of success instead of striving for its conventional image. In fact, many especially from the younger generations find it absurd to adopt society's definition of success measured in terms of wealth and achievements, if it comes at the price they have witnessed in themselves or their parents in terms of stress, performance anxiety, low self-worth, depression, workaholism, dysfunction in relationships, meaninglessness, and loneliness. And it makes even less sense as long as the old definition of success seems to contribute to the destruction of the planet through an unsustainable lifestyle that exhausted overachievers don't have the energy to alter.

Could it be that the new success mindset is to boldly face every challenge life offers; to feel the pain no matter how hard; to dive into the darkness until it becomes Light; and to come out feeling richer, happier, healthier, more fulfilled, AND more compassionate, making us better able to serve the whole?

It's time to ask that question.

First, if our success depends on stable circumstances, we are very vulnerable, because we live in times of unprecedented change. Second, the rules of the game have changed. Long gone are the 1950s when everyone had the same success criterion and tried to live up to a norm that in reality suited very few. Even though most of us are still playing according to the rules of the twentieth century, when success was all about how our life looked from the OUTSIDE, no matter how full we were of self-sabotage, lovelessness, and insecurity, the twenty-first century is here.

Now and in the future, it might no longer be possible to be TRULY successful without FEELING genuinely joyful on the INSIDE. Now we live in a world whose future depends on people following their inner wisdom and acting in harmony with the laws of nature. This means breaking away from illusions and immature mindsets, lifestyles, conventions, and businesses.

If we keep on going as we have done so far, there might be no future for humanity. Scientists are telling us that we are adapting too slowly to the exponential growth of problems such as climate change, the depletion of our natural resources, increasing poverty, human migrations, and so on. The only thing that can alter our common current course is if we make a radical shift of consciousness, since we will not be able to solve our problems with the same paradigm that created them.

In other words: real, deep-felt success now and in the future requires us to change our "success mindset." Redefining "success" is mandatory if we are to survive and thrive.

But how do we do that?

Any type of crisis–from COVID-19 to a career change–is a catalyst. Because crisis forces our hearts open. And then Light–a higher understanding–can enter through the cracks. We can get an experience of our divinely creative essence. An if we cultivate this new level of awareness with new practises, we can access new keys that can dissolve old problems.

In my experience, the recipe for the new success mindset is to shift our focus away from the masculine definition of success to a more feminine one. And then put the feminine foot first and step-by-step let the masculine muscle support and help build a new world.

Here is how that looked in my own case.

After my son died, I spent a few months in what could be called "the fertile void," a phase where I knew I had changed, but was not clear about my new identity and direction. Instead of planning with my mind, I was listening to impulses from within. I still had my business. I had been teaching twenty-first century leadership paradigms for years, but now I knew that I had to work at a deeper and a higher level to make room for all the insight and soul expansion that was occurring after my loss. Three months after my son's death, I conceived the synopsis seeding my book *The Future is Feminine*. This in turn gave birth to my cutting edge Leadership Academy where I connect leaders and take them through a transformational program to become luminous pathfinders, and front-runners of a bright future–for all.

Indeed, I found that the old matter-based concept of success was no longer an option–it had also lost all its appeal. When my son died, so did much of my old ego-identity. I was no longer so concerned with other people's opinions. What was born instead was an intimate connection with my soul and a surrender to those higher realms, which I choose to trust is the new home of my son.

I asked to receive more clues about my new purpose in life, and one day I "downloaded" a new leadership navigation tool with seven facets of twenty-first century leadership. I describe these seven facets thoroughly in my book *Illuminary Leadership*. Because I trained as a scholar, I researched every single aspect of this leadership model thoroughly and found that, indeed, there is scientific evidence for all its facets. The world's most shining people and companies are only truly successful because they live these seven dimensions. I have since tested whether it's possible to apply these new facets to people with leadership DNA who are yearning for less stress, more meaning, a higher purpose, true love, genuine happiness, and more influence with pleasure. I have found that not only do these seven facets give access to a new way of being that feels so much healthier, happier, and better but also they provide people with the ability to turn a crisis into a quantum leap and emerge as illuminating people and businesses.

The seven facets are these:

1. Complementarity–Energizing Leadership. Focus as much on cultivating inner growth such as an increased feeling of peace and joy as on tangible actions and visible achievements.

2. Polarity–Synergizing Leadership. Honor the creative power of the dance between the mature masculine and feminine energies both inside and outside yourself.

3. Proactivity–Empowering Leadership. Take responsibility for healing areas of low self-esteem, so you can take initiatives that lift others instead of reacting, suffering, and passing on your traumas.

4. Authenticity–True Leadership. Stop numbing your genuine feelings and start following your heart so you can be that unique piece that is otherwise missing in the bigger puzzle.

5. Integrity–Reliable Leadership. Align your words and actions with your values so you can respect yourself and enjoy the trust of others.

6. Synchronicity–Inspiring Leadership. Be fully present and co-create the future by listening to evolutionary impulses rather than allowing your mind to repeat the past on autopilot.

7. Totality–Wholistic Leadership. Use all of yourself to serve the whole. It is scientifically proven that you get so much happier by contributing positively to others.

One day I met a holy woman, Outi Kuma, one of the few Westerners who has been initiated into the wisdom of the Mayan culture. She showed me how these seven facets could be combined into a leadership model shaped like a diamond, with the top symbolizing our inner masculine and the bottom symbolizing our inner feminine (to see this model, check illuminaryleadership.com). After participating in one of my leadership trainings, Outi Kuma mirrored to me that what I am actually doing in my programs is helping people polish their "inner diamond" so they can act like beacons of Light and inspire those looking for new and better ways of doing things now that the old world is crumbling.

I have since noticed that the new way of bringing about success is indeed radically different from the old. I used to work very hard to *achieve* success. Now, I focus on my inner work and I seem to *receive* success. I experience it as a sense of being in flow. Whatever I need in terms of people and possibilities seems to come to me in perfect time without having to work hard for it. In fact, it happens that if I use the paradigm which I subscribed to before, the magic and miracles are blocked.

I could never have come so far so fast on my own. It only became possible because I surrounded myself with a network of loving people with whom I have processed both pain and gain along the way. This has given room to more genuine joy in my heart and life.

As we enter what looks like the most crucial decade of this century, in which exponential changes will happen at the speed of technological advances, I would like to point to the power of community. It is scientifically proven that supportive relationships can get us through most challenges.

And therefore one of the most important elements of the NEW success mindset is to surround ourselves with inspiring people who have a compassionate heart and a solution-oriented attitude. This is why networks are a vital element of my programs. Here like-hearted people can join forces for a higher good and help each other make the seemingly impossible possible.

The new success mindset also includes a willingness—even an unstoppable commitment—to conscious evolution. We must strive to not only learn but also to unlearn, because what we used to believe about success and everything else must be turned upside down.

For example, many of our decisions used to be based on fear and separation.

Now and in the future we must recognize what quantum physicists have been telling us for years and what the recent pandemic showed us: we are all connected. Thus none of us can afford to be successful at the expense of others—we are all only truly successful if we create solutions that are a good deal for everybody.

In my experience, these radical shifts are easier to make when we don't walk all the steps on the new path to soulful success alone, but when we help each other. Today I can testify there is an operating system in the world that heals even the deepest pain. It is called Love and I know because it never stopped being present in the form of angels on Earth—family, friends, and new connections who showed me that the Light never disappears, even in the darkest moments. May this new operating system spread like wildfire.

The Dalai Lama has said that the world does not need more successful people; it needs artists, poets, and lovers of all kinds.

This new success mindset is what I am dedicated to help foster through my luminary leadership trainings and networks. Since part of this new mindset is a shift from ME to WE, I freely share a lot of the resources that have helped me on my website, www.kirstenstendevad.com.

My young son's death shifted my success paradigm. Success for me today is the opportunity to use all that I have received and all that I continue to receive in service of a similar profound, paradigm-shifting effect on the world. This way, the loss of my beautiful child can contribute to a common gain and his early death will not have been in vain.

Self-Compassion and the Entrepreneurial Mindset

Steven Seiden

For twenty-five years, Steven Seiden, president and founder of Acquired Data Solutions (ADS), has set the organization's strategy based on four standing principles: (1) people first, (2) customer success, (3) fiscal responsibility, and (4) effective communication. ADS has delivered resilient, robust, and quality solutions throughout the engineering and Internet of Things (IOT) lifecycle.

Prior to founding ADS, Steven earned two masters' in engineering at North Carolina State University and a BS in computer science at American University. He was also a contractor for the US Army Corps.

Steven is dedicated to giving back to his community by providing relevant career development opportunities for low-income residents in the DC region. He served on the board for On-Ramps to Careers, and previously held leadership roles with Byte Back. He has led a summer youth STEM literacy program for DC high school students since 2016. Along with his community work, Steven has taken pride in advocating for mental health for himself along with his staff. During the pandemic, ADS completed its Mental Health Certification from Let's Empower, Advocate, and Do, Inc. (LEAD). He inspired others with his enhanced commitment to his staff's well-being by writing two articles for publications and participated in numerous interviews and articles discussing corporate mental health.

This chapter is dedicated to my wife, who has always supported me during my crazy entrepreneurial journey and for being my rock, and the rock of our family, and to my children who I have tried to show up for every day.

My early life's dream was to start a business after graduate school. I came from two entrepreneurial parents and I always told them thirty years of school, thirty years of work, and thirty years of whatever. So many dreams never come true no matter how hard you work and wish for them. That was not the case for me. Within three weeks of graduating from graduate school, the company I was working for imploded and I was handed the keys to that company and started the business I run now. This year marks Acquired Data Solutions' (ADS) twenty-fifth anniversary, and it's a miracle. The reason ADS has survived for this long is because I've held onto and grown my entrepreneurial mindset.

There are three different elements that make up my entrepreneurial mindset:

1. Never quit until you collapse.
2. Always seek out new information.
3. Practice self-compassion.

I know that the last element of my entrepreneurial mindset may sound unfamiliar to certain generations. When I first learned about entrepreneurship, all I knew was grit and toughing it out. Sayings like "No Pain, No Gain." And this attitude helped and hurt me as an entrepreneur. Discovering and coupling self-compassion with my entrepreneurial mindset has shaped my success mindset in ways that has allowed me to continue this journey for my family, my staff, and equally important, myself.

Never Quit Until You Collapse

I could have never predicted the way my entrepreneurial journey began—nor was I ready for it.

In graduate school, I learned a hot programming language called LabVIEW. After graduation, I went back home to Maryland and became a contractor to a company that used this language. Three weeks after I was hired, the company collapsed and I was presented with two options: take over the business or find another job. I choose to take over the business.

Today, I believe I could work for anybody and be successful; I'm not sure I felt that way when I started my business. There are many issues in life and in business that I could never imagine until living through them. I never got the mentoring or the coaching I needed to run a business. Small businesses rarely do. It is unfortunate that when I started my company, self-compassion was not as mainstream as it is today. All I knew how to do was to drive myself and listen to my super harsh, inner critic.

When you know nothing, everything looks easy because we don't know what the next day brings. From the very first day, nothing was easy and my inner critic grew even harsher. Early on, I felt like quitting the business almost every day. When you start a business, you often don't even know what that business needs. You're in a constant free fall, grabbing for anything or anyone that you think can stabilize the business, or yourself.

My parents and my father's business partner helped me fund the business. Even after my father retired, my father's partner stayed in the business. He has been a constant presence in my life. At a low point early on in the business, I went to him and I said I wanted to quit. "This is too hard," I said. And he told me, "Just keep your feet moving and something will happen. Entrepreneurship is just like climbing stadium stairs. You can quit anytime you want, but only when you collapse. As soon as you collapse, you can quit." He knew I was never going to collapse. I felt like I was going to collapse all the time, but I never did. This was some of the greatest (or maybe not so great) advice I had ever received in business.

Always Seek Out New Information

I was never going to quit—even though I often felt ready to collapse. That is a stressful mindset to live in. In the early days of entrepreneurship, I had a complete stress mindset on top of, and as part of, my entrepreneur mindset. Folded into this entrepreneur mindset of success is the idea that I had to keep my feet moving. I was in a constant manic state. I'm not sure every entrepreneur has gone through this, but I am pretty sure that most entrepreneurs can understand, feel, and visualize the effort it takes to keep their business afloat.

It's hard. Everything about entrepreneurism is counterintuitive. You want to be relaxed. You want to be a human being, but it's a challenge to be a human being when you're constantly having to make payroll. Naturally, I am always seeking, thriving, and looking for the next opportunity. Always on the hunt, always selling, always looking for the next customer or that partnership that makes a difference.

When I started the company, I thought I was the biggest loser in the world if I didn't close a deal every two weeks. That has a huge impact on self. What's more, it has an even bigger effect on everybody else around you. Entrepreneurship weighs on everybody. Yes, there are highlights; I was able to take my family on a trip around the world and check off one of the biggest goals of my life. But entrepreneurship also put its strains on the trip. If you ask my kids what they hated most about the trip, they might tell you that "my dad talked to everybody except us. He was always trying to make a connection." My hope is that someday my children will say, "My parents took seven months out of the hustle and bustle of life to spend with us."

The trip certainly was not perfect. However, my daughter is writing about the trip for her college essay about being comfortable in the uncomfortable. There are always wins in life! Sometimes, you think you're providing for your family; giving your children a once-in-a-lifetime opportunity to travel around the world, but the mania behind maintaining this entrepreneurial mindset and fearing collapse hurts them in the process. Everybody suffers when you're in this manic state: your family, your business, and most importantly, yourself. You suffer the most and you don't even know it because you're too busy denying the fact that you might collapse.

About ten years ago, I hit bottom. I wasn't going to quit moving my feet, but I had no idea how I could grasp back onto the ladder and pull myself up. So, I started seeking answers.

Part of the entrepreneurial mindset is to always be seeking, learning, and exploring. This might help you land a deal, but it can also save your life. I'm lucky—I live in Washington, DC, where there are a lot of resources available to me, like free meditation, recovery groups, and other communities that helped me discover how to forge the entrepreneurial journey without potentially making things worse. I've always known that experience was expensive. And if I didn't hear somebody's story, then I might have the same expensive experience. When I hit my bottom, my wife helped me find places where I could listen to other people's stories. I cannot thank her enough for the opportunity she gave me to help find myself. She certainly saved my life and my family. Without her, there would be no business or certainly no trip.

There was so much I had no clue about, meditation and self-compassion for instance. I had no vocabulary about this stuff ten years ago. I didn't know about codependency. I didn't know about enmeshment. All of these words were like foreign terms to me. But when I hit my bottom, I discovered meditation, self-compassion, and all of these words and practices that I never heard of before. Most importantly, I had to learn how to sit with myself and practice mindfulness, letting feelings, thoughts, and emotions come and go without judgment. Learning how not to react is another full-time job.

Practice Self-Compassion

If you walk up a set of stairs and somebody trips in front of you, what do you say to that person? Usually, you might say something of compassion or ask if they are okay or offer them some help to get back up.

If you walk up a set of stairs and trip yourself, what do you typically say to yourself? Typically, you might say something negative, curse yourself, feel frustrated or embarrassed for tripping.

Why do we give a perfect stranger more compassion than we give ourselves? That doesn't make any sense. For doing something human, we're going to be hard on ourselves and beat ourselves up for something we would help somebody else up with.

I was never taught this lesson growing up and I certainly didn't know it at the beginning of my entrepreneurial journey, but now self-compassion is the key to my mindset. No one in my life had ever heard the phrase self-compassion until very recently. My mother was called out of her first yoga class because she couldn't sit with herself. Self-compassion and awareness didn't come naturally to her, and it didn't come naturally to me. But I learned, as she did, through meditation how to sit with myself and found a way out of rock bottom. By sitting with myself, I was able to relax, slow down, and do the things that I needed to do in order to live like a human being and not a human doer.

I started working with my mindfulness coach about five years ago, when I was still trying to find self-compassion. In fact, I told him that the thing I wanted most was somebody that could (figurately) whack tennis balls at me so I could learn to volley them back so I could get better or in other words NOT REACT when life was coming hard at me. I didn't even want soft shots because I thought only the hard shots would allow me to reflect, think, and process and eventually grow awareness. What I have learned now is that often the soft shots allow me to grow just as much if not more than the hard ones. Sometimes it the subtle things in life that provide the opportunity to practice self-compassion to allow me to move forward and gain the confidence to succeed. I'm going to trip on the stairs. The question is how am I going to learn new coping skills to dust myself off and keep going and react differently?

Through my journey, I discovered that I don't believe in self-confidence alone. I believe in self-compassion. I learned that I cannot build confidence without giving myself the space to fail or trip. If I didn't learn to have self-compassion, I could have never gotten better. When I hit bottom, I thought my life as I knew it was over. In many ways, it was just the opposite. I learned to give myself the space I needed to be able to recover to build back my confidence.

The "U" of Self

"Life is not the way it's supposed to be…It's the way it is…The way we cope with it, is what makes the difference."

When I started my entrepreneurial journey, I felt like I was in a constant state of free fall. Fortunately, through seeking new information and learning about self-compassion, and creating new coping skills, I realized that my journey didn't have to be a continuous free fall. Think of the letter "U." The letter "U" represents self. A "U" has two high points and a deep trough. I have learned that even though building a bridge at the two high points is the most expensive, it is much cheaper than having no bridge and failing to the bottom. Crawling out of the bottom of the U is so much harder and often much more expensive than building the most expensive bridge across the top.

When you do fail or fall, how do you climb out of the trough? I've learned, in my crazy entrepreneurial journey, the only way to climb back up is through mindfulness, meditation, and self-compassion. My entrepreneurial mindset is a combination of self-compassion and seeking that allows me to keep my feet moving and not collapse.

When I meditate on self-compassion, seeking, and never quitting, I am reminded of this quote from the poet Rumi who said: "Your task is not to seek for love, but merely to seek and find all the barriers within yourself that you've built against it." My mindfulness coach constantly reminds me of this quote. It is only now at fifty-four years old that I am truly starting to understand what this quote means. It might take me the rest of my life and maybe into my next one to remove all my barriers.

Like entrepreneurship, life is not a single point. Life is a journey of a series of consecutive points that make a curve with many potential inflection points, similar to a sine curve. I have learned that every point on the curve is an opportunity to slide up or down. I believe if I can live another day, I have the opportunity to succeed. As much as I think I'm going to fail or collapse that day, I know I can do something to succeed and be grateful for the opportunity. This is why self-compassion is at the center of my entrepreneurial mindset.

Everyone Wants to Make It

Catherine Bassick

Catherine Bassick is a luxury real estate market expert and advisor. With degrees in engineering and business, Catherine began her career in satellite technology. Pivoting from a technical role, she served as CEO of one of the biggest music and film companies in the bay area. As her family grew, she switched industries, becoming a real estate agent, and wowing her peers, earning $400K her first year. At Sotheby's, Catherine earned a Top 1 percent rank her first year. She made the first sale of a house over $100M in the history of the US. Catherine is listed in *L.A.'s Business Journal* as one of the Top 40 Women of Influence. She appeared on *Real Trend's* Top 250 Real Estate Professionals, an annual ranking sponsored by the *Wall Street Journal.* She's been listed as a Top 100 agent in the country. She serves as a luxury real estate market expert for the *Wall Street Journal* and BBC. Catherine owns Catherine Bassick Fine Homes and Estates brokered by EXP Realty and ranks as Luxury Home Marketing Million Dollar Guild Level and in the top 0.5 percent in the country in her industry. She continues to increase her knowledge base at Cornell with a certificate in business administration and management and a degree from MIT on developing health-centered communities. For additional information, please find Catherine at www.catherinebassick.com.

Everyone wants to "make it." Human beings are different in a lot of ways, but the American brain can be very predictable. No matter what kind of person you meet, no matter what field, when you shake someone's hand you are shaking the hand of someone who indulges in fantasies of riches, fame, notoriety, and social ascendance. These are the dreams of almost every human being; but why do so many people, in so many fields, instead flounder in dead end jobs with little growth? Because for many, these same brains that fantasize of endless success will also tempt us towards short cuts, laziness, and apathy. One can choose to write this off as cruel irony and succumb to these patterns or push against them at every opportunity—knowing that if you do you will separate yourself from 99 percent of the population. Entering the intensely competitive field of real estate in one of the most cutthroat zip codes in the world, I could have allowed my brain an incredible number of excuses—"I don't know anyone in Silicon Valley!"; "The competition here is just too fierce!"; "I've never done this before, it will be fine if I don't give it my full effort"—and the bitter truth is that others would have enabled me. This is a trap so many fall into when it comes to real estate, but these are temptations that I refused to indulge. I pushed myself to succeed, used my God given savvy to get ahead, and constantly sought ways to better myself—and in 2012, my discipline paid off when I sold the most expensive single-family home in the United States. Yes, everyone wants to make it, but so very few have the drive to create it.

My path towards real estate was an unconventional one; my collegiate degree in physics to residency in LA do not exactly match the pedigree of someone who would go on to sell houses to Silicon Valley bourgeois. I ascribe a good deal of my real estate skills to my background in technology—I left college with a degree in physics from Georgia Tech and a job at Satellite Network systems. Back then, technology was still a somewhat niche field; far from today's saturation of apps, smart phones, and laptops. Instead, technology to most people was still an abstract, vaguely geeky idea. It was this hurdle that helped me hone my skills in sales; I had to sell people their technology, which at that time was like selling a harpoon to a whale. Thus, I developed the invaluable skill of making a client feel comfortable with a product they had limited experience with. I had to make aggressively inaccessible products seem consumer friendly, and my sales expertise grew all the stronger. But I knew tech wasn't my first love, so I took all the knowledge I had garnered and translated it to a field that I would make my millions in: real estate.

Origins in Silicon Valley:

I relocated to Silicon Valley after a brief stint in film, and found myself at a bit of a career crossroads. The atmosphere of Silicon Valley reflected my anxiety—much like all those tech geniuses getting paid in paper clips, I knew that I was on the cusp something great but wasn't quite there yet. I had little guarantees other than my raw talent, immense drive, and a determination to achieve greatness, but it would soon be obvious the path I was destined to take. Before I even took a training class, I would go to open houses every Sunday. I had no reason to go—I loved my home and had no intention of moving—but something about the untapped potential of a house on the market made me infinitely enthusiastic. Eventually, the day came when I put my own house on the market, and I felt an immense dissatisfaction with the personalities in charge of selling my home. This distaste proved to be a surprisingly effective instigator; "If these people could succeed in the luxury real estate market," I thought, "I could kill it." If nothing else, getting a license would ensure I would never have to cede control to an incompetent agent ever again—and that was all the motivation I needed. I studied hard, passed the test, and achieved the status of a licensed real estate agent in the state of California. But I wasn't just starting in your average California town: I was starting in Silicon Valley. Underneath the veneer of peaceful suburbia lay one of the most expensive and competitive housing markets in the entire United States. It was out of the frying pan into the fire, but I was ready to cook.

As a new agent in a new town with few connections and no reputation, I was up against seemingly insurmountable odds—luckily, I was willing to put in the man-hours to spin those odds in my favor. I knew the only way I would succeed in this cutthroat environment was to become obsessed with the work, to never be truly off the clock, and to be more disciplined than all of my competition. I started work early and rarely left before seven. I made every call a priority, always ready in case my cell started ringing. I networked with every individual possible, befriended all of my clients, and never let a Bar Mitzvah, birthday, or wedding go by unattended. I would work with people and build relationships around every house I sold—I would garner not just clients, but friends who would stay in my life forever. And throughout it all I kept a positive attitude and refused to become deterred, constantly reminding myself "nothing worthwhile is easy." Piece by piece, I established myself in Silicon Valley—and though I expected my career to grow, I did not anticipate the dream situation I had set myself up for. I was a great saleswoman with heat in the right place at the right time: selling million-dollar listings at ground zero of the modern tech revolution. My good situation suddenly became a once in a lifetime opportunity. Though I had clients of many different stripes, I had more than a few that developed apps, were social media rock stars, or proudly wore the nerd-genius cliché stereotypical of someone buying a million-dollar house in Facebook founder Mark Zuckerman's zip code. As Silicon Valley grew, so too did my my income, confidence, and love for my profession; culminating in my sale of the most expensive single-family home in the United States. I have since left the Bay Area, but I will never forget the myriad listings, amazing relationships, and impressive career I achieved as the tech capital was securing its identity. Silicon Valley and I didn't just have similar stories—we helped each other write them.

My Secrets:

1. Think positively, and keep at it.

Many new agents have asked me what the "secrets" to being a great salesperson are, or if there's any sort of code that can be cracked. Unfortunately, there is not—but there are a few simple philosophies I stand by that I believe has allowed me to endure in an often-harsh industry. My first philosophy: if things aren't working for you, keep working hard and persevere. So many agents get so discouraged so quickly—the most bountiful period of my life, June of 2011, was also the period I was seeing numerous agents drop like flies. I heard every excuse—"the market is awful!"; "the economy is in the pits!"; "nobody is buying!"—and it would have been all too easy to join the chorus. But I believed in my ability to transcend my circumstance, and refused to join the pity party. And guess what? The discouraging market became a boon for me—my competition shrank, my profile grew, and I turned around and sold the first single family home in the United States for over $100 million.

Negative energy is contagious—not only is it tough to go to bat for the things that you love, but people would much rather read a bad review of a movie than a good review. Peer pressure is a menace—people on the way down will often want to take you with them, which is why it is important to maintain a positive attitude to maintain success. What I have found that with any degree of success, there are a lot of critics. Gain any degree of notoriety and you will find a hundred onlookers poking holes in your positive attitude, cynics telling you why you are wrong to shoot for the stars. These are actions of insecure, bitter individuals who attempt to build themselves up by knocking you down. I only bring this up as a warning: I know from personal experience just how easy it is to be discouraged by negative personalities (or even worse, to start thinking like them). When things seem most bleak and you are met with a chorus of naysayers, do everything in your power to reject negative sentiment and continue thinking positively. This is an important element of my philosophy on perseverance; pursue your goals without an ounce of bitterness. Perseverance is not about hanging around, feeling sorry for yourself—perseverance is about facing every day knowing you are going to win. Negative energy is contagious, but positive energy yields positive results.

I cannot emphasize the degree to which positive thinking has shaped my professional life. I remember in one of my first training classes before I even got my license, the teacher went around the room and asked everyone "how much are you going to make in your first year?" Most people shot low. I frequently heard "$50,000." The dreamers went as high as "$100,000." When the question got around to me, I answered "I would like to make "600,000." I got snickers, some laughs, and was primarily met with condescension. Could I have let this deter me, and let the people I was in the class with make me reconsider my dreams? It would have been all too easy, but I snapped out of it—who were these people, anyway? These people weren't my betters; we were in the same class! They literally knew just as much about real estate as I did! I looked past the facade of superiority that condescension creates, and proved their snickers wrong by making $400,000 my first year. I resolved to never let outside forces dictate my performance—if you don't believe in yourself, nobody else will. Love yourself immensely, and you will attract love. Treat all the people you work with (whether they be other brokers, vendors, or clients) with respect and integrity, and you will be rewarded with good reputation. Think positively, keep working, and treat even your harshest critics with respect; these are principles that are not only good for business, they are good for the soul.

2. Love What You Do

"Love what you do, and you will never work a day in your life." This may be a cliché, but the truth behind it is immense. Love what you do. That, simply, is the secret to success and the second part of my philosophy. Why have I had more success in real estate than any other field? One can credit my work ethic—and I often do—but what has helped me ascend above and beyond your run of the mill agent is my authentic love of houses. To me, a beautiful house is more breathtaking than anything at the MoMA, as escapist as classic cinema. Properties that some might see as mediocre, I often see as the ultimate Cinderella story. To me, there is no greater satisfaction than finding an average house and finding the right buyer; a prince for the shunned step-sister. Anyone can sell a gorgeous house; it was my love for the unwanted orphans that made me stick out, selling properties that had been on the market for over a year. I was recently inspired by actor Jim Carrey's commencement address to Maharishi University of Management's class of 2014. Carrey told a story of his father who made a "conservative choice" in his career, taking a job as an accountant. "When I was twelve years old, he was let go," Carrey declares. "You can fail at doing something you don't want, so you might as well take a chance on doing something you love." If you do not share my sincere passion, obsession, and fascination for being a real estate agent, I advise you to follow a different career path. No matter how great you are, you will feel a time when you're "just not there, just not getting it," and you can allow that insecurity to take over you, or you can utilize your love for the work to power through that slump. Read negotiation books, listen to podcasts, know your market; prove that you love what you do. If you want to sell a $100,000 property, you should know everything about it. Your consistent effort to know everything and better yourself will allow you to become a true champion for your clients. If any of this discourages you from the job, you were probably not meant for it in the first place. The best real estate agents are the ones you could never talk out of doing it, and to them I say: welcome to the club.

3. Live a Life Worth Advertising
My final piece of advice: live a life outside of real estate. This is an easy one to dismiss, but striking a proper work/life balance took more trial and error than any other element of my career. When you are obsessed with work, the first person it's hard to make time for is yourself. If you are committed to the difficulty, time, and perseverance necessary to be a great real estate agent, you face the danger of succumbing to a life of endless work. Workaholism sounds glamorous, but like everything else in life, you need balance. Real estate is a uniquely social industry, and consuming culture purely through the context of real estate is a surefire way to inhibit social interaction. Spending all weekend at the office can do a real number on your Sunday morning charm. Go on a hike before that open house and I guarantee you will exude more personality than if you spent the morning looking through escrow documents. Before you sell a house, you have to sell yourself—and if you want to charm, you better have more things to talk about than real estate. The most rewarding part of my real estate career was the bond I shared with my clients. I became friends with the people I worked with, which turned my work into my life instead of vice versa. But I wouldn't have held on to a single one of them if they never connected with me as an honest to goodness human being. Live a life worth advertising; go to the movies, read a book, go to the gym. Read up on that TV show everyone's talking about, play with your kids, watch the news—all of this will make you more interesting and add dimension to your conversations.

If you take care of yourself physically and enrich yourself mentally, you will be more attractive to everyone you meet. When I moved to Los Angeles, I immediately sought to join the Los Angeles Opera—an organization I now operate on the board of. We currently serve the Los Angeles artistic community and, most importantly, offer 175,000 kids exposure to opera and music education. I am also a member of Women in Film as well as Film Independent, two organizations devoted the raising the profile of under-represented voices in film. I joined these organizations because I emphatically believe in giving back to my country, community, and planet—I would be literally nowhere without them. What made me a good agent was my affinity for the work, but what has made me a great agent is my life outside of real estate. Living a well-rounded life is what builds your personality, what makes you appear as more than a snake oil salesman. Though I found immense success in real estate, none of my hard work, persistence, or dedication would mean anything if I did not feel like a well-rounded person.

About the Author, Catherine Bassick

Though my success in real estate may seem lucrative, it did not come without a grand amount of effort, positive thinking, and hard lessons learned. I made a lot of sacrifice, endured a lot of negative emotion, and faced many moments of doubt; but I endured by remembering that nothing worthwhile is easy, and that persistence is everything. Every struggle I encountered in the beginning were seeds to be harvested a decade down the line, the foundation on which I would sell the single most expensive single-family home in the United States. After that sale, I finally was lucky enough to move to Boston with my husband, now working every day in the greater Boston area. And as I reflect on my intense, crazy journey I realize more than ever that my journey that has yet to end. I still live my dream. I still achieve success. But most importantly, I make the time to love every second of it.

Ten Keys to a Success Mindset

Alinka Rutkowska

Alinka Rutkowska is the CEO of Leaders Press (www.leaderspress.com), a *USA Today* and *Wall Street Journal* best-selling press, where she helps entrepreneurs create books from scratch and then launches them to bestseller status with a 100 percent success rate.

She has helped more than 130 authors get on the *USA Today* and *Wall Street Journal* best-seller lists. Her mission is to help 10,000 entrepreneurs share their wisdom with the world by 2030.

Alinka is an official member of the Forbes Business Council, and her cutting-edge book creation process has been featured in *Entrepreneur* magazine.

To learn more about Alinka, Leaders Press, and how this anthology and many of the solo books of the entrepreneurs featured within were created, visit http://www.leaderspress.com.

The Big Hairy Audacious Goal

It all starts with a BHAG.

What's a BHAG? It's a big hairy audacious goal (a term coined in the book *Built to Last: Successful Habits of Visionary Companies* by Jim Collins and Jerry Porras). In other words, it's a clear and compelling target for an organization to strive for.

What has been my largest BHAG so far? A seven-figure business.

When defining targets like this I also make sure they are SMART (a term used in Peter Drucker's Management by Objectives approach), meaning specific, measurable, achievable, relevant, and time bound.

Have I reached my BHAG? Yes, and my goal for this chapter is to analyze what allowed me to do so.

Long before hitting seven figures I've been studying seven-figure entrepreneurs and joining groups they've joined (as soon as I met the requirements). I've been requesting meetings and picking seven-figure entrepreneurs' minds on how they achieved what they achieved. In fact, you'll see many of these documented in my previous anthologies titled *Supreme Leadership, Supreme Leadership Habits*, and *7-Figure Minds*.

Now I get to join the club.

Looking back, how did it happen? Here are my ten keys to help you achieve your BHAG, whatever it might be.

Key 1. Share your goal only with the right people.

Key 2. Make it a series of smaller goals.

Key 3. Track it.

Key 4. Make adjustments.

Key 5. Drive your vision.

Key 6. Work on your emotional intelligence.

Key 7. Know your values and communicate them.

Key 8. Associate yourself with successful people.

Key 9. Center yourself.

Key 10. Cultivate a success mindset!

Key 1. Share Your Goal Only with the Right People

Who should know what you're after?

You.

And the people who can help you get there. That can be your coach, your mentor, and very likely it will be your team.

Who shouldn't know what you're after?

Potential downers.

You can't tell your friend or family member who works at a low-paying job that you're working on seven figures this year; that's for two main reasons. The first is that you'll likely be met with incredulity, laughter, and immediate resistance. They can't imagine that type of goal becoming reality, so they can't be your supporter or ally.

The second reason is that you immediately create envy and you do so twice. Once right now for daring to dream and the second time once you've achieved your goals.

I'd recommend keeping a low profile with people who are not mentally and emotionally where you are.

Key 2. Make It a Series of Smaller Goals

At school, I remember I had to go through a 270-page grammar book. That's a pretty tough task for a school kid. So I took out my calculator and divided those 270 pages into 90 days, the time I gave myself for completing it. That resulted in going through three pages a day.

So that's what I did, religiously.

If one day I could only do one page, then I would do five pages the next. And if one day I had more time, I'd do four or five pages to be ahead of the game.

I do the same with my current goals. As an example, $1 million USD is $19,230 a week. Now that's a number that's much easier to digest and work with.

Just like with the grammar book, if I have a bad week and only generate $9,320 then I'll aim at $29,230 the following week. And I'll always try to generate more than the target to be ahead of the game.

Key 3. Track It

In order to go through three pages of the grammar book I needed an hour, so I would make sure I scheduled that hour in my calendar. In order to generate the weekly revenue I targeted, I needed to have a certain number of sales calls. In order to have that number of sales calls, I needed to have a certain number of leads. In order to have those leads, I needed to generate a certain amount of traffic.

I established targets for each of those measures and tracked them weekly with my team. Each person was responsible for a certain piece and we met weekly to discuss how to improve. Transparent numbers, black on white, with the responsible people accountable for their segments is what allows us to know where we are and to work on getting better and better.

Key 4. Make Adjustments

Not everything works so you need to be willing to learn, test, draw conclusions, implement, and then repeat the cycle. When you double your business every year like I have so far, the learning curve is fast, so you need to keep up and your team needs to keep up. There are moments when team members rest on their laurels and are not able to grow as fast the company is growing. That requires adjustments concerning the team.

Key 5. Drive Your Vision

In order to achieve your goal, you need to drive your vision. Your BHAG needs to be ingrained in your key players' minds. Ask them (often): "What's our goal this year?" If they get the answer wrong, it means YOU didn't do a good job aligning everyone with your vision and you will pay the consequences.

Key 6. Work on Your Emotional Intelligence

Keep your eyes and ears open and read between the lines. When your goal is dependent not only on you but on other players, pay attention to them. Observe their body language, listen to the tonality of their voice. This will allow you to find out if there are potential problems early on and help solve them before they escalate and become much more difficult to solve. Emotional intelligence (EQ) is key. This term (which gained popularity in Daniel Goleman's best-selling book *Emotional Intelligence*) is described as "…the ability to perceive, use, understand, manage, and handle emotions. People with high emotional intelligence can recognize their own emotions and those of others, use emotional information to guide thinking and behavior, discern between different feelings and label them appropriately, and adjust emotions to adapt to environments" (https://en.wikipedia.org/wiki/Emotional_intelligence). Emotional intelligence is crucial in sales positions. It's also indispensable when managing teams.

Mastering it will also help you in your personal life.

I'll tell you a story. I didn't grow up in a harmonious home. On the contrary, there was a lot of tension, so early on I dove into self-help books and adjusted myself (Daniel Goleman's book was one of the first ones I read). Now that I no longer live with my parents and brother, I often forget what that dynamic was like. Just the other day, when we were all together under the same roof, there was a conflict between my mom and my brother. In the past, I would have taken a side and joined the fight. But my outlook has changed (or my EQ has increased). I could clearly see how both sides felt the way they did. I could also see how they miscommunicated what they wanted to express.

When my brother and mom came to me explaining how it got to that point (which I had silently observed), I simply suggested that they think ahead and find a solution to the petty problem they were discussing and helped them put it to bed.

I did not look for a person to blame, I did not look to examine the problem and focus on the problem and how it escalated, I simply directed their attention to the fastest solution.

I'm not telling you what issue it was because it could have been anything.

High emotional intelligence will allow you to live better and lead better.

Key 7. Know Your Values and Communicate Them

I used to think that company core values were a load of woo-woo. Here's why I was wrong: as soon as we developed core values (and they were a "copy and paste" of other companies' at first) and started paying attention to them, we decided to start hiring according to them, promoting according to them, and settling disputes according to them.

One of our core values is respect. Just the other day one of my team members told me she was having an issue with another team member who cancelled meetings with her or came late to them. I saw the issue right away but I needed her to see it.

So I asked: what is the tone of this person's voice when you do meet? What is the tone of the emails? Does this person behave the same way with other team members? Does he behave the same way with clients?

To which she responded, "I guess it's a matter of respect."

Since respect is one of our core values and we rate each other on core values, the conversation and resolution became easy.

Key 8. Associate Yourself with Successful People

You might not be able to hang out with your heroes in person but you can most certainly find out what they read and listen to and do the same! The more, the better!

Key 9. Center Yourself

This links back to emotional intelligence.

You need to be grounded. You need be calm. You need to think clearly.

And you need to find a way to achieve these things.

For me, it's my morning routine (described in detail in *Habits of Success*). Do what you need to do. For me it's qigong, Wim Hof breathing, cold swims, cold showers, meditation, and most recently horseback riding (you need to be calm and determined on a horse!).

Here's the easiest way to begin: before you enter into any interaction, take three deep breaths, really long and deep. This is the start, then figure out what works for you because there are a lot of potential pressures you will face, but they will not seem that big and scary when you are centered.

And lastly…

Key 10. Cultivate a Success Mindset!

How do you know you're succeeding? Define what that means and be self-aware. At Leaders Press we start every meeting by stating our victories, either business or personal. And I meet some of my team members on a daily basis so every day they need to come up with a new victory, and I need to come up with a victory for every meeting!

Do the things that will turn into victories first when you start your day (right after your morning routine).

And when you wind down after your day, mentally go over the day's victories. The more you focus on victories, the more of them your brain will seek out and the more successful you'll be.

It's all in your hands. Say, "I CAN do this."

You *can* do this!

Roots to Fruits

Vandana S. Puranik

Vandana S. Puranik is a builder, brainstormer, and brander. She has worked in a number of complex industries (H&B, F&B, pharma, financial services, oil, tech, Ecommerce) with high-profile companies (P&G, Kellogg's, RBC, GSK, J&J, Revlon, Petro-Canada, Campbell's, Maple Leaf, ++) for well over twenty-five years, and is particularly known for her expertise and enthusiasm in creative problem solving—a seldom taught skill that she authors and advocates for as a passion project. She loves mining insights, architecting movements, and storytelling. Thoughtfully bold, unapologetically curious, and captivated by the unexpected and unknown, Vandana has grown every business she has worked on, often converting chaos into clarity, showcasing an innovative growth mindset. She has developed a flow to help individuals see their own customized success and is often asked to teach and mentor others.

Growing up a child of the world has given her a tremendous respect for diversity and appreciation for the psychology of how people think and act. Living in multiple countries and continents has taught her how to adapt and recalibrate her way to success.

She loves a good laugh and says without sports, cultural expeditions (having spoken or studied six languages), reading, and most importantly her family (including the furry part), her life would not be even a fraction of what it is today.

She is a graduate of Duke University and a Blue Devil through and through.

Her company is Active Ingredients Inc. and she is reachable at Vandana@ActiveIngredientsInc. com. Watch for her upcoming books on skills to enhance business acumen and personal growth. Visit ActiveIngredientsInc.com for further information.

I've been a marketer for well over twenty-five years. I've been an innovator for just as long. I love finding ways to hack problems by turning them upside down and inside out. I've grown businesses when nobody thought they had a chance and also multiplied the growth rate of strong-performing businesses. I've grown businesses when there was only glimmer of hope before abandonment, and I've launched businesses from the ground up. Basically, I've grown every business I've had the privilege of encountering. I didn't actually realize this until a colleague brought it to my attention. Then I had several people ask me how I did it. That really got me thinking. How did I do that? What was it that got me there? Well, what I know for sure is this. There are always options for success and it's really critical to discover and uncover them. I find ways that others may have perhaps missed. I always endeavor to have a mind that absorbs great ideas from perhaps the most unlikely places. And most of all, I'm always curious. The magic about curiosity is that it puts your mind in an active versus passive state, it heightens your interest and focus on the task before you, it forces you to listen and withhold judgement, and it completely opens your mind to a plethora of possibilities. It makes for one helluva good creative problem solver.

So I was curious about what's made me so curious. What is it that made me wonder what more there is to life beyond my current state? How to navigate what comes next? How to be successful on my own terms? How to find play and peace?

I think I've found the answer.

I grew up a child of the world. We traveled a lot. We moved around a lot. Sometimes that was every six months. And we changed cities, states, countries, and even continents. By the time I went to Duke University, I was attending my fifteenth school. No kidding. I never knew a home as defined by traditional culture. The world was my backyard. And life was all about discovering and adapting and evolving. And through that, I learned to make choices. I was a happy kid.

But I was never like the other kids my age—having a lot to do with traditions my parents kept as first-generation immigrants. I didn't look like anyone else. I didn't smell like anyone else. I was incredibly studious and I didn't go out a whole lot. I didn't drink or do drugs. I had early curfews—my parents always thought of the worst risks—influenced a lot by their professions. My parents really didn't and couldn't get what I was going through; they hadn't been through it themselves.

So everything was new, unfamiliar, or unknown. Apparently, when my parents first had the opportunity to immigrate to Cincinnati, they thought they'd watch *The Cincinnati Kid* to get acquainted with what the city was about. You ever seen that movie? It's about pretty much all the vices you can drum up and put in one reel. Disaster. Then, when they first got to the US, they thought spaghetti and sauce was worms and blood. Lord, have mercy. I had to teach them what hotdogs and ketchup and mustard were—after I learned it myself. I can still picture the scene in the grocery store. But we figured it out, and made some changes; we adapted.

Good times.

Because we moved around so much, I never had family around. So friends became family and other cultures embedded themselves into mine. I also never had the stability of best friends, but I had friends everywhere, and the friends I have now are my most cherished assets. I'm so grateful that I had the chance to learn and adapt during that part of my history.

Further along the way, I got to meet so many interesting people. I was exposed to an abundance of revealing and surreal experiences, both good and bad. I learned several languages. I immersed myself in whichever climate surrounded me. I certainly gained a deep understanding and appreciation for different cultures. And most of all, I started to understand the way populations think and feel. At times it was delightful and at times it was vast and scary, but it was always filled with interesting stories and eye-opening possibilities, flooded with insights. In every instance, I felt like my brain was constantly recalibrating with each new piece of information that it would absorb. These were my moments of truth.

I remember when my grandfather told me he was going to die and made me promise not to tell anyone else—it was our secret—a secret I never wanted. I was eleven. And I was living oceans away from my parents that year. From that point on, I could not get the thought of him passing away out of my head and he did in fact pass away exactly two weeks later. He was an impressive man and greatly missed by many citizens. To this day I'm still trying to figure out why he told me, and me specifically, or even why he felt like doing so. That was the moment I grew unwavering faith. I became the support for my grandmother and adapted to a new normal for her. For us.

One of the most striking memories I have is my father breaking down in tears because his passion for his profession had forced us, his family, to live well below an acceptable standard of living for a number of years. I remember wearing cheap polyester pants that my mom lengthened using fabric from other old pants and then pairing those with the dresses that had become too short but could still be used as tops. I remember begging for doll clothing every time we'd head to Kmart and my parents turning me down quite emphatically. I'd even run back and forth to each of them with the hope that one of them might relent. No-go. So I learned to sew and make clothes for my dolls out of old socks and scraps of clothing. We made it. We adapted.

Have you ever felt hatred or disgust? I've felt it twice. The first was in fourth grade and the cutest guy in class wouldn't hold my hand during our square dancing lesson because I was "different." The second was in ninth grade when I was walking home alone from a track meet, dead tired. I was about to walk across a deserted field and two very aggressive guys came up to me and started yelling and cursing and then spit on me because I was "different." I was in shock. And I was scared. And then I made a break for it and ran like hell. Being treated horribly is going to happen from time to time, but I've learned how to counter that kind of behavior with wit and kindness and curiosity to change the final outcome.

I did have plenty of charming moments too. I met a great guy and moved to a new country yet again. In the beginning, I had a tough time feeling comfortable in my new environment because graduates still came back home for a few years after university. So they had their established relationships and they didn't really need another friend. My husband's friends were a godsend to me at that time because they embraced me like one of their own. I will always remember what they taught me and I have adapted my behavior to make others feel welcome.

Then I started working. A lot. Seven days a week, twelve hours a day. So ridiculous. But I was young and had just gotten into an elite company in its most prized department and I was a work horse–damned if I was going to let anything hold me back. Then something changed. I was missing my life. So I cut out working on weekends. And I adapted to that new change and learned to find more efficient ways of getting my job done. Then I cut out late evenings and I adapted again. I found so many creative solutions at accomplishing tasks much faster. And that growth still serves me to this day.

At another time in my young career, I was in the midst of launching three new products into the market. BIG products, worth millions. I had to fly into a small town, visit a factory, and then present the initiatives to the board the next morning. My director and president were arriving that morning to support me. But their plane got fogged in. That morning and the whole night before I was super sick to my stomach to the point that I thought I was going to pass out. Unbeknownst to me, I was pregnant for the first time. Petrified about doing the huge presentation on my own and feeling incredibly sick, I somehow found a way to pull myself together only to realize that the financials I had been provided were wrong. I had to have the HQ Finance group send me updates–and thankfully got them just in time for my meeting. Keep in mind that mobile phones and PowerPoint were not a big thing yet–it was all land lines, admin assistants, and acetates for me. Believe it or not, we secured full support. Those three launches carried the company that year. You might even see them kicking around stores today.

I share these stories to make a point. Even the most personal, provocative, and mundane moments have a role to play in our lives. They teach us to pivot as needed. We all have these times. And they punctuate each of our stories.

Each of these moments began to form the scaffold that would build my future. I learned to expose myself to many experiences and to take chances. That's the adventurous side in me. How will you ever know what you like or how you'd react to something otherwise? As I got older, I realized I have control over the choices that I make, and EVERYTHING is indeed a choice. This thirst for adventure combined with the desire to uncover and influence my choices made me always set my goals higher. But here was the dilemma: what would I do when I reached each goal? Was this moment's goal IT? What was beyond it? What would I want to do next? So the search for these answers made me set further goals. What I realized is that I don't really define goals as numbers or statuses or levels or states—I define them as recalibration points. So once I've gone down a path that satisfies my initial curiosity, I recalibrate and redefine where I go next.[2]

This process has come to mean pushing milestones. It has taught me that success is not a destination. It's an everchanging path. It's moments of discovery. It's an iterative process. You progress as you complete each cycle. Success is not final; we just continue to seek answers and find solutions every day. It's a number of moments strung together. Our own moments. It's an evolution. It makes life so fun and interesting. I never know what's coming next and I love that. How boring would life be if everything was predictable?

So let's see if we can reverse engineer all this and recap it into a simple diagram.

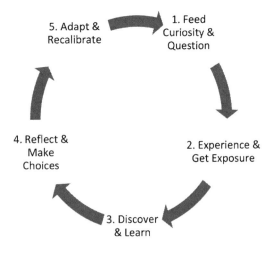

[2] "Emotional intelligence," Wikipedia, last modified September 17, 2021, https://en.wikipedia.org/wiki/Emotional_intelligence

I call it my Roots to Fruits Cycle of Success. And it has never failed me. It is completely composed of my life experiences. And your path will be composed of your own. What I love about this is that it's totally adaptable to any situation. Whether it's business, teaching, rocket science, sports, mental health, recipe creation, weight loss, etc. The steps will be the same, but each individual situation will precipitate customized and relevant results.

One of the things I love about this cycle is that it always presents options. There is never only one right answer. There are always choices. And thus, nothing is final–you always have alternatives.

I would be hard-pressed to believe there's anyone who can't see results based on this path.

There is one more thing I'd add about making choices. It requires you to make decisions. Learn to make them fast. You will never have all the information. You will never have zero risk. You will never please everyone. You will never have only applause. But what I know is this. A decision is better than no decision. Because making a decision allows you to move forward. And that truly is success.

If there were only a few takeaways I could share, they would be these.

1. Life is about making choices and making connections. That's it.
2. Other than death, nothing is final (and even that is debatable).
3. There are always options. There are always solutions. None might be what you were expecting, but there will always be routes that announce themselves as you progress. Possibility is an infinite gift.
4. Always be curious and always be learning. Always be grateful and live your own path.
5. There will always be a new reality. We must always make choices, adapt, and recalibrate.

I'd be delighted to chat with you further on virtually any topic–find me at ActiveIngredientsInc.com or drop me a line at Vandana@ActiveIngredientsInc.com.

A Ninety-Year-Old Secret to Success

Deepak Syal

Deepak Syal is a co-founder and director of GreyB, a leading patent research company headquartered in Singapore. He has worked with some of the world's top companies in helping them build their innovation strategies. His vision is to enable every company to find innovative solutions to the problems they are solving internally.

He is the inventor of multiple patents and has received numerous accolades including an Edison Award, Singapore Entrepreneur of the Year, and IAM Top 300 Patent Strategist. He loves talking about the success mindset and how to build a great team and a great culture. You can find him on https://bit.ly/deepaksyal.

It didn't feel magical. That's how I felt.

When I was a kid, everybody told me that success meant owning a big house and having a huge bank balance. After graduating, I worked hard and did everything that was required to achieve this goal. I managed to buy a house within three to four years and had a good bank balance. However, it didn't feel as magical as I expected when I got all this. In fact, the feeling was nowhere even close to magical. I was not able to figure out what was missing.

Then I thought to myself—maybe I need to go after something even more significant. Perhaps then I can call myself successful. Successful businesses like Ogilvy, McKinsey, and Ideo inspired me to shift my focus from owning a house to building a large company. I worked endless days and nights, put in whatever it took to kickstart a company. Eventually came a day when I had a large company with offices worldwide. It has many Fortune 500 companies as clients. I received many awards and was recognized globally. I had everything we all aim for when we are young.

Despite this, I felt that something was still missing. I realized that something somewhere was wrong.

I asked my grandfather, who was ninety at the time and a very content and successful businessman, what I was missing.

He said, "People have been misleading you. Success won't bring you that magical feeling."

He then asked me, "Why are you so obsessed with success?" I answered, "So that everybody knows I am successful." He then asked, "Why do you want everybody to know that you are successful?" I had to think for a moment as I never thought why I wanted to be successful, and nobody told me what I would get after it. So after a few minutes, I said, "If I have money and fame, I can buy anything I want. I can buy a big car, any phone, any house. I do not have to think of anything before buying."

He again asked, "Why do you not want any constraints on your desires?" I said, "I do not know. I never thought about it. Maybe it will give me a sense of freedom. It will make me feel happy." After a minute of silence, he said, "So you are doing everything so that you can be happy in the end. Can I say your end goal is to feel happy?" I hesitantly said, "Yeah...."

I felt as if he knew what I was going to say, like he had been through this process before. He said, "To be happy, you don't need to have a lot of money or luxuries, and you don't need to prove to anyone that you own them. We are made to think that achieving big things will bring us happiness. We make them our primary goal and run after them. And, during this chase, we forget why we are running and what our end goal was."

"Yes, success makes you feel happy, but its momentary. You buy a new car, you are happy that day; the next day, you feel nothing. I am not sure why people do so much to attain momentary happiness. Let me tell you about my days."

He then started sharing his story:

"I worked at a lot of menial jobs when I was young. In the late 1930s I started as a helper in a truck tyre store. I might have been around ten or twelve at the time. We were really poor. It was a demanding job working at 47° C under the hot sun for seven days a week. You might be thinking I was crazy and nobody would want to do such a job. Well, there was nothing I could do about the sun. Maybe I was too young to complain. I just focused on what I was asked to do and I used to enjoy it."

"Think of it like when you were a kid. During your summer vacation I remember you used to wake up early in the morning to play cricket. The whole day you guys used to play in the hot sun. Did the sun ever bother you? You used to lose some days and win some days. But every evening you were excited to tell everyone at home what happened on the field that day. You could not wait for the day to end so that you could go back to your game the next morning.

"Am I right?"

I said, "Yes, because we used to enjoy playing cricket."

"That's how I used to feel. There were bad days too, similar to when you used to lose the cricket match. You do feel sad on such days. But the outcome of the match is not going to change by feeling sad. So like you I used to start the next day always fresh and happy."

He continued, "This thought process made me always enjoy the job I was doing. When you are happy, you want to do that thing more. I was always curious about new things at work. This indirectly helped me perform better. People always wanted to keep me around. Like the truck drivers around the shop taught me how to repair trucks. Slowly I learned how to drive a truck. I then started taking driving contracts. I had to be away from home for long periods but sulking about it or being sad wasn't going to help me. I started enjoying driving. With the money I earned I bought my first truck. One truck was followed by multiple trucks. I kept going regardless of what came my way, good or bad.

"As for money, it started coming in by itself. I didn't specifically work for it. The thought of earning money was not the core of my being anymore. It became the result of the work that I enjoyed so much."

I could see from his face that he was reliving his life in flashbacks while telling me about it. He continued, "One day, in 1947, during the partition of India, we were asked to leave our town. The whole town was asked to shift. We were asked to move to a new city with nothing in our hands. Millions of people had lost their homes. People were angry, sad, grieving from serious losses. Despite all the pain, there was nothing we could have done to avoid this from happening. It was not in our control. So I decided to not let this affect me. I was not happy, but I was not sad either. I focused on what I should be doing next. So, I found whatever small job was available during the time and was happy with myself even if it got us just some bread to survive on."

With curious eyes, I asked him, "What happened after that? How did you build this big business?"

He replied, "I followed the same basic thought process. I enjoyed whatever I was doing and kept moving forward. I kept learning new things. I spent twenty years doing various types of jobs, from grocery store manager to driving trucks, working in a shoe store to many other things. Today we own a big movie theatre. If you had asked me when I was a kid if owning a large movie theatre was what I wanted, or if the movie theatre would bring me more happiness than anything else in my life, my answer would have absolutely been no. Although I was the first one to bring movie theatres to the town, it didn't make me any happier than I already was.

"I do not think about success like everybody else. I think about being happy. The secret is happiness is a feeling. It originates from inside. Therefore, I could feel happy when I used to work at a truck shop, and I feel happy even today with our movie theatre. If you can change your mindset, you can start feeling happy and content independent of your circumstances outside.

"If you do not have control over your happiness, you will find it very difficult to be happy even if you own the greatest thing in the world. I call it the happiness mindset."

After listening to his story I was intrigued. I asked him one more question which was constantly popping in the back of my mind. I asked him, "Does this mean I should not be aspirational? According to this theory, we should feel happy with whatever we have and nobody should think of achieving anything big in life?"

He took a moment and then replied, "Different people want different things from life. Some people just want happiness like me. Some want to do more like creating something big. Let's call them dreams. Dreams are like a new world that we wish to create for ourselves. We want our dreams to turn into reality because they would give us joy."

I could not stop myself and said, "So, you're saying it is ok to think big and try to make it big, but not link our happiness with it?"

"Yes," he replied, with a sparkle in his eyes.

Motivated by this conversation, I asked him again, "So, let me ask you one more question. Do you also have a way of thinking on how to make your dreams come true?"

He smiled, but then replied, "I never dreamt of anything big, but my father used to share this with me. He used to say that there are very few people whose dreams turn into reality. Majority are not able to realize their dream because they do not think backwards. We all are taught to make plans looking forward. His way was to start with your dream and then work backwards. This way you can see the milestones you need to achieve and the skills you need to gain to achieve your dream."

"Thinking backwards." I had never heard of that. I interrupted him again and asked a follow-up question. "Wait…this is getting too philosophical now. Can you explain this with an example?"

He took a minute and replied, "These days a lot of kids have a dream to become a CEO. We all know becoming a CEO is not easy. So let's think this through backwards. Visualize a CEO that you aspire to be. What do you see him doing? Addressing the media? Talking to customers? Trying to convey the company's vision and how the products may change the industry? This means the CEO has to be a great public speaker to talk to the media. This also means he has to be good in sales to be able to sell his vision. If he has to also be responsible for framing the future vision of the company, he also needs to be an avid reader so that he can see how the industry is going to change in the future.

"Most of the young kids I have seen think unidirectional. They would focus so much on their core work that they never think about the need to overcome their fear of public speaking. They feel sales to be an inferior quality. Sadly, they do not realize the need to learn these skills until eight to ten years have gone by and their growth has stopped. Thinking in reverse helps them understand the relevancy of these skills and learn them much earlier in their career.

"What else does a CEO do? Address the whole company? He should be able to brainstorm with the team members on technical grounds on how the product may fulfill the vision. This means that to brainstorm, the CEO himself should have good technical know-how. He should be able to resolve conflicts and ego clashes that may arise between team members. If competition overtakes, he has to be fearless and confident. Most young kids these days avoid conflict. When something bad happens to them, they get demotivated. These are the weaknesses that would stop them from attaining their dream."

I loved what he said. First about success, then happiness, and also about the concept of reverse thinking to reach your dreams. I learnt a lot more from him and I now share those learnings with everyone through different platforms.

Stop Being Ignored

Kris Safarova

Kris Safarova leads a private equity firm that manages a portfolio of companies including the largest strategy and consulting practice development training platform in the world, StrategyTraining.com and FIRMSconsulting.com. She is a best-selling author and manages two top-ranked podcast channels, *Strategy Skills* and *Case Interviews and Management Consulting*. She is also a speaking coach who studied under Roger Love. She holds an MBA from Ivey Business School, and was on the dean's list with highest distinction. Prior to her MBA, she worked in management consulting. Post-MBA, she was a corporate banker managing a portfolio worth over a billion US dollars, and a management consultant in Toronto, Canada. In her early career, Kris was a master classical concert pianist and an official representative of the Russian Federation who toured Europe.

"No" Often Does Not Mean "Never"

I lived in Russia until I was twenty-one. From an early age, I noticed many people treated my family differently because my father was Azeri.

One evening, my father went to take out the garbage and came back with blood all over his face. He said he fell. Later, my mother teased an explanation from him. Our neighbors beat him up, and when they finally let him go, they told him that we should leave Russia.

There were many similar incidents. Like any great country, a few nasty people can make the lives of many intolerable.

When the former Soviet Union collapsed and many people immigrated, I urged my parents to move out of Russia. They told me we couldn't because it wouldn't be better elsewhere.

Those were tough years. I remember standing in line for hours to buy one pack of margarine.

When I was around six, I was rejected from a music school. After being rejected, my mom left me in the hallway and reasoned with the teachers to admit me. I saw my mother not taking "no" for an answer, and I realized then that "no" often does not mean "never." If you don't give up, you may get to a "yes."

I studied at that music school for the next seven years. By age thirteen, I was selected to represent the Russian Federation as a "gifted child of Russia." I performed in Europe as an official cultural ambassador of the Russian Federation.

I also wrote my own music. One day, a famous Russian composer named Mark Levyant overheard me playing my own composition. He contacted my parents and insisted that I continue my musical education. This is how I ended up at DG Shatalov Music College.

All We Have Is Today

At DG Shatalov, I challenged myself with complex pieces that required hours of practice each day. Yet, I knew I wasn't passionate enough about music to dedicate my entire life to it.

I got a full scholarship but still needed money for food, clothing, and medical expenses. So, I performed at weddings and restaurants. Despite my hard work, I only earned about $2.50 per day.

There was a particular event that forced me to pick my own path. When I was sixteen, about two months after I started at DG Shatalov, I awoke with my face blown up and swollen on the left side. I was hospitalized, and the doctors diagnosed me with a severe and likely fatal allergic reaction. It was most likely caused by a recent vaccination, which hadn't been properly tested. I remember being surrounded by doctors who were saying, "She will not live until the next day. As soon as this blown up part of her face will go down to her neck, she will die."

Over the next few weeks, the inflamed part of my face burst, and the swelling went down to my neck and eventually disappeared. I left the hospital with a big scar on the left side of my head, which I still have.

This experience taught me that all we have is today. You have to push boundaries while you still have time. At this point, I was even more determined to completely change my life.

Approach Business as Your Own

Leaving Russia wasn't easy. It was possible to get a visa to South Africa. I received a three-month visitor's visa and arrived in Johannesburg with my savings: $1,000.

Initially, I lived in a tiny, cockroach-infested place. I struggled to find a job because I didn't have any business skills, I didn't speak English well, and I had a music diploma from a music college respected in Samara, Russia, but unknown in the West. Yet I was happy because I knew I was moving up in the world.

I searched for a business job for eight months and had some very bad interview experiences that included being locked in a small room in the back office of a gas station during an interview gone horribly wrong.

Just at that low point in my life, things started improving just a little.

I started working as a receptionist at a small manufacturing company that served high-profile clients in the defense industry.

The salary was only about $500 a month. There were many days when I had to count coins to decide if I should buy something to eat. But I had a foot in the business, and I was learning. I approached that business as if it was my own. I did whatever had to be done, often without being asked.

I learned to always drive for results. I renegotiated prices with hundreds of suppliers and drove the cost of goods sold down by 25 percent. Within one year, I became the owner's right-hand person with a broad portfolio of responsibilities.

I also started my part-time undergraduate degree in commerce and economics at the University of South Africa. I studied at night and on weekends; I also worked full days teaching the piano and translating documents into Russian.

I would study with my dictionary, as I did not understand most of the words. When I received the results of my first exams, I was very surprised. I was initially afraid I would not pass. Instead, I was at the top of the class.

During this time, I was invited to a dinner sponsored by several companies, including a major international consulting firm. I was just so happened to be sitting next to the local managing partner of the firm. I mentioned that my goal was to go into management consulting. Later, he offered me a position in a research department. I accepted immediately.

Get the Job Done

Although it is rarely mentioned openly, no one respects a research department, and I was the most junior person there. One business analyst wouldn't even return my greetings in the hallway once he realized I was part of the research department.

Soon after starting this role, I tracked down a partner who was helping a large multinational financial services company enter the Eastern European market. Knowledge of the Russian language was the one advantage I had. He agreed to let me work on the project in my free time. Eventually, I was leading big parts of analyses.

Within a few weeks I joined his team full-time. The project grew to become a pivotal study for the firm. I received accelerated promotions, first from research department to business analyst within the strategy and innovation practice within weeks after joining, then from business analyst to consultant less than a year after joining that practice. I was promoted again to senior consultant about five months later, at which point I was at the same level as consultants who joined the firm with an MBA.

This taught me the importance of just getting the job done. It became a pattern that I would routinely be placed on tough studies; I always aimed to do the best possible work.

Play the Cards You Are Given

I was studying during early mornings in the parking lot before work and on weekends. Ultimately, I managed to graduate with a distinction in every exam. But it was a journey of blood and sweat.

The Eastern European financial services project gained a lot of momentum. We visited Russia to meet with potential investors and strategic partners. Eventually, we met the CEO, an owner of multiple companies in various countries and a close friend of Nelson Mandela. During that meeting, the CEO spent a lot of time with me. He and his wife invited me to dinner. I think he appreciated that I approached a conversation from the angle of what was important for him and addressed his key concerns and the apprehensions of his team.

I was twenty-six years old, and I was at the point in my life where I wanted to be professionally.

But while I loved South Africa, I realized I needed an MBA to move ahead. I selected the Ivey Business School because of their reputation for producing the most CEOs, bankers, and consultants in Canada.

During my MBA, I committed to reading and studying everything the professors assigned, even though many professors told us that it was humanly impossible to do so. I was determined to make the most of that year and to learn as much as possible. My English was still not strong, so this was difficult, but I read every case, book, and article assigned.

Despite receiving a partial scholarship, I spent basically all my money on this degree. There was a point during my MBA when all I had left in my bank account was $76.

Despite my poor English, I graduated on the dean's list, with distinction in every subject. I was also president of the public sector club and editor in chief of the public sector journal. I was happy to have done so much in just one year. It made everything seem worthwhile.

Post-MBA, I was a corporate banker managing a portfolio worth over a billion US dollars, growing portfolio revenue 11.4 percent beyond target annual growth, and receiving quarterly Best of the Best awards. But I decided I missed the problem solving aspect of management consulting, and I rejoined consulting. I went through multiple interviews and joined a major professional services firm at the management level.

I felt I needed to work harder to prove I deserved the larger title. The firm was understaffed, and this turned out to be a particularly stressful period. Due to years of prolonged stress and long work hours, my immune system became particularly weak. I became very ill and had to take time away for treatments.

I decided I wanted to do more important things and work on issues that mattered. It was a similar wake up call to the one I had at age sixteen. Both times there was a very big possibility that my life was over, and both times I realized I was on the wrong path.

I started looking for a more impactful role because I realized that if my life had ended there, it would have been a waste. I was not on the path that would help me evolve into the person I intended to be, or the path that would allow me to do my life's work and truly make the world better.

This realization led me to commit to building FIRMSconsulting.com and StrategyTraining.com full time.

FIRMSconsulting is a private equity firm. We invest our intellectual capital to co-develop high-potential businesses. I have expanded the business into publishing, podcasting, media, document management, and other sectors. We run the largest strategy and consulting practice development training platform in the world, StrategyTraining.com.

Throughout this journey, the biggest lesson I have learned is how important it is to be on a path that is meaningful to you and will help you evolve into the person you want to be and leave a legacy you intend to leave.

That also means you have to play the cards you are given. Being a minority–speaking Russian as my first language, my music background, and being a woman in business–did have its advantages, and I used those advantages for my benefit.

No matter what position I was in, I took ownership of the role. I never treated the work as if it was below me, and that opened doors to pursue greater opportunities.

Helping Clients Unlock Their Full Potential

Throughout my life, I have focused on helping people unlock their potential. Now, as CEO, I have an even bigger opportunity to change the world. Our goal is to help our clients unlock their full potential and make a meaningful positive impact.

When I committed to FIRMSconsulting full time, there was a period of disrespectful behavior from some clients and partners which I felt was driven by the fact that I was a female. But as I always do, I focused on doing the right thing and I knew that in time my work would speak for itself. A pivotal moment for me was when Bill Matassoni, one of the most revered McKinsey and BCG former partners, responded to an email by saying, "We should only do it if Kris agrees." He valued my views because I always focused on making sure our work made a difference and to ensure there was a win-win for all parties.

FIRMSconsulting is just getting started in making its impact on the world. A few years back I had the idea of exchanging equity in businesses in return for offering detailed advice to start and build a business. After careful vetting of some ideas, we are now running an auto, mining, and luxury brands business.

We also published multiple successful books, and *Succeeding as a Management Consultant* and *The Strategy Journal* are #1 bestsellers on Amazon. Our podcast channel, *Strategy Skills*, is a top podcast for careers in many countries. And just last week, after years of studying under Roger Love, I became one of the few people in the world who is certified to teach Roger Love's method for speakers, a new powerful skill we can now add to our clients' toolkit. Roger Love is recognized as one of the world's best vocal coaches and has coached professional speakers such as Tony Robbins.

It hasn't been easy. Take heart in knowing that even if you are twenty-five years old, barely speaking English, with no degree and working as a receptionist only earning $500 a month, you can go very far.

We get in life what we have the courage to think is possible for us. I'm here to support you in summoning the courage to ask for the life you want to live, deserve to live, and then help you get it.

Stay in Touch

If you would like to receive a free chapter from my book and weekly emails with advice, insights, and resources I don't share anywhere else, I would love to have you join me on FIRMSconsulting.com/promo.

Rethinking Success

Paul O'Mahony

Paul O'Mahony is a speaker, author, entrepreneur, trainer, and husband and father. His companies, ReThink Academy and FUNancial Freedom, help people of all ages master crucial skills in money, mindset, and marketing. His books have earned him the title of best-selling author twelve times over, and he is a multi-award-winning international speaker. When he is not helping people *ReThink and Grow Rich*, he runs a foundation with his wife, Sarah, to help children with autism spectrum disorder and other disabilities.

Learn more about Paul by downloading his free book, *ReThink Social Media,* or watching any of his videos on YouTube.

At thirty years old, I began the process of "rethinking" what a success mindset meant to me.

From the outside, looking in, it appeared that I had it "all." Yes, "all" the trimmings of modern day "success." I had a great job, two houses, an MBA qualification, and even a BMW. Both of my parents were teachers, so I followed in their footsteps of the traditional model of education. I qualified through university and received a degree in industrial biochemistry (you read that right), and then took the corporate route for my career. I was living the dream, right?

When I reached that milestone birthday of thirty years of age, I took a moment to evaluate my situation. The two houses and the car that I had weren't exactly the signals of wealth that they appeared to be. I owed €500,000 to the bank in negative equity alone; I was a slave to debt. During this time in my life, I was what I call "rich-poor." I was rich on the outside, but truly poor once you peeked under the hood and saw the details of my bank account.

I decided that something needed to change. I felt that I had done everything I was supposed to do but now at thirty years of age I was much worse off financially than I was as a five-year-old child! How could this be? How could this be seen as "success" for so many? I started to look around me for answers. In 2009, I went to my first ever "motivational" event, hosted by Tony Robbins. These types of events were new to me and were not exactly aligned with my natural skeptical nature. It ended up, however, having a significant impact on my life. That same year, day one of the event, I quit my corporate job.

Yes, people thought I was crazy, and they were absolutely right to think so when viewing my decision through a regular person's perspective. I, however, wanted to completely change direction. Within four months of starting an online business, I was making the same amount of income I had been making at my corporate job. By following the recommended path, it took thirty years to reach $10,000 a month; yet it only took four months on this new, less-tested pathway to match the same level of financial "success." I started asking myself, why do we all do what we do if in fact there is a much faster and easier way to achieve the same goal? This question became a trigger for rethinking my life, business, and success mindset.

Before I turned thirty, I would never have thought that this shift was possible. I was very confident in my view of the world from behind my corporate desk that anything other than the traditional path was second rate at best. I believed that a corporate career was the only way to go. When I stepped out of the corporate world, I started to see a very different world where you were paid per value provided, not hours worked. I saw people younger than me making twenty times more money and working less hours than I ever had in my career. These people don't have to get up at 7:00 a.m. on a Monday morning and sit in traffic for an hour to get to work. They have a different type of freedom. They have confidence about them and seem to just "know" that they have the tools to survive any knocks to the economy. They have become self-sufficient. The people who have walked down this new path not only have control of their lives, they also seem to have control of their minds.

In retrospect, I don't blame myself for having my previously-held views, but I've learned to understand the challenges that arise when you're surrounded by people that think the exact same way as you. You can completely fall into groupthink. When I embarked on my personal development journey, everything began to change. I learned how to master key skills such as building a business, building a successful team, and aligning the values of the team members with the organization. I quickly learnt that the fastest way to get results was to find those who had done it already and pay them to teach me how to do the same. It paid off. Today, I am a twelve-time best-selling author, an international speaker, and an entrepreneur. Our organisations invite people to rethink their lives, their mindsets, their measures of success and their results, and empower them with the tools to completely shift their lives' trajectories.

The audiences that I speak to can relate to my journey. I have met so many people who just weren't happy, especially considering the sacrifices they had made to do everything "right." They did what they were supposed to do, just like me: they went to school, studied hard, got a corporate job, but then they woke up in their mid-forties with two children, two cars, and a house, all owned and being paid for by the bank.

I understand their journey because I lived it. I, too, have asked myself, "Is this what living the dream really looks like?" We expected so much more; we were wrongly sold a dream. By rethinking, we have been able to make the shift and actually live the dream that we thought we had been working toward for so long.

What Is the Risk?

When I tell people I walked away from my corporate job, they commend me on the "risk" I took. But looking back, I ask myself, "What was the risk?" If I had not succeeded in my online business—if I had been desperate—I could have always applied for another job. How is that any different than working in any other career? When you work at a corporation, you don't own the business. Your superiors can fire you any day that they want. Walking away from your job today to start your own business puts one- or two-months' salary at risk, but you can end up in a much better situation than you're in today. At least you have addressed the "what if" that may have been sitting at the back of your mind for so many years.

Don't misunderstand me: I'm not anti-job. I'm pro-jobs, but I want to give you the opportunity to shift your perspective. In my view, the biggest financial risk people are making each day is the risk they take when they nonchalantly believe that keeping their job is not a risk at all! When you hold onto this mindset, you're banking your entire future on a business or a government that you've no control over. You're holding yourself back from the possibility of creating and owning your own income sources–of controlling so much more than you ever could in a corporate position.

A mentor introduced me years ago to the idea that "hell on earth" was meeting that person you "could have been." That really resonated with me. I am very grateful to have made this shift when I did and took back the freedom over my life and career; but most people don't. Warren Buffett often warns us that the binds of debt are too weak to be seen before they are too strong to be broken. It's not easy to release the shackles of what people expect of you, but it's also not any easier to stay stuck and miserable! Most people, if asked honestly, would agree that they have never gotten out of second gear, so fearful of the very thing that could make them more content and fulfilled.

I understand why we fail to shift. For so many years, I was anti-entrepreneurial. There was no entrepreneurship in my family and I believed that 90 percent of new businesses fail, so what would be the point in creating one? What I didn't understand was that the rate of failure applies to traditional business models. The entrepreneurs that open a brick-and-mortar business, borrow money, get into debt–they're acquiring debt until death and are more likely to fail. The word mortgage comes from the Latin word *mortem*, meaning "death." Would you like some debt until death, sir? No thanks, you might say, I would like a mortgage. But they are one and the same. No wonder mortgage brokers are pleased that Latin is no longer very commonly understood.

If this life is the only shot that we have on this planet, I personally don't want to spend it paying off debt. Debt, or at least "bad debt," is slavery under a different name. When you build an online business, you don't have to live this way. There is no mortgage to take out or heavy debts to acquire. You wake up, turn on your computer, follow the rules of the game, learn how to add value, and start earning money directly in line with the value you provide. Before I started making money on the Internet, I spent money on the Internet without a second thought! I was helping somebody else make money. When I changed my attitude and understood that the shift from making somebody else money online to making money for myself online wasn't a big shift, I was able to stay in my pyjamas while matching my previous salary. Best of all, this proved only to be the beginning. In just ten years, we smashed through the $50 million revenue mark across the seven companies, hiring close to one hundred people.

As you read this, it is likely that your thoughts are beginning to kick in. They will start reminding you about your circumstances, your story, your history, your issues, and your fears. Please start to appreciate that this "mind chatter" is nothing more than a work of fiction. Your ego is the author. The reason why "it's ok for them but not for me" is a story that we use to protect ourselves. Everything that you tell yourself about the growth of your business, the challenges you face, and the life that you want to live is a mental game. This is the ultimate mindset for success: seeing and hearing your mind chatter floundering with excuses, smiling at it, and then writing a better story with you as the hero, not the cowering victim.

As Henry Ford said, "Whether you think you can, or you think you can't–you're right." Years ago, every time I heard anyone say anything negative about entrepreneurship, I used it to reinforce what I believed to be true at that time. Now, when I hear people saying these same negative things, I use it differently. I use it to remind myself about the power of mindset.

You Are Not Your Thoughts

Today, I sing a different tune. I believe that the last thing the world needs is more compliance. We need more leaders.

I want to help people rethink all areas of their life. This is about more than just starting a business online. Everything we do at The ReThink Academy ultimately comes back to your mindset. If you're fighting a losing battle with your mindset, you are not going to see anything around you as a win. The first battle that you have to win is to understand that you are not your thoughts. There is a difference between the world your mindset is creating and the world around you. The moment you start to see the "madness" of your thoughts is the moment you can start to redirect them and then reprogram.

We spend so much of our time listening to the negative groupthink that surrounds us. If not the gremlins that live in the chasms of our mind, this groupthink can come from our families, friends, partners, children, or colleagues. It's hard to escape! When you turn on the news, what do you hear? Good news? Success stories? Profiles of everyday people making millions of dollars? Hardly! The news we hear day in and day out is deeply distressing. We turn off our TVs or podcasts in some degree of panic—we freeze. If you want to leave this state and move forward in your life, you have to break out of the negative mindset that the world has created for you. Garbage in, garbage out. In order to let the flowers of your mind thrive, do some weeding!

I know that this sounds somewhat grandiose, but you can move toward big changes by shifting your mindset with small decisions. Focusing on one decision at a time can take you farther than you might have previously imagined. When you plant seeds and water them carefully, nature will take its course. It's time to plant these new seeds.

Although we know this, we don't always behave accordingly. Take the typical man who may not have been to the gym for a while. He comes back to the gym and decides to reach for the heaviest weights. Can you guess what happens? He completely overdoes it and gets injured! Don't give into the temptation to pick up the biggest weights. Start small and build from there.

One of the most toxic elements of today's society is the need for instant gratification. We want everything yesterday! We want the muscles, the millions, the perfect life. But if you want to grow your muscles, you have to pick up the smallest weights within your ability first. If you want to live the life that you have always wanted to live, you have to make small decisions first. I'm a huge fan of habits: creating small, daily habits and practicing persistence until you get into a natural routine. Natural routines help you hit goals. They help you improve your physical and mental health, putting you in prime position to do your best work and live the version of your life that you have always wanted.

There is always going to be someone fitter, healthier, or richer than you. There is also always going to be someone with more debt or less healthy than you. A success mindset is about having the humility to know that, no matter where you are, you are on a stepping stone leading to the goals that you have set for yourself. It's not a race; no one else's goals are better or worse than yours, although they may be less well-defined. If you learn to enjoy the journey, these stepping stones are beautiful places to be. Learning to be at ease with yourself and experiencing joy daily in the areas you are already successful will help you experience more flow.

A success mindset is having the wisdom to know that you are already successful. In fact, everybody is successful. We are all uniquely successful in specific areas of our lives already, but you are quite possibly blind to it.

Break life up into the eight areas that I use at The ReThink Academy:

1. Relationships
2. Earnings
3. Tao
4. Health
5. Investments
6. Networks
7. Knowledge
8. Fun

Now ask yourself, "In which of these areas could I perceive myself to already be successful?" You will find at least one! If you perceive you are lacking "success," it is probably in an area that you have naturally neglected. For example, if you constantly say "I am terrible with money," don't expect that you will somehow be a success in the Earnings category. You might have instead found success in your children, the relationship with your partner, or the ability to care for your parents. You've invested time, effort, energy, and money into these areas and aren't identifying the benefits that you have been reaping as success. The universe, on the other hand, has seen you plant those seeds; you are now seeing the fruits of success in that area.

See that success, be grateful for it, and know that it's relative. Then, ask yourself, "What seeds do I want to plant now, and what weeding needs to commence?"

Finding Joy on the Journey to Success

Karl Shaikh

Karl Shaikh has a never-ending thirst for learning. He is curious. He challenges perspectives and enjoys identifying new hypotheses to test. At the heart of his curiosity is the question: how, in a world of uncertainties, can we be successful and unleash our potential?

Karl has held strategic roles in many large corporations and started and grown businesses. He has taught at graduate schools. He has also advised many entrepreneurs and assisted the boards of many nonprofit organizations, gratis.

Karl is currently writing a series of books on the topic of being strategic, for both individuals and organizations. The most recent is titled *Stop, Change, Grow*.

If you lead people, whether your family, your community, a non-profit organization, or a business, and are interested in the topics of growth and unleashing your latent potential, he welcomes you to get in touch. For additional information, visit www.1unknown.com.

Are you finding challenges on your path to success? Wouldn't it be nice if you could actually enjoy the journey, and not just the destination?

Success is not easy, whether it means getting that dream job, career progress, mastering a skill, starting a new business, building or scaling a business, nurturing a family, helping your family through tough times, helping your community, or any other pursuit.

The underlying premise of this chapter is not only that success is within your reach, but also that the journey is more rewarding if what you believe is aligned with the success you desire and the path you have chosen. Those three variables must be aligned—the success you desire, what you believe, and the path you have chosen. Finding alignment will bring you superhuman energy and joy for your journey to success.

In this chapter, I'll show you how to discover what you believe is the path to the success you desire. You may think you already know what you believe. And perhaps you do. This chapter will help you peel back the various layers of your own beliefs to get to the beliefs you hold, deep down, which influence the joy towards success. Once you arrive at your deeply held belief about the success you desire, you'll be empowered to either change what you believe or change the success you aspire to–or how you try to achieve it–and bring joy to the journey.

Let me share an example from my own personal experience. It highlights the impact of becoming aligned and how that alignment generated immense positive energy towards the success I desired.

Improving the Odds of Success

In the last year of my university experience, like many fresh graduates, I hoped to begin my career in a good job. However, the country was in deep recession. It was clear that there wouldn't be many jobs for new graduates. The prospect of job hunting seemed futile. **I did not believe that my job-hunting actions would lead to the success I hoped for,** even though I was chasing success by those actions. And what I believed came to pass. I did not find a job.

Then, within a few weeks of returning home from university, life hit me with a sucker punch. My life changed instantly. I was knocked completely off my feet.

For the purposes of this story, it doesn't really matter what happened, but I can tell you that I woke up the next day with a herculean desire to be self-sufficient. I suddenly felt an enormous need to pay my own way.

Overnight, my belief had changed. I now believed that even though the odds of success were against me, **if I worked hard enough at it and increased how many applications**

I filled out, job hunting would lead to being able to put a meal on the table, pay rent and other bills, and support myself.

The journey became like a game, and I still recall it fondly. I went from submitting three to four job applications per week to submitting as many as thirty to forty applications on some days. I worked harder to get a job than I had only weeks before. And in just under two months, I had two job offers. Later, my new boss admitted that I was the hungriest job hunter he'd seen in years.

You don't have to wait for a life-changing event like mine to achieve the success you desire and, more importantly, to enjoy the journey. Instead, follow the rest of this chapter to uncover your beliefs, ensure alignment by creating your own Success Mental Model, and enjoy the journey.

What Are Your Mental Models?

Mental models are how people simplify and make sense of the world, often without realizing they're doing it. They are your deep beliefs about how the world works and how things "ought" to be. Mental models simplify complex things so your brain can reason through them. They are based on a small set of fundamental assumptions that enable simplification; they're shortcuts through the noise to your expectations. Mental models represent the underlying beliefs that dictate **why** you expect what you expect.

Because mental models are so basic to understanding the world, people are hardly ever conscious of using them. You use mental models to make good decisions without needing to know everything about a situation. You even use them to cross the road without knowing the exact speed of and distance away from approaching vehicles. You use mental models all the time, without being aware that you are.

Even though a baby may not understand what a mental model is, they know that **crying leads to being fed**. It works! But if you were an orphaned baby in a neglectful orphanage, the mental models you developed would be entirely different. Either case, your mental models would influence your decisions.

As a society, our collective mental model of what to expect from smoking cigarettes has changed. Back in the 50s and 60s, smoking was considered sexy. Today, cigarettes are seen as cancer sticks.

I've discovered a unique type of mental model, which I like to call **the Success Mental Model**. The Success Mental Model comes into play when there is alignment between **your belief of what actions will lead to what outcomes**. As in, I believe hanging out at the museum will lead to finding someone with whom I can have a rewarding relationship.

Identifying Your Success Mental Model

I recommend opening a blank document or getting out a pen and a piece of paper for this exercise. You don't have to, but doing so will let your brain know that you expect it to do at least a little bit of thinking.

Ready? Now, think about what success you aspire to. Look deeply into your soul and consider: what actions do you believe will lead to the success you desire?

Try it by filling in the blanks in the following statement, and please, do multiple versions:

I believe _____ (action) leads to _____ (outcome).

This is a brainstorm, so you can try to write multiple versions of this, and settle on whichever version feels right to you.

How did that feel?

Don't worry; I won't hold you to the words you came up with in this first draft. This first draft of your unique Success Mental Model is just there to warm you up.

If you were feeling playful and wrote something like: I believe buying a lottery ticket leads to becoming a multimillionaire, then thank you. You've given me the opportunity to provide more guidance on critical parts of creating your statement.

First, your "I believe ___ leads to____" statement can't be superficial. The statement has to be something you believe to be true, deep down inside you, down to your soul, down to your bones. And yes, **believe**, not wish, not hope. Your belief must be based on something you hold to be true. You need to do your homework so that what you believe is not based on a loosely-held claim.

Second, if you want success, your belief can't be borrowed or adopted from others. Often, we carry "I believe ___ leads to___" statements we've grown up with, or that belong to our family, the network of our friends, or even the wider community. Without even realizing it, we may have adopted others' statements, but like some borrowed clothes, they may fit poorly or be uncomfortable. For example, marriage leads to happiness, or having children leads to happiness. These statements may represent wishes others hold for you, but if you don't truly believe them, don't write them down.

It's okay to adopt someone else's "I believe ___ leads to___" statement if it feels true to you, and feels authentic deep down in your soul, your heart, your gut, your bones, or wherever you deeply feel things.

One way to test if a belief really feels true to you is to challenge it. Look for opposing arguments. If, upon serious challenge, you see chinks appear, you need to either evolve your statement, or perhaps abandon it for something else.

By now, you should be noticing that although the Success Mental Model sentence seems so simple, you must reflect deeply to identify a statement that really represents what you believe to be true. It's the deep guided reflection that makes all the difference. For some people, this entire exercise may take hours; for others, weeks, or even months.

Taking Your Success Mental Model to the Next Level

Let's now create draft two of your Success Mental Model. The trick here is a combination of authentic self-reflection, compassionate iteration, and fine-tuning.

Now, still in your brainstorming mode, revise your prior statement as you read and understand the significance of each of the elements of the statement. Read each element, revise the prior version of your Success Mental Model, based on your new understanding, and then move to the next element. In each section, the square brackets [_____] in the statement mark the area to brainstorm around, before moving to brainstorm around the next element.

"*I believe _____ leads to [_____].*"

This word or phrase represents the success you aspire to. It can be short-term or long-term success. It can also represent stepping stones. Recall from my earlier example that I didn't know what job I wanted, but I knew I wanted a job! If the success you aspire to requires a long time horizon, then be **less** specific in describing the destination. For long horizons, clarity of direction is more powerful than specificity of destination.

It's highly likely that what you have written down in your brainstorming so far are a set of "have" outcomes. You have probably written down outcomes that you aspire to have or achieve. Like have a job. Or have a family. Or have a house in a particular neighborhood or achieve a certain revenue target and so on.

"*I believe _____ leads to [being _____].*"

Now I have introduced the word "being" in the above statement that wasn't there earlier. I want you to now convert the success outcomes you wrote earlier into what behaviors or ways of being you will exhibit in your desired future state once you are successful at your goal. This is a really critical step, and can be difficult at first. But once you have tried it a few times in your brainstorm, you'll notice it really takes you much deeper into what you really desire. Do you really desire to be a teacher, or do you aspire to help children live their dreams? Do you really want to achieve a particular revenue target for your landscaping business (or any type of business) or do you want to help people spend more of their time outdoors enjoying nature?

In my earlier example, I went from wanting to have a job, to being self-sufficient.

Starting with the behavior outcome and working backward allows you to avoid the limitations that arise when you focus on solving today's problems.

"*I believe [_____] leads to being _____.*"

The underlying action can be an immediate action that will trigger other dominos to fall, and/or a continuous action that creates the momentum that drives home success. What action will get you started in the right direction? What action will have the most impact? What actions will overcome the biggest hurdles? The 80/20 rule is really helpful here.

"I believe [being _____] leads to being _____."

Now that I have introduced the word "being" here also, I'll ask you to convert the actions you previously wrote, to how you will be "being." In other words, how do you need to "be" today to achieve the being outcomes you desire for the future state? Again, it seems difficult at first, but try it a few times, and it starts to feel better.

By "being" happy, loving, loyal, open, compassionate, and a good partner you will begin "doing" things differently which will allow you to "have" things you never would have had otherwise. **Be** the person now who you would be if you already had achieved your goal, then you will naturally do the things that a successful person would do, which will allow you to have what you want.

"I believe being _____ [leads to] being _____."

The words "leads to" in the middle represents the cause and effect relationship between the two parts of the statement. Be literal here. You want an explicit clarity. Will the immediate ways of being you wrote down explicitly cause the effect (your desired success way of being)? Or will it improve the chances of success happening?

Will being calmer, when your kids are squabbling, allow them to see a role model of calmness and also allow their mirror neurons to reflect your calmness, such that their tendencies towards squabbling diminish, thereby making parenting easier for you? There must be a clear and obvious relationship between the cause and effect. The stronger and more reliable the tie between the cause and effect, the better.

"I [believe] being _____ leads to being _____."

The word "believe" is powerful when you use it wisely. It reminds you that you must really believe in the cause and effect relationship you stated. It's not okay to write wishful, hopeful statements like in the lottery example earlier. You must be able to support the cause and effect relationship you commit to. If you don't believe your statement, wholeheartedly, or if you believe a variant of what you've written, you'll feel like you're swimming against the current. Success will feel illusive or, at best, harder than it needs to be.

In my earlier example, I went from believing there to be a low probability to job hunting success, to believing that sheer number of applications would overcome the low odds.

> As **a cautionary point**, don't let yourself add the word "in" to your "I believe" statements. Try it, fill in the blank: "I believe in_____." Even though the "in" is a small deviation, it will typically bring to mind forces outside your control. Just keep "in" out of your statement.

"*[I] believe being _____ leads to being _____.*"

The word "I" makes the whole statement unique to you–your personal Success Mental Model. The statement doesn't have to be true for anyone other than you. It has to be what you believe. It has to be personal. And as long as you wholeheartedly believe in the cause and effect relationship you explored and committed to, that's what matters.

Yet, you can also replace the "I" with "We" if you're creating the statement for a team working on a collective Success Mental Model. If you're working as a team, allow extra time for the various team members to co-create the statement. Each of you can also devise personal iterations that fit within the collective statement.

And remember, this is an entirely iterative exercise. You probably have many sub drafts along the way to creating draft two. As you refine your Success Mental Model, you can revisit it as often as you like to make sure it still holds true. Adjust it as required.

Making Your Success Mental Model Even More Powerful and Joyful

Let's do this again to create draft three of your Success Mental Model, to give yourself even more power and joy for achieving the success you desire. Now, challenge yourself to go deeper.

I said earlier, "Mental models represent the underlying beliefs that dictate **why** you expect what you expect." You are going to go deeper by making explicit to yourself **"why"** you believe what you believe. Why you believe the cause and effect relationship you have stated above to be true.

With the most recent draft of your "I believe being _____ leads to being _____" statement in mind, ask yourself, "**What** are my **expectations**?" of the cause and effect relationship? And follow that with a "**why**" question, such as, "**Why** do I expect **that**?" Answers to "**why**" questions offer fuller, more meaningful understandings.

Asking the **"why"** question only once is never enough. You'll typically find that the first answer to "**Why** do I expect **that**?" isn't meaningful enough, which is why you'll need to ask repeatedly "And **why** do I expect **that**?" of each preceding answer. When you feel you've gotten deep enough, then ask yourself, "**Why** does that **matter**?"

In most cases, people end up answering with words like "because I believe being___leads to being___" with sheer conviction. You'll get a feeling like: "This is it!" You'll also feel an urge to get started. You'll have extra energy. That's when you know you've discovered your own Success Mental Model. This version is what you try on for a while to see how it resonates with you. You might need to sleep on it and see if you still feel that feeling the next day. Adjust it as required.

And that's when I will know my job here in this chapter is done. Your **journey** towards your success will itself bring you just as much **joy** as the ultimate success you aspire to.

Sandbox Activity

Try the Success Mental Model approach yourself on stories from this book. Which stories did you most like or connect with? What do you think the author of that story expected to happen and why? What role did their beliefs play in their success? As you get better at identifying Success Mental Models in the success stories of others, it will be easier for you to identify or refine your own Success Mental Model.

> Mental models are what we mean by "wisdom." When someone is "wise," they're just using mental models to generate insights—whether they realize it or not. (Adapted from Julian Shapiro.)

Mental Model Evolution

Just as most people are unaware of their mental models, we are also oblivious when our mental models evolve. Now that you're an adult, you've learned you no longer need to wail when you're hungry. You can help yourself when it's chow time without actually needing to think of that as an evolution of your mental model.

Some mental models evolve through outside intervention. Imagine that over a series of weeks, and perhaps months, you find yourself eating, eating some more, and then eating some more. You're constantly hungry, and food is not satiating that desire. Surprisingly, you're not even gaining weight. On the contrary, you're losing weight.

After a visit to the doctor's office and a battery of tests, you find out your thyroid is hyperactive. Your doctor informs you that your metabolism is extremely high. You're burning way more food than is healthy for you. Through this experience, you evolve to a new mental model. Your doctor has helped you evolve your mental model to a hyperactive thyroid leads to high metabolism, which leads to weight loss.

Adapt, Evolve, Become–Challenge Accepted

Raghavan V. Venugopal

Raghavan Venugopal is currently an executive director, a member of the C-level team at Wiwynn International Corporation, an industry leader in cloud infrastructure integrator segment partnering with Top 10 Service Providers in the world. Prior to this he was the director of engineering and product development strategy at HPE, responsible for Cloudline servers that catered to the service provider segment. Throughout his career he has transformed organizations with his unique customer-centric approach to success resulting in a 250 percent increase in revenue, a 40 percent increase in time to market, a 30 percent efficiency in costs, a 50 percent improvement in quality, and forty-two new patents in three new technologies.

Raghavan holds a bachelor's in engineering from Annamalai University, India, a master's degree in electrical engineering from Tennessee Tech University, and an executive MBA from Jones School of Business, Rice University. Raghavan holds twenty-seven patents and has twice been published.

Defining A Success Mindset–A Knack to Creating An Environment That Delivers Value

1. 250 Percent Increase in Revenue
2. 40 Percent Faster to Market
3. 30 Percent Cheaper
4. 50 Percent Better Quality
5. 42 New Patents in 3 New Technologies

Does the above sound like a definition of success? If yes, please read on.

At the very basic level, success involves a transaction of two parties, one providing something of value to the other. The party that delivers this value by understanding a need extracts a price for the service or the product. To constantly keep delivering value, the party needs to understand the dynamic changes and interests of the customer and be aware of the competition that is also going to be vying to provide a similar value to the same customer.

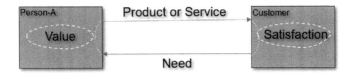

A leader with a success mindset can create a conducive environment where every individual in his organization is able to consistently find a personal growth path that is aligned with the organizational goal to deliver value for their customers. A successful mindset further gets emphasized when the probability of such occurrences is higher than normal and is repeatable in different scenarios and environments with different sets of individuals.

What is the driver for this success mindset that delivers not only a strong purpose and meaning but also, more importantly, lasting value to the customers?

Life's Curveballs

When I think of success, a mosaic of several key moments in my life conjures up in front of me. All stitched together abstractly evoking a medley of different hard to explain emotions, like water teeming out of a cloud burst...

One such event is when an ambitious, naïve, fresh graduate, bubbling with optimism, entered a swanky twenty-third floor office located on Marine Drive, Mumbai, The Financial Capital of India, to make a presentation about the front-end user interface of the banking software that he was stationed to commission in three months. He was brutally critiqued, rejected, and scarred.

Is Challenge Accepted to Act?

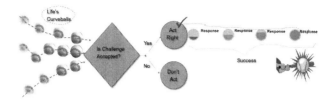

Life keeps throwing curveballs at us. They come in hard, fast, and in ways that we are not expecting and as seen above, in my case, at different stages with different ferocities from all different directions. When we tend to be frail, emotionally drained, and hopeless.

Are we going to accept the challenge, stand, deliver, and open that door of possibility standing between us and an opportunity? Or are we going to be meek and choose not to fight?

If you have chosen to take up the challenge, you have made the right call. Read on.

Now that you have chosen to act on the challenge, how are you going to respond? What are you going to make out of this challenge?

Know that success is nothing but a series of actions that are well thought out responses to challenges life throws at us. So, it is very important to understand the basis for a well thought out response as it often leads to success that is sustainable. If you are looking for shortcuts, I am sorry to disappoint you. I do not have any to offer, and the content contained here is not for you. You can stop now.

Cultivating to Act Right As a Virtue–The Five Dimensions to Act Right

It is awesome that you have made it this far. I am very proud to have you as my audience.

To be action-oriented is a virtue. However, to act in haste would lead to chaos and waste. So clearly while being action-oriented is in itself something that we need to practice and cultivate, it also behooves us to act with a reasonable amount of thought that allows for some level of planning. It is also prudent to express thought as words to a limited audience with know-how on the topic of our action so some level of feedback has been built into planning that action.

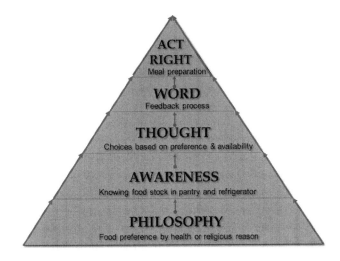

Thought, word, and action need to be harmoniously aligned and synchronized so there is no contradiction.

However how does a thought first germinate? Thoughts do not arise from a vacuum, they come from our consciousness that is built over a period with an evolved awareness about ourselves and our environment.

Is there a stage prior to awareness? Isn't a philosophy a key component to our awareness? This philosophy shapes our needs, likes, dislikes, and our practices. So a philosophy that is rooted to act with a purpose and driven by self-motivation towards integrated growth is instrumental in enabling a mindset that is destined for success.

What Is Integrated Growth and Why Is A Conducive Environment Essential to Achieve It?

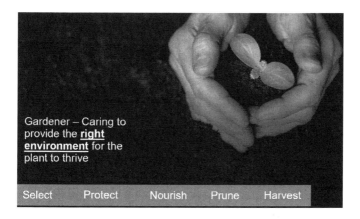

Gardener – Caring to provide the **right environment** for the plant to thrive

Select   Protect   Nourish   Prune   Harvest

Using an example of a plant, integrated, healthy, and wholesome growth occurs only when the gardener understands the unique nature of the plant and provides a conducive environment so it thrives to its fullest potential.

INDIVIDUAL   ORGANIZATION   COMPANY

Apply the above analogy to the growth of individual.

1. An individual who is part of a team.
2. A team that belongs to an organization.
3. An organization that is part of a company.

Shouldn't work that takes up a significant portion of an individual's waking time be enabling them to thrive at all the levels linking the individual, team, organization, and the company?

Shouldn't integrated growth account for the needs of all four of the dimensions of an individual namely body, mind, intellect, and soul? Shouldn't a leader be responsible for creating an environment that nurtures and harnesses the potential of all these areas and ensures that the growth of all these facets are mutually complementary versus contradictory?

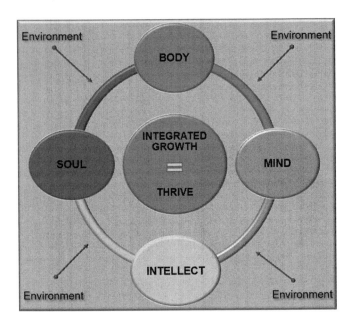

Philosophy of integrated Growth on the path to Unite with purpose to Serve (iGUS™)

This philosophy is strongly rooted on three pillars: integrated growth of an individual as the objective, finding customer value as the path, with the purpose to serve oneself, the customer, organization, and the company.

Integrated Growth. We all yearn to grow, achieve, solve problems, and derive satisfaction out of this process. This growth and transformation need to be an integrated one along four vectors—body, mind, intellect, and soul.

iGUS

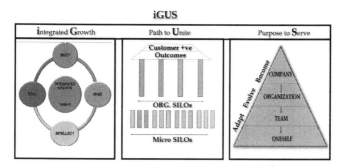

Path to Unite. This is the path where the individual gets connected with his team and the extended organization. The connection is found in the path to find an outcome that is of value and is the common ground among a heterogeneous set of disparate disciplines. This path while recognizing the uniqueness of each of the functions also clearly sets the positive customer outcome as the unifier and the end goal.

Purpose to Serve. The third pillar sets the growth of the individual along the purpose of service. First at an individual level where one is focused on self-development learning to harness one's own potential, then at the level of a leader, able to influence a larger set of people. In an organizational setup, the three stages can be seen as an individual contributor, mid-level manager, and an executive. The three distinct stages are elaborated below.

Serve Oneself, **Adapt**. The first stage is how an individual can understand the subtleties about oneself and learn one's strengths and weaknesses and, as a result, learns to serve oneself better.

Serve Near and Dear, **Evolve**. The individual learns to apply the harnessed potential in the previous stage and decides what areas to extend it to. The individual is humble to listen to the differing needs and acquires the skills to tame those challenges and evolves to empower and serve those that truly are looking to be heard and becomes their voice.

Serve a Community, **Become**. The individual becomes a leader who is capable to answer why an action needs to be performed and aligns it to be a positive impact to all that are involved. The leader brings about a transformational change by applying all his learnings to perfectly align everyone to the common purpose.

What Does iGUS™ Mean for Businesses?

Why is this philosophy important for business? The three pillars of iGUS™ morphs to three foundational business principles of growth mindset, differentiated value, and continuous improvement. These principles allow for businesses to achieve higher revenue, market share, meaningful innovations, higher margin and quality, while achieving superior operational excellence with shorter time to market and lower cost. These directly contribute to enhancing customer experience that leads to loyal customer base that is supported by a purposeful and satisfied employee base.

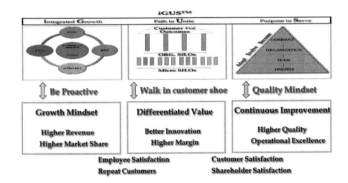

iGUS™ Philosophy to Management Policy

A philosophy is important to learn, understand, and embrace because policies stem from them. Policy is the equivalent of awareness of a business. The policies that are borne out of iGUS™ are grouped into the three business principles of growth mindset, differentiated value, and continuous improvement.

Key policies are illustrated below.

iGUS™ Philosophy to Management Policy

iGUS™ Policy to Processes–How Does Policy Convert to Processes In An Organization?

Policies matter as they set the cornerstone for how different processes are established in an organization. Processes control the thoughts, words, and actions of an organization. Processes are the rhythm that sets the beats of an organization and how its members are functioning to achieve a specific outcome.

Key processes are illustrated below.

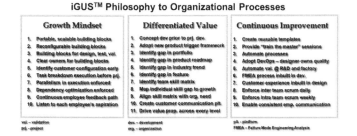

iGUS™ Philosophy to Organizational Processes

How Does iGUS™ Build Leaders and a Leadership Pipeline In An Organization?

Who is a good leader? What are the virtues of a good leader? A good leader is one who thinks beyond himself, listens to both the customer and the employees, and produces results for the customer by leading from the front, taking necessary risks, overcoming any challenges.

iGUS™ builds leaders within the organization who are imbued with the above characteristics. Given below are the virtues that iGUS™ builds in the leaders of the organization.

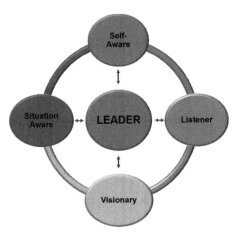

The way that iGUS™ provides a continuous integrated growth path is by setting the path of the leader along the following concentric spheres with the innermost sphere being the self.

1. Self
2. Team
3. Organization
4. Company
5. Industry
6. Country
7. World

There are six core pillars of development that a leader goes from the innermost sphere to the outermost. They are captured below in the 6K™ approach to success:

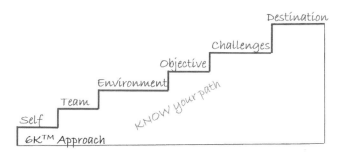

In summary the four fundamental qualities that iGUS™ instills in leaders are self-awareness, situation-awareness, humility that sharpens listening, and a vision that lucidly and simply connects, inspires, propels, liberates, and sets everyone on the path of their integrated growth.

The Guiding Compass to a Success Mindset–4S™ Compass

As the individual goes from the innermost sphere of knowing about oneself to extending outwards to learn about the team, organization, company, and the industry, in each sphere there are four stages that iGUS™ uses as the compass that guides the individual in the right direction as illustrated below.

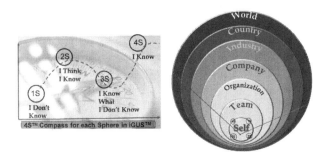

How iGUS™ Develops the Ingredients to A Success Mindset–People, System, Process, Metrics

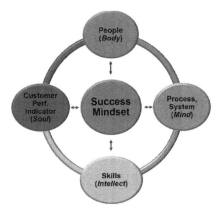

<u>**People (Body)**</u>. The single most important ingredient to the success of any process is the people that are part of it. We need to build this key resource based on the aptitude, attitude, communication capability, and the fit for the role.

<u>**Processes, Systems (Mind)**</u>. Another key ingredient that is required during this journey is a candid assessment of what existing systems need to be reengineered or new systems that need to be put in place to enable people to achieve their goals. A framework of processes with owners

who are accountable to drive clear and transparent goals that are assigned to an owner is fundamental to achieving success.

Skills (Intellect). We need to build this key resource based on a skill set versus focusing on products or services that are being delivered. Focusing on the skill set allows for the company to not only drive satisfaction to the employees and provide a continuous growth path but also allows the company to be flexible to adapt to changes.

Customer Performance Indicators (Soul). Customer Performance Indicators (CPIs) are the gel that connects all the different functional groups within the company towards a positive customer experience. The final step is to connect the CPIs with Key Performance Indicators (KPIs) of the different functional organizations. The right CPIs connect each individual to the organization and provide a strong purpose. When this connection is made people (employees) become more aware, committed, satisfied, and highly productive.

Key Takeaways for a Success Mindset–No Need to Guess, Here Are the Answers

A success mindset begins with an intent to act. Below are the key takeaways:

1. To act right we saw how the five elements–philosophy, awareness, thought, word, and action–need to come together. The unique philosophy that we discussed in this essay is called **iGUS™**, the abbreviation for integrated Growth on the path to Unite with a purpose to Serve.
2. With this philosophy, there is no need to guess, and it has the answers to create a success mindset. An action backed by a strong purpose to serve, that puts an individual's growth at the center, guided by customer

value is the magic mixture that creates an environment for a success mindset.

3. We also saw the policies and the processes that are borne out of **iGUS™**. A leader who walks the talk with this approach will have four key virtues of self-awareness, self-governance, listening, and is a visionary.

4. The four ingredients that are a part of the environment to propel successful outcomes as a habit are the right people, right processes and systems, right skills, and right CPIs.

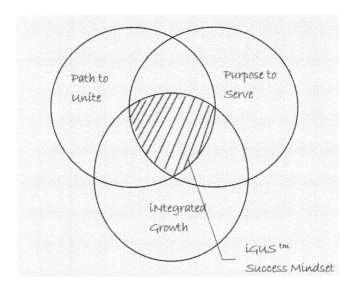

At the beginning of the chapter I mentioned a medley of images of myself facing some of life's curveballs. Upon completion of this chapter, what would I tell myself about a success mindset?

Buckle up, **fight back**, do not wallow in self-pity and sorrow!

While fighting, understand that success is a **journey** and not a destination.

Also understand what you truly want and go after it, with **self-awareness**.

Realize that your **effort** is the only thing that you control and focus on that.

Learn to **listen** more and understand your environment as you undertake this journey.

Cultivate **attributes** and **skills** along this journey and be ready to be surprised, humbled.

Adapt, Evolve, Become, Accept the Challenge and Keep Seeking....

Lessons in Success

Arvind Sharma

Arvind Sharma is vice president and managing director of Lear Corporation. Lear Corporation is ranked #166 on the Fortune 500. He has thirty years of experience in the automotive, manufacturing, and high-tech industries and has implemented several complex projects and innovative strategic solutions. For additional information, please contact smartarvind@gmail.com.

Enrolling in the School of Experience

The secret to success is that there is no secret to success–or, if there is, it is an open secret. We succeed because we learn from our successes, from our failures, from our continuous re-evaluation of what constitutes success. If I have "succeeded in succeeding," it is through learning from the wisdom acquired through experience and through attention to the sage advice of proverbs and clichés. While certainly not an exhaustive how-to guide, the following anecdotes may offer some insight into the ways I have learned to evaluate my own victories–and defeats.

Balancing Vision and Action

An ancient Japanese adage warns that "vision without action is a daydream; action without vision is a nightmare." Like everyone, I have some aspirations that I have cherished since my earliest years and have longed to translate into realities. At crucial junctures in my life, I have disciplined myself to treat myself as a smart executive treats his business: in need of careful evaluation, a mapping of skills, assets, goals, possibilities, and steps to be taken.

For instance, after having worked six years in my native India, I decided to fulfill a lifelong yearning to explore the world outside my familiar scope. With my physician wife, Sadhna, I produced a personal mission statement, considering which cities around the world were most likely to welcome us and to benefit from what we had to offer. We sifted and narrowed our choices, and, after long deliberation, relocated to Singapore.

Five years after settling into our new home, we were established both financially and professionally. I decided that the time had come for me to pair another vision with action and fulfill a lifelong desire to become an entrepreneur. When (as I will describe) my attempt did not work out as hoped, a new mission statement had to be drafted and become the foundation for a new course of action.

Once the objectives outlined had been met, we reassessed our aims and our means and, again, reformulated our life plan. As our children grew, we asked them to share their own visions so that we could take the actions that would transform those daydreams into facts. Such routine reality checks require unbiased, clear-headed appraisals and calculations and the resolve to act according to objective truth rather than wishful hopes. Because we have undertaken the cold analysis and willing sacrifice called for, though, we have accomplished "visions" that might otherwise have remained in the realm of fantasy.

Even now, as I near retirement, I am revising my updated mission statement to reflect our new circumstances and goals. I believe that such scrutiny and planning is essential to any type of success.

Getting Back Up

After more than a decade in business, the time seemed ripe to become the entrepreneur I had always longed to be. With $150,000 in savings and years of experience in the automotive sector, I settled–after extensive investigation–on becoming a franchisee in a car repair chain in Orange County, whose citizens seemed to spend much of their lives on the highway. My savings fell short of the $250,000 price tag, so I took a bank loan to cover the rest, persuaded that I had found a "sure thing." To make certain, once I had transferred the entire amount to an escrow account, I took the eight weeks of vacation I had saved and headed to the US to do due diligence. For six sixty-hour workweeks, I studied the numbers, actual and projected, and reviewed the actual business only to end up stunned and profoundly disappointed.

Intense review of the financials revealed the truth: the projections had no relationship with reality. The business was not viable. And, effectively, I was broke.

My savings of eleven years was wiped out. The hefty exit load in the escrow account's fine-print provisions amounted, incredibly, to $250,000. On top of these penalties, I now had to pay back my high-interest unsecured loan. In six short weeks, I had lost all that I had and, even worse, more than I had. My dream was shattered. I had failed.

Or so I thought. My family was my true wealth. My plucky, sensible wife devised three alternative plans for us to regain our financial footing. We would, of course, both continue to work at our current jobs, but Sadhna outlined options that would allow us to emerge from debt. There was an element of "Goldilocks and the Three Bears" in the alternatives. The aggressive plan required cost-cutting to the bare bones, skimping on the quality of the children's education and living a spartan, no-fun, no-help lifestyle. That was too hard, although the quicker repayment was enticing.

The relaxed plan was too soft, although it's easier circumstances made it attractive. We could choose simply to use the money we were accustomed to saving and use that to settle the score, leaving our lifestyle and budget otherwise untouched. It would take us five years, though, to get clear of our debt.

Ultimately, we selected the "just right" Baby Bear option that necessitated thrift, but not miser-like hardships. Without compromising the education of the children and by making modest cutbacks, we paid back what was owed within three years.

Best of all, I learned a great deal from my "failure." Another Japanese proverb reminds us to "fall down seven times; get back up eight." In other words, we haven't truly failed unless we surrender to despair and inaction. This lesson had a profound impact on my attitude toward subsequent setbacks.

Apparently, I am not alone in this School of Hard Knocks degree. In a 2019 study, three researchers from Northwestern's

Center for Science of Science & Innovation concluded that failures early in one's career actually lead to a greater record of success afterwards, echoing Nietzsche's assertion "what does not kill me makes me stronger." My own experience suggests that there is indeed value in failure–so long as one scrambles back up after being knocked down.

While I did not become an entrepreneur, I did progress rapidly in the corporate world, and my confidence in my abilities grew accordingly. Even more important, my insight into when calculated risks are worthwhile became more acute and my perceptions of what elements to look for before leaping became sharper.

Becoming a Champion

After a few years of progress and stability, I recognized the stirrings of some old dreams. With a renewed faith in my potential and a lingering wanderlust, I decided to revise my mission statement again. Investigating emerging markets, I discovered that opportunities were proliferating and compensation soaring. India had become an attractive destination for an ambitious businessperson. I decided–based on rational considerations and careful planning–to return home.

Many friends and colleagues were shocked and appalled by what they viewed as folly. My move

meant leaving a secure, prestigious position in one of the largest corporations in the automotive sector and beginning "all over" with a midsized firm generating a comparatively tiny revenue. The risks could not be denied, but I mitigated them by making practical arrangements that ensured that I had an exit strategy if my Indian gamble did not work out. My previous lesson had taught me a great deal.

When we returned to India in 2004, the greatest challenge in the automotive sector was growth management. Financial institutions were bullish on India, and industry and the market were growing rapidly. Mergers and acquisitions options were burgeoning. One cross-border prospect proved particularly appealing to my new employer's CEO.

I was more cautious. I noted that not only was the customer base European, but that manufacturing had to remain in Europe as well. Furthermore, we had no leadership competent to manage operations in Germany. I urged a judicious approach, seeking a joint venture with globally established players pursuing a feasible entry strategy into the Indian market. We identified a top-tier German firm with forty billion euros in revenue searching for just such an opportunity and persuaded its CEO to consider partnering with us.

Naturally, other obstacles had to be overcome. The CEO wanted to focus on Indian exports for the components and systems to be manufactured. In contrast, I urged strategizing based on "local" (Indian) business, as is wise for emerging markets. Focusing on manufacturing capability, operational excellence, and the relationship between Indian customers and original equipment manufacturers was the course that I recommended. Fortunately, our German partner—and, ultimately, my employer—agreed with my advice. Within six months, we signed our first joint venture. Within the following year, a North American joint venture, built on the same paradigm, ensued. We had chosen a wise course and I had been taught yet another lesson. In the words of Sugar Ray Robinson: "To be a champ you have to believe in yourself when no one else will."

Finding a Way

Becoming the champ, though, does not mean hanging up the gloves. There is always another round to fight.

My firm sold hub assemblies to manufacturers of motorcycle wheels, and these assemblies accounted for 35 percent of our sales revenue and nearly 50 percent of our profits. It was worrying to discover that sales volumes were declining, and continued declines were projected, despite a significant boom in the motorcycle market. A speedy response was imperative.

Finding that alloy wheels were now greatly preferred to the hub-and-spoke variety, I felt that we desperately needed a partner who manufactured such wheels. As Honda controlled almost 75 percent of India's two-wheeler market and constituted nearly

100 percent of our two-wheeler sales, the alloy wheels had to be Asia-based and Honda-approved.

I identified a potential partner in China and quickly hired an experienced automotive engineer able to communicate in both Chinese and English. With his help, I pushed through a joint venture agreement in a record three-week timeframe. We assured our new Chinese partner that he would be the sole supplier of the equipment we needed, which helped build trust. In return, he counseled us about how to maintain profit margins in the competitive alloy wheel market. The major cost driver, we were told, is the cost of energy consumption per unit of alloy wheel. To optimize profit, he suggested using recycled aluminum in the alloy manufacturing plant. By melting down scrap, we could avoid buying aluminum alloy ingots. A 40 percent reduction in energy cost allowed us to maintain profit margins in a highly competitive market and build a sustainable business model.

As Ryan Blair asserts, "If it is important to you, you will find a way. Otherwise, you'll just find an excuse." Finding excuses plays no part in success.

Staying Committed to "The Family Firm"

Neither my professional nor my personal journey has ended. I subsequently relocated to Shanghai, working for a multinational with twenty billion in revenue, and, as I near retirement, I am looking for opportunities in the United States, where both of our children now live. I'd like to end my meditation on success, though, by mentioning what may be the most important element of all. I am certain that, important as money is, it is not the greatest measure of success. A close, loving, supportive family is.

Trite as it sounds, *my* success is really *ours*. My wife, my son, and my daughter have been just as invested in and dedicated to "the family firm" as I have. At the nadir of our financial well-being, we discussed the circumstances, the consequences, and the possible ways forward and we decided together how to adapt our mission statement and to turn hopes into facts. I remember how touched Sadhna and I were when, during our hardest time, our children proudly announced that they had set aside their greatly curtailed pocket money to treat us to an ice cream extravaganza.

Success is a slippery term, but of this I am certain: it requires planning, and persevering, and continually adapting to circumstances. It demands faith in oneself and learning from one's missteps. Perhaps most of all, though, it relies on one's staunchest, most dependable allies: family.

Find Your Business Partner and Take That Chance

Nedra J. Barr and Sharon L. Ross

Nedra J. Barr, chief executive officer at Spyder, Inc., is an award-winning "C" level technology executive. She has received a "Top 10 Most Impactful Women in Technology" award from Analytic Insights, a "Top 50 Tech Visionary" as well as a "Top 50 Tech Leaders" award from Intercon. She is an accomplished speaker, author, and sits on numerous advisory boards. She started her insurance career at age sixteen in Fort Scott, Kansas, and has been in the insurance/financial services industry her entire career. Nedra made her move into insuretech/fintech in 2000.

Nedra served as a chief revenue officer for a fintech firm in the wealth management space and helped lead and guide tech firms throughout her career in fintech. She designed the first-to-the-market annuity payout illustration solution.

Sharon L. Ross, chief operating officer at Spyder, Inc., has more than eighteen years in financial services and fintech. Sharon is a versatile, collaborative, and strategic executive leader with proven success in continuous improvement, operations, organic firm growth, client management, customer experience, needs analysis, project management, governance, and corporate initiatives. Sharon supports a client centric approach to business development with an emphasis on execution while building and maintaining positive and productive relationships.

Sharon spent a decade as a compliance director for a registered broker-dealer, developing strong risk management capabilities with a solid structured approach. She has managed corporate governance and development for a financial service digital platform provider. She served as project manager for a multimillion-dollar broker-dealer and technology company joint venture that was established to create software solutions for the alternative investments industry.

Sharon Ross

I first met Nedra when we were fellow employees at a tech company. I was put in charge of a growth initiative, so I held a meeting with the movers, shakers, and champions of the organization. Nedra was one of those people.

I began the meeting with a standard corporate icebreaker. The task was for everyone to share their results of a personality quiz that determined what "color" they represented, thereby showing strengths and differences in the group. The standard answers were one word: blue, gold, orange, or green. When it came time for Nedra to share her answer, her response was so much bigger and bolder than her simply stating her color. She told the entire meeting who she was, what she did, and her intentions to take the company to the next level. And she said, "When I'm done with that, I'm going to become a CEO of a tech company."

Everyone in the room was confused–did this woman just come in and say that she was taking their boss's job? But I was impressed. Her confidence was tremendous, and her answer was strong and different. I knew I liked her with that one response. I followed up with her after the meeting, and over time our mutual appreciation of "getting things done" fostered a business partnership that has led us to start multiple companies and move toward the success that we had set for ourselves today.

I was never the kid who was sure of what she wanted to do. My family members all knew what profession they preferred from an early age, but I wasn't that person. I liked all things that involved taking chaos and creating "order" with variety in task and high sense of urgency, but that didn't seem to all fit into one professional bucket. My path was largely undetermined, and success would be nebulous. The "choose a career" lightbulb never went off, even as I finished high school, finished college, and entered the corporate world.

In this world, someone dictated my path for me. I excelled at every task I was given and reached every position that someone else labeled as a benchmark of success. Clearly, I was valued, but I wasn't walking down a path of my own. Eventually I began to question why I put all my energy into others' dreams and concluded that to be successful, you need to be fulfilled. You must take a chance and trust you are every bit as much of a rockstar navigating your own path as you are walking down someone else's.

Coincidentally, around this same time Nedra saw that I was on someone else's path–that I was living other people's dreams. There had to be a better way for us to reach our personal idea of success. Nedra told me about her idea for Spyder, Inc., and why it was the right time to pursue it. We had just lived through the first few months of COVID-19; while the rest of the world was trying to figure out how to continue business, the tech industry worked day and night to help the world adapt to lockdowns. Nedra and I looked at each other and said, "If we're going to work this hard, if this is what it takes, and we are already doing it–we should do it for our own dream, going forward together."

Every single day, you drive by a Starbucks. Starbucks wouldn't exist if Howard Schultz hadn't decided to pursue his idea. You log into Facebook, which wouldn't exist if Mark Zuckerberg and company hadn't decided to pursue their idea. Why would the idea for Spyder, Inc., be any less great than either of those two? Why would your idea be any less great than the idea for Starbucks, Facebook, or any company that is succeeding right now?

There will come a time when you finally recognize that others have been dictating your future for you; from the time you come out of school, or even in high school, parents, teachers, professors, coaches, managers, your friends are telling you what you're supposed to be. If you have an idea, and you think that you've got value, take that chance. Move forward. Go down your own path. If you're not comfortable with totally going the path alone, and you have an opportunity to join forces with a person who complements your components, take the risk. You will spend the rest of your life regretting that you didn't take the shot.

When you have this mindset, nothing you do will be a failure. Even if the venture does not financially succeed, you succeeded in taking a shot and taking a chance at something that you never would have done before.

Nedra Barr

Before I came into the tech world, I was in the top fifteen producers of a big insurance company that had thousands of advisors. One time, we were in Bermuda for the Chairman's Council. The chairman of the board finished one of our meetings by going around the table and speaking to every male about what they thought could make the industry and the company better. But he didn't ask me. I was the only woman in the room and he didn't address me. I spoke up; I said, "Excuse me, but you missed me."

Being a 4'11" female was a hindrance in the corporate world. For my whole career, I've worked around men who are 6' and tower over my petite stature. Because I was "vertically challenged," others may not have seen me for all that I am, but my mindset helped me through these obstacles. There were plenty of times when I had to demonstrate self-advocacy and set an example for others—that I would not be overlooked for my contributions that were just as important as others that were being recognized. My mindset doesn't allow me to let anyone make me feel less than or not be heard.

I realized early in my career the challenges of being female in a male-dominated industry, and I set out to change the game. I've always had to let my personality shine and show that I know what I'm doing, so I started speaking up at a pretty young age. When things weren't going the way I wanted them to go, I self-reflected, reevaluated, and started walking my own path.

And that means I have always had to put in the work. My dad always told me, "If you get yourself into it, you get yourself out of it." My whole life, nobody's ever pulled me out of any messes. I've pulled myself out of my own mess. And that lesson was a huge part of developing my mindset. You've got to learn how to solve your own problems, and how to do it fast and in the right way.

I owned my insurance practice for about nineteen years; I've also owned a car wash and a consulting company before I went into tech. When I met Sharon, I was at a point in my life where I was determined to be a CEO of a tech company.

But my path wasn't always smooth sailing. I had a bad accident in 2006–I broke my neck and my back and I didn't get to work consistently for quite a few years. Fortunately, I've always loved work, and I had a strong enough mindset that told me to get well, push through, and get back to what I love. I worked hard on my recovery, got myself where I needed to be mentally and physically, and came back to work stronger than ever in 2016. I have killed it ever since.

I have overcome these challenges because of my mindset. Success is all about mindset. You've got to know what you want and you've got to fight for it. Nothing worth it comes easy in life. Master your belief in your "want;" that focus powers enough will to fight for it.

Not everyone wants to take the chance and start their own company, but Sharon and I are forging ahead. We're stepping out with a great opportunity to build a dynamic company that will have a social impact on a community in need of economic growth. We are going to give it our all. The path we are on is our own, which means it will have twists and turns that we are prepared to tackle. No journey is ever perfect; along the way, I remain humble and listen to people with more or different expertise to navigate that path. This is what makes up my success mindset, and what encouraged me to take those first few steps toward entrepreneurship.

One of those steps, for me, was to find a good business partner to make this dream a reality. We have a big mission to fulfill at Spyder, Inc., and one person can't do everything to reach the goals that we've set. It's true–one person can't do everything. Business partnerships need to be balanced for success. When these partnerships are lopsided, the relationships will struggle to survive. Some people think when setting up a business partnership, they can get away with having 90 percent of the company and giving their partner 10 percent. That's not a success mindset. If you're partners, you're partners, 50/50. And that's how Sharon and I approach our businesses.

Sharon Ross and Nedra Barr

We have found great joy in working in a business partnership. Entrepreneurship isn't easy; it can be lonely. When you're on the path with somebody else, you will have more fun. Having a success mindset as an individual is important, but so is having someone who can encourage you to move forward. There are days where you're going to feel the weight of the mission that you're trying to fulfill. The right partner will help you carry the load. Find them. A lot of people don't believe that that person is out there, but you've got to take the chance; just like you're taking the chance to walk on your own path. Look for your business partner. You will find your other half.

For us, this meant being self-aware and recognizing what the "Yin" to our "Yang" looks like. Before you can go out and find the right business partner for you, you must validate that you and your partner are on the same page. You must know what you want in a business partner and what you need them to be and do to move ideas forward. Even when we're dealing with small obstacles along the way, we find a way to joke and laugh about it. We know how to help each other get through the day and that will help us succeed.

We know we are Yin and Yang; we're polar opposites. One of us is risk-averse, and the other one prefers to calculate their risks. When one person is anxious, the other is reassuring. But we think alike. We value each other's opinion, and we trust each other. When you can find the person who matches and completely opposes your personality in the right ways, you can create a great environment together. When you have the ability to create a great environment, you're going to find that more doors open for you and that your career is going to run on overdrive.

Of course, this doesn't happen immediately; you have to do your due diligence. Vet your potential business partners. You're not looking for a reflection of yourself–you are looking for someone who can complement you. Don't hire or partner with somebody that's the same as you. Hire or partner with somebody better than you are and that does something different than you. That's how you grow as an organization. If you select somebody that's less than you, they're not going to be able to help you. If you select someone that you see on the same level as you, you're not going to grow. Select somebody better than you, with different skill sets.

Looking beyond your skill sets, you should find someone who allows you to be heard. We admit, that's not always easy to find. You need to be looking at somebody who can walk the path alongside you, whether you're in the sunshine or the storm. If you both have the mindset that you succeed or fail together, you will have a much higher chance at success. A true partner doesn't walk away when times get tough. A true partner is in it, 50/50.

We believe that when the fighting starts, the business partnership is over. That's the reality of running a company together. When we first got into business together, we made an agreement that we don't fight; we hear each other out and then we move on. Once it's over, and we've come to a decision, then it's over. There's no remorse, there's no retaliation, there's no revenge. We move on.

Coming to a decision without fighting can be a big challenge for business partners, so we believe that you have need to have a tiebreaker. We work differently than a lot of other business partners, so our tiebreaker might look different. But if you're equal partners, there must be some kind of tiebreaker. One pair's tiebreaker could be found in a legal document where another's could be a game of Rock, Paper, Scissors. A board of directors or a legal advisor could be the person who calls the tiebreaker. Chug a beer to break a tie–it doesn't matter. When you hit that impasse, if you have an established tiebreaker, you will have a much easier time making a decision and moving on without fighting with your partner.

Every business has to do this. Quite honestly, we believe every friendship and relationship needs a tiebreaker, too. A tiebreaker allows you to stay positive, hold onto that success mindset, and be kind to each other even when decisions are hard and someone "loses out" on something. A tiebreaker, with the right business partner, keeps your head right when times get tough.

If you're not right in the headspace with the person who's by your side, how can you lead and guide a company?

We started working together for the same reason that we are writing this chapter together; we hold this success mindset and we're dedicated to making our business partnership and our company work. Throughout our careers, we have seen all sorts of things that leaders have done that fail to provide a great employee experience. As leaders ourselves and as people building a business, we want to change that. We know that by having our mindsets right and setting our company up with the right core values and a welcoming culture, we will make our company and our people thrive.

The world has changed; corporate America is an ever-changing terrain. Everything's competitive, but if you can still thrive and have a great mindset, you can do good and succeed.

We want people to see that your dreams and aspirations are possible. Your path is possible. If you want to be successful, do your due diligence. Don't take an uncalculated risk, and really find the right person that can help you walk your own path. But once you've done all of that, take that chance. Take that chance! You've lived in somebody else's dream before–when it's the right time, live in your own.

Success Mindset of a Marathoner

Randy Green

Randy Green is an American who has lived in China since 2004. A member of Toastmasters International for over twenty years, he has published several books, created the blog randy-green.com, and contributed to Medium.com and other writing platforms. He has lived in Chongqing since 2016 with his wife and son. In 2021, he founded Mind Fleet, a company to introduce Western educational and quality of life products to Chinese consumers.

In 2003, living in his home state of Missouri, he received a life-changing invitation to come to China and teach English to university students. In accepting, he committed himself to a life both satisfying and mystifying. After seventeen years in China, his experiences include: university-level teaching of spoken and written English for eleven years; being chosen for publication in two books of essays by foreign teachers in China; being issued a rare Permanent Resident Permit (green card); riding a bicycle on crowded Chinese streets; fourteen years with a Chinese wife; eight years with a bilingual, bicultural Chinese/American son; extensive travel throughout China; and living in three large cities in different regions of China. Somehow, he survived all of the above. For additional information, he can be contacted at mindfleet.cn.

In ten years, 96 percent of today's new businesses won't be in existence. This is well-documented, and even though it might sound grim, these figures have been a reality for a long time. Many years ago, in a parallel example, Earl Nightingale asked us to imagine 100 people in their mid-twenties, full of optimism and energy. By the time they were sixty-five, Nightingale said, only *five* of them would be financially secure.

How can we separate ourselves from the 96 percent? How can we ensure that decades from now, we are financially secure and our businesses are thriving?

We have to hold the mindset of a marathon runner.

Before I started my online business, I had been working toward an entirely different goal: running a marathon. But are these goals so different? Sure, you must wear sneakers to complete one goal and should opt for more professional shoes while achieving the other. You can still run a successful business while eating a fast-food diet or pulling all-nighters; marathoners will find more success by eating more leafy greens. There are, however, many similarities between starting a business and running a marathon. I took some of the habits and the mindset required to complete a marathon and mapped them onto the habits and mindset required to successfully start a business.

I suspect that a comparable failure rate would apply to the large number of people who get excited and want to run a marathon, but never complete one. Suppose *you* want to run a marathon. You want to be one of those people who proudly wears a t-shirt proclaiming to the world that you completed a 26-mile race. The path to success seems simple enough: run the race, get the t-shirt. To get that t-shirt, however, you must first complete the 26-mile course–and to do that, you must change your life. You make preparing for the marathon a daily high priority. You take action steps–lots of them, literally. You read books and articles about training, equipping, and eating for a marathon. It is beneficial if you can find some kindred spirits to go on those training runs and the 5K and 10K weekend races as you build up to the marathon distance. In fact, it helps if you can immerse yourself in the marathon world in every way possible.

But those are not the *most* basic action steps necessary to complete a marathon. Yes, if you are going to run a marathon, you should do all those things. But their purpose all supports and fine-tunes your daily training runs. The most basic thing you can do to run a marathon is get your butt out of bed a little earlier every morning and start running. The most basic thing you can do to build a business is get your butt out of bed a little earlier every morning and start working. If you can do this every day without quitting, you are more likely to separate yourself from the 96 percent.

Somewhere in this long, daunting, uncomfortable process, most aspiring marathoners quit. That's why you will be damn proud to wear that t-shirt and why you will share an unspoken bond with others who have also earned the right to wear one.

As I've built my online business, I've found many parallels between earning the t-shirt and getting my business to a point where I can look at it with a similar amount of pride. I have had to change my life: taking action steps, reading and absorbing information every day about entrepreneurship, and finding kindred spirits who are willing to "run the race" with me as partners or contributors. But the *most* essential requirement for starting and building my online business has been getting out of bed and working. I have been able to do that because I have the mindset of a marathoner: I won't quit until I've reached the finish line.

Don't Be Surprised By Surprises

Not everyone training for a marathon gets up every day with the full confidence that they will cross the finish line. Often, we second guess our decisions. After we start something, we create rationalizations for quitting. Even during the hours that it takes to run 26 miles, a marathoner may be thinking about how they can justify dropping out of the race.

But consider this. You wouldn't tolerate someone else tempting and confusing you with such conversations. If you had a personal trainer tell you that you couldn't meet your fitness goals, you'd probably fire them. So don't do this to yourself. Drop the conversations where you tell yourself you can't push forward. Instead, remind yourself that you have made the decision to start a business, run a marathon, or achieve any goal on your list. Follow through! Life becomes more peaceful and simpler when you eliminate discussions about quitting. Life becomes more exciting when, every day, you choose to get up and not quit until you've crossed the finish line.

This doesn't mean that obstacles won't pop up. Surprises are an occupational hazard in starting up a new business. They pop up

272 | Success Mindsets

almost every day; I call them the *crisis du jour*. Marathoners wake up with sore legs. Entrepreneurs wake up to rejections, doubts, and challenges. When I began, I thought starting a very small online business should be a pretty short and simple process. I wasn't even close. As you start out, know that crossing the finish line is much easier when you expect surprises and inexplicable delays.

I didn't realize that everything it took to get my business up and running would take so long to complete! I was not familiar with all of the requirements or even the obstacles that came with creating a website. Many of these obstacles were unexpected. In addition to the long list of requirements, there were so many things I had to personally inspect and approve. I thought building a website would be a simple task: describe the page layout, write the text, then send the directions to the designer. But the actual process of building the website involved long notes about changes and adjustments, checking my work, making more changes, and then checking them again. I got so tired of reviewing every page over and over. And, to do it right the first time, I had to review everything, keystroke-by-keystroke; anything I didn't notice, some sharp-eyed, suspicious customer would see in the future.

During these moments of frustration or impatience, I thought back to that 26-mile behemoth. While running a marathon, I wanted to hold onto the mindset that each mile marker I passed meant I was one mile closer to completion. Yes, there might have been 25 miles to go, but I completed one, and that meant I could complete 25 more. The ancient Roman army had a similar mindset, leaving milestones along their route to measure how much progress they had made. When starting a business, we can use both concepts to track our progress and remind us of how far we've come. Each step completed is a mini-achievement. Each future step will also be a small achievement.

If I were to start another business tomorrow, I would start with the expectation that the process would be long, difficult, and sometimes painful, and there would be numerous surprises and disappointments. I would know everything would take longer than expected. But even though I was surprised by many obstacles along my journey, my mindset helped me to keep going. Each obstacle that I faced was just another mile to run. If I could run one mile, I could run 26. And at the end of each day, I knew I could cross the finish line (literal and proverbial) because I had seen other people cross the finish line. If other people can do it, I can do it.

"Seek First to Understand"

I would not have been able to run 26 miles without the help of trainers, running club members, and experts who showed me the right shoes to buy and diet to eat. In order to run a marathon or start a successful business, you have to ask for help and consider the opinions of others.

Yes, being the CEO means that you are the one that has to make decisions for your company. But does that mean you should isolate yourself? No! You have to consider that because other people have crossed the finish line, they can help you do the same.

One of the biggest challenges I encountered when starting my business was listening to others, even when their advice contradicted what I thought was right. Early on, I was paying for a service. The people working for that service insisted on doing things their way. This was frustrating, but I realized finally that I was paying for this advice! They were the experts; not me. Besides, letting them have their way required only a few small changes. Getting the job done was more important than getting the job done my way.

Only my ego has kept me from accepting that someone else might have a better idea or superior knowledge. If you want to build long-term relationships that will last throughout the lifetime of your business, you have to let your ego go.

The more I encountered obstacles as an entrepreneur, the more I learned just how important the cooperation and contributions of other people were to my decisions and strategy. So many entrepreneurs have faced the hurdles that you and I will face as we continue to grow our businesses. As Newton says, we are standing on the shoulders of giants. Don't ignore the giants or you will lose your footing.

Everything I was attempting to do, someone else had already done–and documented it somewhere. I am not an expert when it comes to running an online business, and I certainly wasn't when I started! I have learned that I gain so much more when I listen to others who have cleared those hurdles and kept running. Role models, mentors, and other sources can help you understand, but you can also seek out this information in other places. I like to spend some time each day reading or listening to relevant materials. Do whatever you can do to learn, every single day. As Stephen Covey says, I try to "seek first to understand." Listening more and speaking less is so crucial to success.

My most notable achievement while training for a marathon or starting my business has been adjusting my mindset. By letting go of ego, I have come to realize there are no limits except those that I accept for myself. I cannot control the world around me, but I can control my response to what happens around me.

In some cases, this means accepting the surprise obstacles that are bound to pop up every day. Once these obstacles are cleared, I try to recognize the steps that I have taken and how they will contribute to my overall journey (no matter how long that journey takes.)

In other cases, this means stepping back, listening, learning, and considering the people who have come before me. Every obstacle that I faced or will face has been cleared by someone else before me. If I listen to their advice or let them teach me something new, I will be more likely to clear anything in my path.

With this mindset, you can achieve any goal. You can run a marathon. You can start a business. This mindset is what will separate you from the 96 percent. Whatever "finish line" you want to cross, you can cross with a success mindset.

A Scientist's Success Mindset

Hans Keirstead

Dr. Hans Keirstead is an internationally known stem cell expert and serial entrepreneur who led the development of a treatment that restored movement and sensory function to people with quadriplegic spinal cord injury, and a treatment for cancer that has saved the lives of people with melanoma, brain cancer, and ovarian cancer. He has also led therapy development for immune disorders, motor neuron diseases, and retinal diseases, as well as a vaccine for COVID-19. He has founded four successful biotechnology companies, each returning significant value to investors and treatments to patients. He holds board positions in several prominent biotechnology companies. He was a full professor at the University of California, Irvine, where he founded, directed, and erected a building for the UCI Stem Cell Research Center. He was a founding advisor of CIRM, a $3 billion dollar stem cell fund. He has been a long-time advisor to several governments.

Dr. Keirstead received his PhD from the University of British Columbia in Canada and was awarded the Cameron Award for outstanding PhD thesis in the country. He was elected as Senate Member of the University of Cambridge and Fellow of Downing College and was the youngest member to have obtained those positions.

I have always been a big thinker. As a young child, the idea of outer space intrigued me—I was always thinking about what was beyond our planet and our atmosphere. Physics and astrophysics fascinated me. On a more terrestrial level, I found myself wanting to explore the oceans, consumed by the vastness of our planet and how much was left undiscovered.

The focus of my curiosity and intrigue continued to shrink until I reached the human body. At eleven years old, a lightbulb went off: I knew that the human body is the most extreme miracle that we can see. Nothing on land or underwater, in the sky or the larger atmosphere, can compare to the wonders of sperm, egg, and the human being they create when they come together.

The most extraordinary unknown is the human body. Yes, we know that when a sperm and egg get together, we're well on our way to growing a full-size human. But no one really understands what happens in that pivotal moment. No one has yet been able to replicate life in a single cell or even grasp the complexity of the human brain.

If I could come one step closer to understanding how we are made, I realized, I could change someone's life. Best of all, I didn't have to stop exploring along the way. At such a young age, I understood I could be the explorer that I wanted to be, but do so in a way that was meaningful; one that shaped my career and legacy.

This molded the mindset that I now have as the CEO of AIVITA Biomedical, Inc. We have dozens of patents to our name and we continue to change the lives of people around the world. This continued success is due to knowing that everything is possible, knowing that people are everything, but above all, maintaining the innocent intrigue and happiness that science first sparked in me as a child.

At age eleven, I told myself that I was going to heal someone of disease or injury; I was going to generate a treatment that would change or save someone's life. I've always had the confidence that I could do that.

First, this meant going to medical school for a very long time. Being so immersed at such a young age, I didn't think too far ahead of that first, life-changing moment in which I would change or save a life. I thought that after I did save or change a single person's life, or generate a treatment that saved their life, I'd retire. My priorities would shift and I would run a country store somewhere far away from the city, living a slower life with the knowledge that I had accomplished what I wanted to accomplish. To me, changing the life of one person from disease or injury was the best thing that I could do. It was the finish line, rather than a checkpoint.

I crossed that finish line. I invented a spinal cord injury treatment that was applied to humans. Timothy Atchinson was the first person to receive it—he was a full quadriplegic with no motor or sensory function from the chin down. Through the treatment, he regained full motor and sensory function of his hands and arms.

At the time, I really did consider retiring to that little country store that I had envisioned as a youngster. I helped that one human meaningfully—I had done what I had set out to do. But on my journey, from age eleven to the moment I saw Atchinson's results of my treatment, I learned that I was exceedingly happy inventing therapies. The lifestyle suited me and I was good at it. I put the country store on the backburner and got back to work in the laboratory.

It's important to remember that there is more to a scientist's mindset than exploring and pondering with intrigue. When you really think about what a scientist does, you realize that they fail for years. Scientists might even spend decades running experiments trying to prove their hypothesis—and sometimes they can't. The experiments mess up. They have to invent a technique. Biology is smarter than they are. There are all kinds of reasons why it takes years to cross a finish line. And even when you establish a process or prove your hypothesis, it can be proven wrong *years* later.

Once these lines are crossed, other scientists don't always want to revisit them to verify the end of the race. People get fooled by their own science even if they're the world's leading experts in their subject. Science is tough, and it is pure exploration—sometimes, exploration and intrigue are the only way to push through the years of working to prove a hypothesis or the struggle of revisiting "truths" already established in the field. Exploration, intrigue, and the idea that anything is possible, however, can truly change the way that we view the world.

Before I had applied the treatment for spinal cord injury to humans, we were applying it to paralyzed rats. Initially, the treatment allowed the subjects to get up and walk again. We considered the treatment a success and took the next steps to apply the treatment to humans. This takes time –at least a year or two, often many years. And during this time, just as we thought we were making progress, the rats stopped walking. They were paralyzed once more. We couldn't figure it out. Why did the therapy stop working?

The dogma in the biology community at the time had established that stem cells were immortal and they never stopped dividing. But in our lab, looking at these paralyzed rats, we held onto that innocent intrigue of a child who believed that anything was possible. We kept our eyes and ears open, and looked for evidence that stem cells behaved differently than we had been taught, that perhaps they *weren't* immortal. Of course, this wasn't received well by many in the scientific community, but what we found turned out to be something that no one in the world had ever seen before. We discovered, through pure exploration of an idea that had previously been thought of as fact, that stem cells aren't immortal. That was extraordinary. We repeated our experiments using younger stem cells, and paralyzed rats walked once again. Three years later, Doug Melton at Harvard published a paper that confirmed that stem cells are not immortal. The dogma in the field was dramatically changed because we opened ourselves to the idea that anything is possible.

All it takes is one moment to change everything: a life, a tightly-held belief, or the direction of your career. One moment.

I'll never forget those rare moments when I looked through a microscope and realized that I was the first human in the world that had ever seen what was happening in the petri dish–I had just made a discovery! As a scientist, you're lucky if you ever get that moment. If you're really good, you might get two or three over a twenty or thirty-year career. It doesn't always happen, but I can tell you that you get to these moments because you have that innocent intrigue and because you *know* that anything is possible. Scientists can fail for years–or they can have the mindset that rather than failing for years, they are on the road to their next big discovery. Your mindset determines how far you are willing to go until that discovery is made.

The difference between holding these two mindsets, more often than not, depends on the people around you.

People are everything. Every transition in my life, every advancement, every "aha" moment, and every moment that wasn't so marvelous, were all the result of an interaction with an individual. The high points in my career were brought on by others. The lowest points in my career were brought on by others. My ability to step aside and continue forward was sharpened only through the help of others.

People are everything. If you don't make this realization in your mind and truly believe it, you will never succeed–I guarantee this. You will never be a quarter of what you can be if you don't have a support group around you that you empower and who will empower you. It's reciprocal; people need you, and you need people. If you don't understand that, you will never succeed as a leader.

I made the switch from academia to entrepreneurship because I needed this support group. I don't have time to go changing everybody's view or responding to naysayers who only want to bring me down out of jealously, malice or self-aggrandization. I'm certainly not going to change the academic system. When I found myself in an environment that was not cheering me on in my innocent intrigue, I had to change the environment that I was in.

I believe that people bury themselves; you don't have to assist. You don't have to put naysayers down–they're taking care of that themselves. Just step aside and keep going down your own path. Instead of lingering on the people who doubted you, you have to surround yourself with people who have the same mindset as you–who believe that anything is possible.

I eventually quit academia entirely once I was able to build a multimillion-dollar laboratory, in a private facility of my own design, that exceeded the capabilities of the academic lab. Yes, this took me a little while, but I had to change the environment I was in. The scientists I work with today share my vision; they aren't wallowing in politics, career advancement, or their inflated egos. My team has become so good that rather than writing the whole recipe for different tasks or processes, I can now come up with half the recipe and they cook up the rest. Some of them are so good that I can just come up with the idea and tell them they need to make the recipe. They are inventors themselves.

The company owns the patent when these inventions are made, but only because of the amazing people who make up our team.

The one challenge with switching from academia to entrepreneurship is balancing the delicate roles of scientist and CEO, but I've always tried to nurture my ability to be a great scientist. Whether I'm wearing a scientist's hat or a CEO's hat, I keep my eye on the science side of things. I'm very aware that science can suck up every hour of my day, and no matter how hard I work, I'm always behind. CEOs feel the same way.

In order to be productive as a scientist *and* as a CEO, the secret is the same—you have to be happy. You have to have the intrigue of a child, to be in a place where you *can* believe that anything is possible. That is the secret to succeeding, no matter what hat you wear or industry you are in.

Scientists, especially scientists dealing with treatments designed to save lives, know the importance of this. You see, I'm surrounded by death. I have been developing therapies for diseases and injuries that kill people. Cancer, spinal cord injuries, and spinal muscular atrophy…these are horrible, horrible things. But I can only run a company that helps beat these horrible things if I can maintain that entrepreneurial, bright-eyed spirit of discovery. I do this by not surrounding myself with people that are dying, but with people that are trying. I surround myself with people that are on my team, see my vision, and are all working towards the same thing. This keeps me happy and keeps the sense of innocent intrigue alive.

Ironically, I only allow myself particular times to interact with patients *because* I'm so compassionate. I need to see patients, but I know that if I have a call meeting with a patient in the morning, I will feel sad for the rest of the day and can't do what I need to do to help that patient and hundreds more survive. I schedule these sessions at very particular times of the day when I know I won't have need of a happy and energetic brain for any massive, productive work afterwards, because I know I'm going to be emotionally down when I interact with patients and families who are fighting so hard to live. Whether you are dealing with patients, investors, board members, or competitors that threaten to derail your focus, you have to be able to compartmentalize.

Fortunately, there are a lot of tools that entrepreneurs can use in order to compartmentalize different tasks so they are handling everything at the right time of the day. I compartmentalize the chill, quiet time when I'm feeling a little bit burnt out; I sit down in meeting rooms that are comfortable when my team downloads to me.

Even if you are an entrepreneur that doesn't deal with death and dying, you can still apply these tricks to your daily schedule so you are happiest and most productive when you need to be. One of my tricks is scheduling a 10 percent administration rule. I look at my day, and I do not do more than 10 percent of administrative tasks that bog me down. I can certainly take five to ten minutes each day to answer emails or take on boring tasks, but if I'm doing hour after hour of administrative tasks, I will be so unhappy that I can't pick myself back up. Cluster balancing tasks that make you happy with your other tasks to keep yourself at peak form.

I also cluster (or batch) my activities so that I'm not bouncing from one thing to the other all day. If you are able to control your activities, batch the ones that are similar. If you can't, throw this advice away. Do what works for *you,* to help you stay happy and in a success mindset. Get intellectual in the mornings, if that's when you think best. Relax in lounge chairs all afternoon and cluster your meetings during times when you are mentally tired out, but able to listen. Do what works for *you,* to help you stay happy and in a success mindset. Keep yourself fit. Keep yourself excited and even scared from time to time. Keep your brain young, maintaining that innocent intrigue. This will help keep you balanced; more important, it will help you succeed.

That's the key to success. Find the tools that maintain your happiness and be very diligent about filling your days with them while weeding out the ugly and boredom from your life. Only surround yourself with people who have the same mindset as you. Nurture your innocent intrigue so that you're always keeping your mind open, challenging your own assumptions, and believing that anything is possible. You can treat spinal cord injury. You can treat cancer, even though your own colleagues and supporting institutions tell you that you can't. Don't listen to them. Be happy, stay intrigued, and you can do everything that you set out to do and more. A whole lot more.

Learning Your Way to Financial Independence

Rick Orford

Rick Orford is an author, investor, mentor, and finance writer. His work has appeared in several high-ranking media placements, including *Good Morning America*, *The Washington Post*, *Yahoo Finance*, on MSN, NBC, FOX, CBS, and ABC News. His passion is personal finance, and he works tirelessly to deliver content in an easy-to-understand manner.

Born and raised in Canada, Rick is known as a respected influencer that brings a proven ability to translate vision into reality. He is also the author of *The Financially Independent Millennial.*

From a young age, I was attracted to wealth. I grew up in a middle-class community in Montreal. My parents weren't wealthy, but they worked hard to buy their own home. Then, a car; next came a boat. That meant taking on debt, which I didn't understand at ten years old. At the same time, I had family members who seemed "fabulously wealthy." And, I gravitated towards the "fabulously wealthy" lifestyle.

Since a young age, I've been interested in business. In elementary school, I had a paper route. In case you're unfamiliar with what a paper route entails, you wake up at four o'clock in the morning to deliver papers to forty or fifty houses. When I discovered that double the houses meant double the money, I expanded to three paper routes and eventually learned about outsourcing labor–for the first time. Working hard came naturally to me. I understood hard work was essential to obtaining my goal of living like my "rich family members."

A vision of success was born: a big home, in a warm climate, and a fancy car. That was my perception of success at age twelve. I wanted to be "rich." I did not yet realize there was a difference between "rich" and "wealthy."

Ask Questions, Risk Failure, Learn from Mistakes

Even with that paper route, my foundation for success was already present. I've never shied away from asking questions. I've never been afraid to fail. I've always tried until I got it right. In fact, I have failed so many times, I've lost count. The key is learning from mistakes and not repeating them. If you stop because of a failure, your story ends there. Failure is what will be remembered. You have to keep going. Being willing to risk making a mistake is one of my pillars to success. I recently conducted an interview with twenty-five different millionaires (and a billionaire) who all said basically the same thing: success didn't just happen for them. They made mistakes until they eventually figured it out.

Of course, success doesn't come from excelling at just one thing. To be successful, one needs a recipe, like baking a cake. For a good cake, you need flour, eggs, butter, and sugar. If you use too much of an ingredient, or not enough, you'll end up with a cake, but it may not be good. Success has been similar for me. I was never afraid to ask questions of people who were more successful than me. Even today, I still ask for outside perspectives. Almost to the point of driving the people (I'm asking) crazy. I have always gravitated towards older, smarter, more experienced people. And today, I realize that I prefer to surround myself with smarter people.

This goes back to when I was growing up. I always felt a little more "mature" than my peers. I left high school after completing Grade 10 to start my own business. Many would say that's a recipe for disaster. In my case, I made it work. At sixteen, I started a business selling computers and services. Convincing customers to buy computers from someone as young as I was no easy feat, but I adjusted and earned their trust.

The Path to Getting "Rich"

At age twenty-two, I moved to Vancouver. First, to escape the cold climate. Second, to have a fresh start in a city rich in tech opportunities. Thousands of kilometers from my family, this was the first time I truly moved away from home. My first challenge was finding a job. That was harder than I'd anticipated since I didn't even have a high school diploma. Well, I made looking for a job "my job." In the fall of 2000, I spent eight to nine hours daily, six days a week, searching for a job. And, while I was ghosted by many, it wasn't long before I landed a job as a sales rep at an engineering company. I was fortunate to discover the job paid more than twice what I was expecting!

I was on the path to getting "rich." But life is full of challenges. In fact, life is a bit like Tetris. Remember that game? We were all addicted to it in the 90s. Tetris gives the player a series of pieces falling from the sky, and you have to configure them to make complete lines. As you master the game, it changes speed. Life is no different. Every day, different challenges crash down on us. As we get better at solving these challenges, more are just around the corner. And, when it comes to money, we remember the surprises. Think about the last time your car broke down unexpectedly, or when you had to spend hundreds or thousands of dollars on an "emergency."

Growing from Failure

I've taught myself to prepare for these kinds of situations, personally and professionally. For instance, in 2012, my company discovered an ongoing theft of nearly $50,000. The loss was uninsurable. We had to cover it ourselves. That was a lot of money for our business. Instead of closing the business, I learned how to prevent such a situation from happening again. I consulted other companies on how to avoid the same problem we encountered. In the long run, I chalked it up to education through first-hand experience.

As disappointing as that experience was, I hit a low in my personal life around the same time. I had a good salary, and my business was successful, but I didn't feel wealthy yet. Further, I was in a toxic relationship that prevented me from achieving the kind of success I had wanted since I started the paper route. We did not have the same goals. I wanted to save and invest, while my partner was eager to spend. Healthy relationships feature partners on the same page, sharing in the success. It sounds simple, but most of us marry hoping that our partner will change for the better "some day." They believe exchanging vows and signing a marriage license will change them. In my experience, the only way to change…is to change. You cannot change someone else's life. Only your own.

Experience has taught me that trial and error is the only way to succeed. Success without failure is luck. It's no different than winning the jackpot on a slot machine. Winning a million dollars at a casino is pure luck. Getting "rich" that way is pure luck. You can get lucky once, but counting on it to sustain your success is unwise. In my experience, luck can't be replicated.

When I was younger, I was not aware of the "financial independence" movement. My eyes were opened when I realized being rich wasn't all I expected it to be. Having the never-ending appearance of richness is unsustainable. Being wealthy and living within one's means is far more sustainable. After my first marriage ended and my second business sold, I realized that I no longer wanted to be "rich." I wanted to be wealthy. Being wealthy means being financially independent. And, it's more than making money, it's sustaining that money.

By the summer of 2012, I realized that showing off material "things" was unsustainable. The spending was never ending. And it needed to stop. That's when I learned how to create a monthly surplus. By spending less than I earned, I found a way to scrape money together. From there, I learned how to grow my money by investing it.

Intuition as a Sixth Sense

Reflecting on that time, I developed a healthy risk appetite. Taking calculated risks is an important part of becoming and remaining wealthy. Not all investments will be winners. And, keeping a hands-on approach has worked well for me. I've learned that intuition is the foundation of one's experience. My experiences have given me a "sixth sense," the intuition to navigate through life today.

Intuition led me to marry someone who shares my goals. Together, we started a new technology company. More specifically, a VoIP telephone company—and I knew little about the phone systems we were selling. However, we listened carefully to our customers' needs and adapted the offering in the way that our customers expected and wanted. In other words, we gave the customer what they wanted, and offered them value. Fast forward five or six years, the product that earned us the most was not what we thought it would be. We listened to our customers' continuing needs and changed our business to fulfill this demand. In business, being flexible and willing to adapt is key. Giving the customer what they want rather than just what your business can provide is a pillar to success.

For example, say your business is selling bread. If your customers are gluten-free, there won't be much demand—unless you use gluten-free flour. Sell something your customers actually need.

Reflecting on my experience, perhaps if a mentor had been guiding me, my path to financial independence would have been faster. However, I was forced to figure things out myself. Fortunately, I like figuring things out on my own. In the end, I'm wealthy because I arrived at these conclusions on my own.

Wealth Inspires Sustained Success

Financial independence is possible for all of us. All one needs is time, energy, and desire. And sprinkle a little willingness to learn. To me, success is being fearless in how you approach learning. You have to be willing to make mistakes, even if only to learn from them. Also, live within your means and spend less than you earn. For those who aren't used to it, that's easier said than done, but it must be done. Reduce your expenses, increase your income, and invest the surplus. Finally, share your life with someone who shares your vision. If you're not on the same page with your partner about what kind of cake you're looking to bake, life might not be as sweet.

Ultimately, learning and being willing to fail fueled my success mindset. It led to three notable achievements. Take away any of these achievements, and my life would be a lot different. First, I sold my first company. Selling a business is often the biggest wealth builder an investor will achieve. Even with a seven-figure exit, much of the money ran out after two years. So, I started a second business (the VoIP telephone company), and it was there when I learned how to live within my means. When I sold the business, I realized success was reproducible. If I had not discovered I could sell a business, I might not have believed it was possible. I would not be where I am today.

The second achievement was figuring out how to manage my money. And how to invest properly. Spending less than you earn can be challenging. Society encourages us to keep up with the Joneses. Even if it is a race to the bottom. Learning from the mistakes I made after selling my first business, I started investing my monthly surplus. The magic of compound interest has my money working for me.

The third and arguably most important achievement was marrying someone who shares my success mindset. My partner, Andrea, pushes me to stick to my goals, even when I'm tempted to put work off until tomorrow. It's tempting to get bored staying on a tried and true path, especially when it comes to money. Together, we keep each other on the plan.

And today, our reward is sustainable financial independence—exactly what this kid was looking for when he started a paper route, all those years ago.

Realizing Your Potential...With a Success Mindset

Kermit S. Randa

Kermit S. Randa is a results-driven CEO with extensive experience driving sustained profitable growth through customer-centric transformation, cultures of accountability, and positive employee engagement. His career has included leadership positions throughout the software and technology space, principally in private equity environments. Most recently, he served as the CEO of Syntellis Performance Solutions. Under his leadership, Syntellis achieved significant customer, operational, and financial milestones while earning numerous industry and third-party recognitions. Outside of the office, Randa is a board member, investor, volunteer, and a very grateful father of three beautiful children.

There's no way around it—the world is getting more complicated by the minute. Everything is changing and evolving: the way we live, work, buy, sell, entertain, and socialize. The only constant thing in our lives these days is change and the pandemic accelerated the pace of that change. To navigate and realize the potential of all this change requires an equally constant focus on keeping a success mindset.

We too must evolve...and it is hard. With the pain and disruption caused by change, it is incumbent on each of us to unlock the potential that lies beyond the obvious challenges. In the business world, it doesn't matter what position we hold or what level of the company we are in; we can't look at what is happening around us and simply shrug our shoulders. We must see beyond the current circumstances. We must look for the greater opportunities that lie ahead, create an action plan, and execute on that plan until success is realized. Outside of work, you have the opportunity right now to make meaningful changes at home, in your community, and in the world. This mindset is an absolute requirement to realize your full potential, regardless of the moment you may be experiencing.

I wasn't born with this mindset, and I didn't begin my career as a leader in the technology space. I grew up in a blue-collar town full of smart, humble people who cared for their community. As a kid, becoming a CEO was not on my list of dream jobs. I didn't even comprehend it as a possibility! The reason I was able to develop and realize these dreams was the support from my family, friends, teachers, and mentors in that town. They taught me the value of humility, hard work, a formal education, and common sense. Most importantly, they helped me synthesize these components to become the leader I am today.

Throughout my journey, I have learned how to see past the current conditions, unearth the true potential of the moment, and passionately push forward toward the realization of that potential. This is how I define my success mindset; it is at the center of every decision, strategy, and approach that I use to lead, participate in a team, and even parent.

See Past Your Current Situation

When people ask me for career advice, they are often considering a new role or switching companies. I always start from the same place: "It is never about the job; it is about the job after the job." Your current situation is always a stepping stone in a much larger journey. Taking a job or making a choice because of dollar figures is a tragic error. Think beyond the money. Ask yourself: how will this next role or company equip me to use and grow my capabilities? Will this teach me something new? Can I use this opportunity to help myself or the people around me? When we don't ask ourselves these questions or look beyond our current situation, we lose focus and make moves that take us off the track entirely. You have to strive to know your position, understand how you are truly processing your decisions, *and* where you believe you are meant to go.

I learned this lesson the hard way. In one of my earlier sales positions, I was working a very, very large deal. I had a history of closing deals this size due to my constant focus on the client and what it took to realize *their* vision.

Given the size of the deal and where I was in my life, I did something I had never done before: I calculated what my commission would be if we closed. From the moment I saw that number–which would have been more money than I had made in the past four years–I was off my game. Instead of driving to win, I was playing not to lose. I was blinded by my current situation instead of seeing past it and focusing on the client's best interest. Every decision I made was based on *my* results and how they would change my financial situation.

Unsurprisingly, I lost the deal; from then on, I never calculated a sales commission again. The lesson was clear. In order to succeed, you *have* to look beyond where you are today and focus on realizing the future wins. That doesn't mean your individual economic success isn't important–it is. However, I have found that if you focus on doing the right things, the economics will follow.

Our current circumstances are just a point in an evolving journey. Where we are right now does not have to be where we are going; there is a better future ahead. In order to get there, we need to invest our time and be honest about what that future looks like.

Understand Your Potential

Everything and everyone has the potential to grow, improve, and succeed. Naysayers will disagree and focus on what is broken; you can't let this type of mindset cloud what is possible. This has been the driving force behind my entire career. When I work with teams, we analyze old problems with fresh eyes and find new ways to drive value for the employees and the investors. We challenge the status quo, ask hard questions, reward our "truth tellers," and lean into what is possible. This mindset works outside the office, too; when we make the no-nonsense commitment to do the work, we find potential growth pathways for ourselves.

We start to see these pathways when we are young, if we have the right mentors and leaders guiding us. Think about your favorite teachers as a child—I can still remember the names of mine. As I made my way through school and led a top-tier ed-tech company, I learned a critical lesson about teachers. Our favorite teachers are always people who see the potential within their students and open their eyes to what is possible. These teachers make their students feel comfortable and confident, and provide a sense of accomplishment.

To this day, I remember my fourth-grade teacher as this kind of educator. I so vividly remember reading *The Lion, The Witch and The Wardrobe* in her class. I was nervous to read aloud in front of my peers, but she encouraged me. She made me feel like I could stumble and stutter—that it was all a part of improving my skills as a reader and public speaker.

A few years later, I had a physics teacher who encouraged me in the same way. I'll admit I wasn't a top student, but he didn't let that define me. He had confidence in my ability to work hard and took the time to push me a little further. I remember the pride I felt from all of my hard work, and it's all thanks to a teacher who helped me see that I was capable of success.

The first moment I believed I could be a CEO was due to a leader much like the excellent teachers who challenged me in school. In graduate school, the dean of the program believed in each of us and held us to an extremely high level of accountability. He had a clear expectation that we would all be successful leaders. As part of his philosophy, he believed that if we were going to be chief executives, we should dress that way. While other students at the university wore flip-flops and shorts to class, students in my program were required to wear a suit and tie whenever we were on campus. The experience was surreal; people opened doors for us because of our attire. Hearing and living up to that expectation every day ignited a spark in me. It was a clear signal that it was our job to understand and achieve our full potential. That expectation created a level of confidence that I never had before, and with that confidence I was able to build the career that I have today.

This mindset has now come full circle in my personal life. When I started to see some larger financial returns from my career, I didn't prioritize paying off our mortgage or buying new cars. Instead, I put that money into my kids' college savings accounts. I want to know that each of those three amazing individuals have a clear-cut path toward unearthing their potential and understanding that it is unlimited. Being able to go to their top school isn't the only way that will happen, but it's a great start.

At work, at home, or in your community, you must get in the habit of looking for potential. There is always the potential to learn from challenges, repurpose roadblocks as stepping stones, and offer what you've gained to the people around you. Opportunity is everywhere, and often it is hidden in plain sight. Get creative if you have to. Think outside the box and look for what others may not see. When you start to develop a mindset that is always looking for opportunity, you will see past the headwinds, have the courage to move past the naysayers, and confidently enlist others on your journey.

Realize Your Potential

Once we understand our potential, it's time to realize that potential. And our success mindset is the fuel that propels us forward through challenges, uncovers the best in ourselves, and helps others do the same.

The best leaders that I've worked with continuously offer their team opportunities to grow and learn because they see the future, and that future contains success. They stop at nothing until that success is achieved and their potential is realized.

I try to see my team like the great leaders and teachers in my life saw me. Great teachers do not stop at helping a child understand their potential; they take the necessary steps for the child to *realize* their potential and achieve success. No matter what roadblocks are in the way, great teachers and leaders believe everyone will overcome them. With this mindset, every opportunity becomes a chance to show that you can live up to your potential. That's the kind of perspective that keeps you moving forward through obstacles and reassures the naysayers who want to quit along the way.

All of our experiences, good or bad, teach us a crucial lesson; when you do the work, embrace setbacks and push forward, you will be more prepared to take on bigger challenges. You will know that you have the potential to overcome them! That's why it's so important that we encourage ourselves and others to take on these opportunities and move forward. So many people give up because they don't believe they can push through. As a leader, you have to invite them to follow you–just a little bit further– to see how far you can really go. Commitment to this mindset separates leaders and helps achieve outsized results. Trust me; at the end of your journey, those who once doubted you will appreciate you.

"If we did all the things that we are capable of, we would literally astound ourselves." My teams know this Thomas Edison quote because I have shared it for years. Just like my favorite teachers and employers have encouraged me, I try to encourage my team: one more phone call. One more brainstorming session. One more ounce of effort that could unlock everything that you've been working toward. I know they can achieve more than they think is possible; they are exceptional people. I know they have the potential to do more than what they are doing right now. I try to see them like my teachers and mentors saw me. When an employee tells me that they want to be a VP, I ask them why they don't want to be the CEO. They have the potential to reach the goal and they shouldn't limit themselves, ever. No one should. And you know what? When they look back at all they've done, almost always they are *literally astounded*. In my experience, that realization has changed the course of careers for the better, it has improved companies that have pushed past challenges and provided better results for their clients and created new jobs and innovations.

Again, the same holds true outside of the office. If we take the time to help people realize their potential, they get a light in their eyes, they radiate energy, and the best part…they help others do the same. It is one of the most gratifying feelings in the world.

If the world needs anything right now, it is leaders, future leaders and strong individuals who have the courage to look past the circumstances of today, have the resolve to imagine the incredible potential of what can be done, and make the commitment to drive hard to realize astounding and powerful results. In reading some of the other chapters of this anthology,

I am equally humbled and inspired to be part of this amazing group of contributors. I see how their mindsets have helped them realize their potential and make our world just a little better. I am hopeful that my small chapter in this inspiring collection will somehow connect with a reader and encourage them to look past current circumstances to uncover and realize the limitless opportunities ahead of them.

Seeing people realize their potential is one of my favorite things in life; it is the cornerstone of my leadership approach and my success mindset. I believe that this is at the center of our responsibilities, not only as a CEO, but also as a parent, a mentor, and ultimately and most importantly, as a fellow human being.

Epilogue
by Alinka Rutkowska

Let's check in with your mindset. Do you see success on the horizon? Do you believe that, no matter what challenges have been thrown your way, you will reach your goals?

After hearing from so many inspiring, successful people, it's hard not to see the tasks and challenges in front of you in a brighter light. Continue to shine this light and use it to see what success lies ahead for you. That light doesn't come from money, customers, or status–it's just your mindset. Shine it brightly for the world to see.

I wanted to share some of the most powerful lessons I collected from reading these chapters.

There are billions of people on this Earth.

You just read the stories of people who may have been complete strangers to you before you opened this anthology. In their stories, you weren't just introduced to the authors; in many cases, you were introduced to the people who influenced them and shaped their mindsets. One of the most beautiful takeaways of our anthologies is just how many inspiring, successful people are out there.

There are people who are doing things that seemed impossible twenty years ago, five years ago, or yesterday.

There are people who came from nothing to achieve great success.

There are people out there who are ready to help you along your path to success, even though you haven't formally met them yet…

…and I'm just talking about the people who contributed to this anthology.

We so often get caught in a mindset where we compare ourselves to other people. We look at our neighbors, our colleagues, or the people making headlines in the news. But they are just a handful of the billions of people on this Earth who are struggling, succeeding, learning, losing, failing, winning, changing, or holding themselves back from their potential because they are comparing themselves to others.

Don't live in that mindset. Don't let the people around you be seen as a measuring stick for your personal success. Switch to a success mindset that acknowledges the humanity in other people, but also allows you to reach your potential, even if no one else is focused on helping you succeed. You could find yourself with a chapter in our next anthology if you do.

Failure is only a failure if you fail to learn.

Failure. Loss. Honest mistake. Lesson. Stepping stone. A challenge that got the best of you this time. Temporary setback. Your mindset determines which term you use to describe the events that may have prevented you from moving forward on your journey. Your mindset may even tell you, "You haven't stopped moving forward—you're just moving in another direction, but you're still heading toward success."

A failure can be a dead end or an opportunity to pave a new trail—the answer just depends on your mindset. Every single person who has achieved some level of success has also encountered setbacks. People have doubted them or people have stolen from them. They have made the wrong choice or taken too high of a risk. What they did, or what was done to them, ultimately doesn't matter. What does matter is that this person did not see the event as a stopping point. They kept going, pushing forward no matter what. Eventually, they reached their definition of success. Who says you can't do the same?

You can change your mindset right now.

It takes one person, one win, one quote, one failure, one world event, one personal event, one moment to shift a person's mindset significantly. This happens to people every day—one thing changes their entire view of the world, the people around them, or themselves. Yes, this can have negative consequences. But thinking with a success mindset isn't about focusing on the possible negative outcomes. What one thing can you do to shift your mindset to a success mindset?

Can you connect with someone on LinkedIn that you admire? (To break the ice, you can recommend the wonderful anthology that you just read!)

Can you forgive yourself for a mistake of the past, or let go of an event that darkened your mindset?

Can you take a deep breath and set the intention to change your mindset from here on out?

Big or small, one thing can change the way that you see the world.

What one thing will you do right now to step into a success mindset? Go out and do it.